Bad Education

Debunking myths in education

Bad Education

Debunking myths in education

Edited by Philip Adey and Justin Dillon

Open University Press
McGraw-Hill Education
McGraw-Hill House
Shoppenhangers Road
Maidenhead
Berkshire
England
SL6 2QL

email: enquiries@openup.co.uk
world wide web: www.openup.co.uk

and
Two Penn Plaza, New York, NY 10121-2289, USA

Open University Press 2012

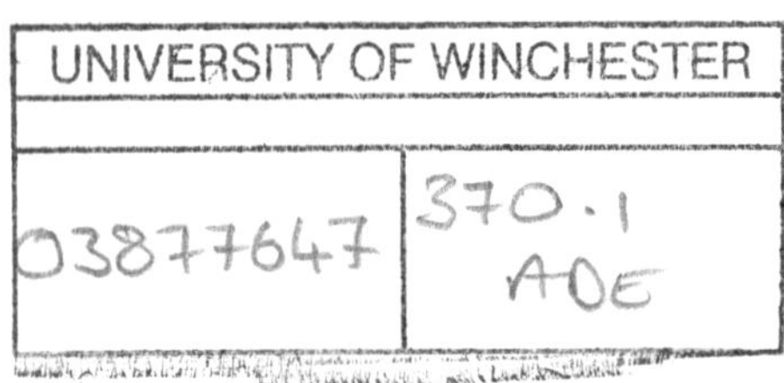

A catalogue record of this book is available from the British Library

ISBN13: 9780335246014 (pb)
eISBN: 9780335246021

Library of Congress Cataloging-in-Publication Data
CIP data has been applied for

Typeset by Aptara Inc., India
Printed and bound by CPI Group (UK) Ltd, Croydon, CR0 4YY

The McGraw-Hill Companies

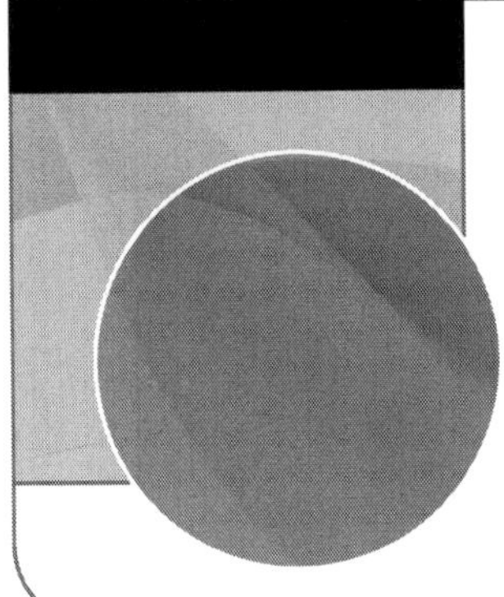

Praise for this book

"As education policymakers it can be difficult to resist the comfort of our own experience and gut instincts or the lure of populism. *Bad Education* is an invaluable myth-buster that tears down common misconceptions and serves up hard facts in their place. This is a politically unpalatable guide to the evidence that will challenge policymakers, the press and parents alike."

—Dale Bassett, Head of Public Policy, AQA

"Kenneth Baker describes in his memoirs how education policy was influenced by Margaret Thatcher's hairdresser and possibly her cleaner. More recently policy has been justified by the selective use of research in an attempt to create legitimacy for policy changes

Bad Education seeks to address some of the most important issues facing education without resorting to the rhetoric of ideologues or detailed statistical analysis. Instead an acknowledged expert in each issue facing education looks carefully at the available evidence. These issues range from how schools are organized, to teaching methods and learning. Each of the issues examined is one that has many 'myths' associated with it.

The authors show, in an clear and compelling way, that too much of what is being done in schools is being decided upon based on the selective use of evidence. Vocational education, ability grouping, class size, use of teaching assistants, synthetic phonics, learning styles, brain training and dyslexia are just some of the issues where the evidence is presented, in an engaging and easy to digest manner, and where all of those in education should take notice of the conclusions. In some cases the evidence is helpfully conclusive. In others it is inconclusive and messy.

As we constantly seek to redefine what is best for the next cohort of children to enter education Adey and Dillon, in this highly readable and well edited book, provide us with the evidence as to what does really does make a difference. Perhaps more importantly they move the debate on from gut instinct and myths to looking at the evidence.

This book should become a manifesto for change for all of those in education who want to ensure our children do not receive a Bad Education. Every Headteacher should buy a copy for every teacher and hopefully somebody might even place a copy under the Secretary of State's Xmas tree."

—Gary Phillips, Head Teacher, Lilian Bayliss School

"This is a welcome and important book. It takes apart the myths which support the dearly held convictions, simplistic assumptions, prejudices and irrational certainties of both politicians and teachers. Admitting that education is not itself a science, but demonstrating how both neuroscience and psychology have become available to inform educational policy and practice, it should provide food for more careful and well-informed thought to all who can influence what happens in our schools."

—Baroness Perry of Southwark

For Ayesha, Kamilah, Saffron and Leo representing all children who are experiencing the educational system

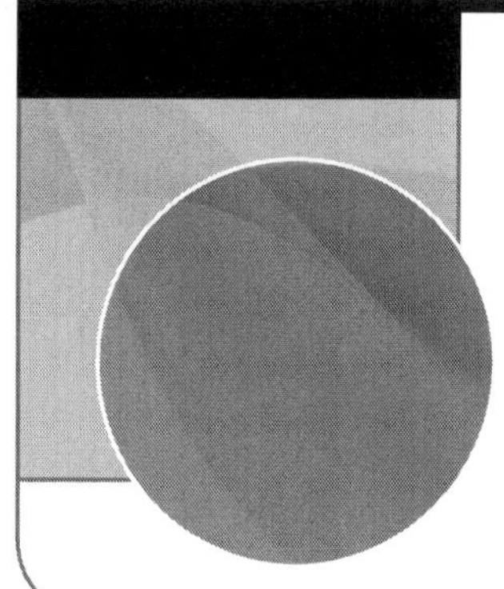

Contents

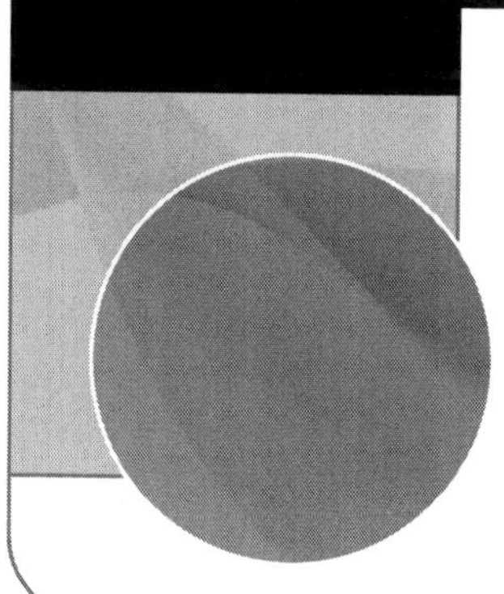

Notes on contributors

Philip Adey is Emeritus Professor of Cognition, Science and Education at King's College, London. He taught chemistry in a secondary school and then became involved in research into children's understanding of scientific concepts. He was one of the originators of the cognitive acceleration programmes.

Mike Anderson Winthrop Professor Mike Anderson is Director of the Neurocognitive Development Unit (NDU) at The University of Western Australia and Research Director of the Project KIDS research program. His 1992 monograph on the Development of Intelligence continues to provide a blueprint for his research and for that of his many students at the NDU. Over the past 18 years Mike and his colleagues have developed a unique child-friendly research methodology for investigating cognitive, social and emotional development in school aged children. This program is known at Project KIDS (Kids Intellectual Development Studies) and has involved work with more than 2,500 children.

Ed Baines is Senior Lecturer in Psychology and Education at the Institute of Education, London. He has an extended record in educational and psychological research and has a long-standing interest in teaching and learning in classroom settings. Ed has undertaken research on grouping practices in primary and secondary schools and was the main researcher on the SPRinG project that focused on improving the effectiveness of pupil groups in classrooms and was funded as part of the ESRC Teaching and Learning Research Programme. Ed co-wrote a training and resource book for educators on promoting effective group work in classrooms. He has also researched and written about peer relations and break- and lunch-times in school.

Paul Black is Emeritus Professor of Education at King's College London. He has made many contributions to curriculum development for science in the Nuffield projects, and as leader for the science surveys of the APU in the 1980s. He was chair of the Task Group on Assessment and Testing in 1988 that formulated advice to the UK government on the new national assessment system. He has served on committees of the USA National Research Council, and as Visiting Professor at Stanford University. His work on formative assessment with Dylan Wiliam and colleagues at King's has had widespread impact.

Peter Blatchford is Professor of Psychology and Education at the Institute of Education London. He has received numerous research grants from research councils, Government and charitable trusts, and has had 10 books and over 70 peer-reviewed journal papers published. He recently directed the largest study yet on the deployment and impact of support staff in schools (the DISS project), and prior to that directed a pioneering longitudinal study of the educational effects of class size differences (the CSPAR study), and co-directed a large-scale ESRC-funded study on the development and evaluation of a programme of collaborative group work for school pupils (the 'SPRinG' project). His work on social life in schools and school breaktimes/recess is well known.

Margaret Brown is Professor of Mathematics at King's College London, and has been involved in membership of national committees on the mathematics curriculum in England for over 20 years and under both main political parties. She taught in both primary and secondary schools, and then moved into teacher training and research. She has directed over 25 research projects on mathematics learning, teaching and assessment in all phases, from infant to university, including adult numeracy.

Guy Claxton is Professor of the Learning Sciences and Co-Director of the Centre for Real-World Learning at the University of Winchester. He is author of many books on learning, creativity and expandable intelligence including *Hare Brain, Tortoise Mind, The Wayward Mind* and *What's the Point of School?* and co-author (with Bill Lucas and others) of *The Creative Thinking Plan, New Kinds of Smart* and *The Learning Powered School.*

Frank Coffield is Emeritus Professor of Education at the Institute of Education, London University. Together with colleagues he produced a systematic and critical review of learning styles. His latest book, written with Bill Williamson, is *From Exam Factories to Communities of Discovery: The Democratic Route*, published by the Institute of Education in 2012.

Justin Dillon is Professor of Science and Environmental Education at King's College London. He taught in London schools for 10 years before joining King's in 1989. Justin is Head of the Science and Technology Education Group at King's and his research interests include school science teaching and learning inside and outside the classroom. He has co-edited a number of collections including *Becoming a Teacher* (OUP, 1995, 2001, 2007, 2011), *Engaging Environmental Education: Learning, Culture and Agency* (Sense, 2010) and *The Professional Knowledge Base of Science Teaching* (Springer, 2011). He is an editor of the *International Journal of Science Education* and Secretary of Bankside Open Spaces Trust.

Julian (Joe) Elliott is Principal of Collingwood College and Professor of Education at Durham University. Initially a schoolteacher, he subsequently practised as an educational psychologist before entering higher education in 1990. He is a Chartered Psychologist and an Academician of the Academy of Social Sciences. He appears regularly in the popular media discussing issues surrounding dyslexia, special educational needs, and the management of children's problem behaviour.

Simon Gibbs has been an Educational Psychologist for 25 years. He is now Reader in Educational Psychology and Programme Director responsible for training educational psychologists at the University of Newcastle. He collaborated in research in the field of reading interventions with colleagues at the University of York (where he is an Honorary Research Fellow) and is currently investigating teachers' beliefs in their classroom efficacy and well-being.

Jeremy Hodgen taught mathematics in primary and secondary schools before joining King's College London where he works to improve the teaching and learning of mathematics. His research interests include assessment, the learning and teaching in algebra and multiplicative reasoning and international comparisons in mathematics education. He currently coordinates (with Louise Archer and Justin Dillon) the ESRC's Targeted Initiative in Science and Mathematics.

Neil Humphrey is Professor of Psychology of Education at the University of Manchester. Over the last five years he has been actively researching and writing about social and emotional learning and mental health promotion in educational contexts. To this end, he has led (or been involved in) a number of major studies, including the national evaluations of the primary SEAL small group work element, secondary SEAL programme, and the Targeted Mental Health in Schools initiative.

Annette Karmiloff-Smith CBE FBA, FMedSci is Professorial Research Fellow at the Birkbeck Centre for Brain and Cognitive Development, University of London. She has a *Doctorat en Psychologie Génétique et Expérimentale* from the University of Geneva, where she studied with the famous Swiss psychologist, Piaget. She is the author of 10 books and of over 200 chapters and articles in scientific journals, as well as a series of booklets for parents on different aspects of foetal, infant and child development. She has two grown-up daughters and seven grandchildren.

Bill Lucas is Professor of Learning and Co-Director of the Centre for Real-World Learning at the University of Winchester. He is author of many books on creativity, learning and change including *rEvolution: How to Thrive in Crazy Times* and *Power up your Mind*, and co-author (with Guy Claxton and others) of *The Creative Thinking Plan, New Kinds of Smart* and *The Learning Powered School.*

Bethan Marshall is a senior lecturer in education. She specializes in issues relating to the teaching of English and assessment on which she has written extensively including her book *English Teachers: An Unofficial Guide* and *Testing English: Formative and Summative Practice in English*. She was a co-author of *Assessment for learning: Putting it into Practice* and *Learning How to Learn: In Classrooms, Schools and Networks*. She hopes to do research on the differences between the way English is taught in England and Scotland.

Brian Matthews taught science in secondary schools in London for 19 years and then trained science teachers on the PGCE at Goldsmiths and King's College, London. He has always been interested in finding ways of increasing pupil's interest in science while approaching equal opportunities. He has researched ways of developing emotional literacy in science classrooms and has published *Engaging Education. Developing Emotional Literacy, Equity and Co-education* with McGraw-Hill/OUP. He started the Engaging Education Consultancy (www.engagingeducation.co.uk) to help schools in these areas.

Corinne Reid is Associate Professor in the School of Psychology at the University of Western Australia and Clinical Director of Project KIDS. As a clinical psychologist, Corinne brings practical expertise to the investigation of developmental trajectories in childhood. Currently at Project KIDS she is working with children with Type 1 Diabetes, children born extremely low birthweight, children with complex mental health presentations and neurological conditions. Corinne also works with four remote indigenous communities supporting parents and teachers in preparing children for school. Corinne trains postgraduate students in the art and science of working with children and families.

Rob Webster is a researcher at the Institute of Education, University of London. He worked on the Deployment and Impact of Support Staff project (the largest of its kind in the world), and a follow-up study, the Effective Deployment of Teaching Assistants project. He currently works with schools and local authorities to improve the ways in which teaching assistants (TAs) are deployed. Rob also worked for six years as a TA in primary, secondary and special schools in London and the south-east.

Dylan Wiliam is Emeritus Professor of Educational Assessment at the Institute of Education, University of London where, from 2006 to 2010, he was its Deputy Director. In a varied career, he has taught in inner-city state schools, directed a large-scale testing programme, served a number of roles in university administration, including Dean of a School of Education. His most recent work focuses on the power of classroom assessment as a focus for teachers' professional development, and school improvement.

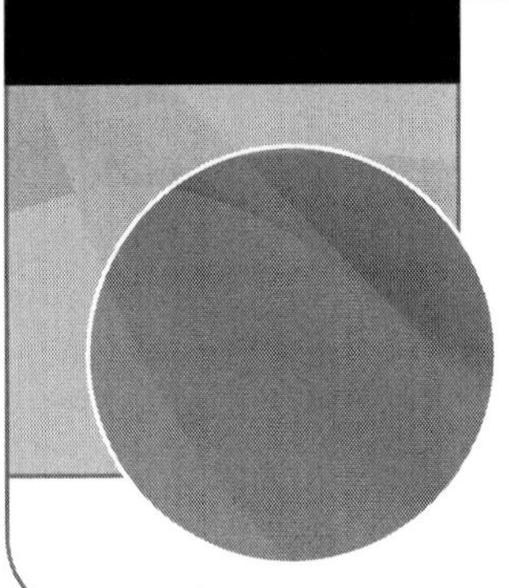

Foreword

For an opening line, I cannot improve on Ben Goldacre's introduction to his book on *Bad Science*:

> *Let me tell you how bad things have become (p. ix)*[1]

However bad it may be in medicine – Goldacre's main topic of concern – it is certainly bad in the case of educational policy-making. A few examples of ministerial opinions serve to express my concern.

'Barmy theories' was the phrase with which the then minister dismissed a proposal presented to him, with the support of the inspectorate, that the department invest in developing a programme to enhance pupils' reasoning skills. The case was based on the work of Michael Shayer and Philip Adey who had produced quantitative evidence that the programme enhanced the test scores of the pupils.

'Complicated nonsense' was the dismissive reaction of another minister to the first trial of SATs produced, under contract, by a university-led consortium: they were built around tasks designed to intrigue and motivate young learners with problems that would require them to apply their skills in mathematics and literacy. These were not what the minister regarded as proper tests, so the contracts were cancelled and 'proper tests' came to dominate the agenda in schools.

'... its approach was suspect' was Margaret Thatcher's reaction to the report of the Task Group on Assessment and Testing.[2] What is significant here was the reason she gave for her suspicion:

> Ken Baker warmly welcomed the report. Whether he had read it properly I do not know: if he had it says much for his stamina. Certainly I had no opportunity to do so before agreeing to its publication... that it was then welcomed by the Labour party, the National Union of Teachers and the Times Educational Supplement was enough to confirm for me that its approach was suspect (pp. 594–5).[3]

There are many more examples of reactions of these types in the chapters of this book. 'Barmy theories' was symptomatic of the way that evidence is dismissed if it does not agree with one's preconceptions – ironic, to say the least, when one of the central tasks of every teacher is to challenge their pupils' preconceptions by encouraging them to consider them in the light of evidence and reasoned argument. 'Complicated nonsense' is equally alarming. On such proposals as the design of a new suspension bridge, or a new regime for the use of a new cancer drug, expert opinion would be trusted. Complexity has to be justified, but to dismiss an outcome without careful attention to its justification is dangerous. Many apparently simple questions cannot be given a simple answer. For such questions as ' Does the choice of school for your children make a difference to their prospects of success?' (Chapter 1) or 'Do setting and streaming between or within schools produce improved performance?' (Chapter 3), the careful answer has to spell out the variety of types of evidence, and the variability in the quality thereof, in coming to a judgement, one to which some reservations would often have to be attached. If a one-word answer were demanded, the response in both cases would be 'No', but this would be misleading and it would be all too easy for any critic to select a particular study, or, sadly and more often, some personal anecdotes, to argue that such a conclusion must be wrong. One reason for such behaviour is that both policy-makers and the public desire simple conclusions that appeal to 'common sense' and make for positive headlines. A related reason for dismissing the judgements of academics is that they will never give a simple answer to the (dangerously simple) questions that are put to them.

A further cause of difficulty is the time-scale problem. Elected politicians have to worry about the next election. Yet there is ample evidence that it takes several years to design and implement any innovation, let alone evaluate its long-term effects. In my field of formative assessment, the Scottish government first consulted the group at King's who had studied the evidence and who had conducted a two-year pilot study in six schools about possible implementation. They then selected a small number of schools, distributed across Scotland, for two years of trials, drawing on personal contributions from both the researchers and the teachers from England. This was then evaluated by another research group, and when that described very positive outcomes, a programme of dissemination, using teachers in their trial schools, was implemented.[4] Two of the temptations that can undermine a good strategy of this type are described in Chapter 9. One was to go beyond the evidence to make the innovation look more attractive. Another was to be committed to and start a trial before the evidence of a pilot study could be evaluated.

This is an important and welcome book. Across its various chapters readers can see the faults of simplistic judgements, neglect of evidence, dismissal of researchers and injudicious implementation displayed across a range of aspects of central importance to the quality of pupils' learning. It is indeed to the credit of numerous teachers that they have ignored, or made some sense of, some of the innovations described here. They deserve better, and better informed, support. Yet the task is a tough one, often for the reason formulated by Goldacre:

> “You cannot reason people out of positions they didn't reason themselves into. But by the end of this book you'll have the tools to win – or at least understand – any argument you choose to initiate . . . (p. xii)”

Yet that quotation also, in expressing his hope for his book, supports hope that I have for this one. Indeed, I would be more positive, yet also cautious, in expressing my hopes in verse, with apologies to Hilaire Belloc[5]:

These findings should be thought about
And seriously taken
By everyone who has the power
To mess-up education

Paul Black
Emeritus Professor of Education,
King's College London

Notes

1. Goldacre, B. (2008) *Bad Science.* London: Fourth Estate.
2. DES (1988) *Task Group on Assessment and Testing: A Report.* London: Department of Education and Science and the Welsh Office.
3. Thatcher, M. (1993) *The Downing Street Years.* London: Harper Collins.
4. The approach used for the same innovation in England lacked most of these positive features, and its effects were never evaluated.
5. Belloc, H. (2004) The Bad Child's Book of Beasts in *Cautionary Verses.* London: Red Fox Books.

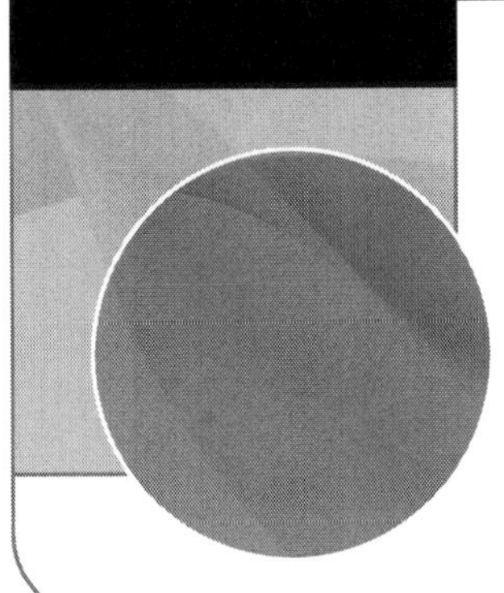

Introduction

On Tuesday, 1 January 2008, *The Guardian* published a letter from one of us (Justin Dillon) in response to an article written by one of their columnists, Tanya Gold, in which she had pretended to be bright at a speed-dating evening and dumb at a 'lock and key' party. She had concluded that men want women to be lobotomized. After pointing out that she might have been more convincing being dumb than being bright, we asked whether it was 'time to add a Bad Social Science column to complement Ben Goldacre's exemplary Bad Science column?' Three years later, following a conversation at the OUP stand at a conference in Reading, Fiona Richman expressed her opinion that 'there could be good potential in a book that exposes the various myths that abound in education (e.g. learning styles, brain-based learning schemes, etc.)'. She even suggested the title, 'Bad Education' and encouraged us to set up 'a team to take me up on this idea'. So we did. And here it is.

But the book has other origins. As observers (and participants) of wave after wave of educational change, we have seen and heard much that has left us despondent, irritated, exasperated and, occasionally, inspired. In his foreword, Paul Black provides an insight into the shocking levels of ignorance so often displayed when politicians are presented with evidence that does not support their policies. The dismissal of sound evidence of the success of educational initiatives as 'barmy theories' and 'complicated nonsense' might prompt outsiders to ask why do people bother doing educational research at all? But we know that there are people involved in education who actually value evidence even if it means that what they have held as an immutable truth begins to show signs of being wrong. We are also aware that there are people who want 'the facts' to support what they believe to be right and others who feel they need to know more in order to engage in the debates about education that really matter. And so our aim in this book is to examine some common myths in education and to expose them for what they are, but also to explore why they are attractive and whether they contain any kernel of truth to which we should attend, and in what way they lead us to think more deeply about the process of education.

Despite the laudable desire expressed by some educators and some policy-makers to base educational practice on evidence, it must be admitted that education itself is not a science. One cannot reasonably expect educational practice to be driven solely by principles that have been empirically established. If you want to build a bridge or put a person on the Moon you are playing for high stakes with people's lives but you also have well-established laws of physics which are reliable and which allow one to design a structure or a rocket with almost entirely predictable properties. Education is not that simple. Lives may not be at stake but the predictability of a specific outcome from any educational practice is generally low. For a period in the 1950s and 1960s Skinner and his followers believed that they had established laws of learning with reliability similar to Newton's laws of motion, but it was an illusion. The messiness and complexity of human nature bubbling with emotions and attitudes continually undermined the behaviourists' utopian view of learners as little black boxes reliably producing responses to stimuli untainted by feelings or social interaction.

Nevertheless, 'education' does draw on science, particularly on scientific psychology and nowadays increasingly on neuroscience. One rich source of 'bad education' is the misuse, misrepresentation or overinterpretation of these sciences; for example, by imbuing a rather vacuous construct such as learning styles with properties of reliability and validity that do not stand up to scrutiny, or oversimplifying the idea that different parts of the brain do different things and then quite unjustifiably extrapolating from this to a notion of multiple intelligences. We could draw on many examples of such misuse and overclaiming from genuine scientific evidence but we might ask also, why are educators so gullible? This is not just a matter of ignorance of scientific grounds for believing something; it is also a result of (1) wishful thinking, what teachers want to believe (e.g. 'everyone is good at something') and (2) lazy thinking, the too-ready acceptance of theories that are presented in nice glossy packages and which promise simple recipes for improving learning (e.g. 'teach each child according to her preferred style'). Included in this misuse of evidence would be misuse of statistics. Statistics show that there is a negative correlation between class size and achievement; that is, large classes achieve higher grades than small classes. But look at the sample: in most schools, top ability sets are typically large because they behave better and are easier to teach, while the small classes are of children who for one reason or another are rather challenging. It is not the size of the class that impacts on achievement, it is the size of the class that is determined by expectations of achievement.

Another source of bad education has philosophical (or at least logical) rather than empirical roots. Dylan Wiliam used to joke 'The way to improve educational standards overnight would be to turn all schools into Girls' Catholic Schools'. This is the *reductio ad absurdum* conclusion from the then Prime Minister's assertion that we should have more Faith schools because they get better exam results (and the uniforms are smarter, too). There is quite a rich vein of such illogical thinking to be tapped.

Many myths in education arise from oversimple categorization and stereotyping. We probably all have a notion of what we mean by 'traditional' or 'progressive' education, but to make any meaningful comparison of the effectiveness of each requires more than a woolly notion. The characteristics of each need to be described, and the influence of each characteristic on educational outcomes needs to be separately assessed. It may prove that the really influential factors are incidental to the main characteristic by which 'progressive' or 'traditional' are defined. We will never stop the popular press from creating misleadingly oversimple headlines, but we should beware of playing into their hands by presenting research conclusions as less complex than they really are.

Over the last 25 years teachers have been subjected to an increasing barrage of instructions, guidance, advice and statutory regulation, all designed by an administration that acts as if the fine details of classroom life can be fully controlled. Teachers have been deprofessionalized by these attempts to impose increasingly detailed instruction on how and what to teach. The National Curriculum programmes of study, work schemes, numeracy and literacy strategies, and statutory assessments are just the bare bones of the mass of instructions issued to teachers, all of which serve to diminish their freedom to exercise their own judgement and erode their professional capability. Governments and the inspectorate behave as if the process of teaching can be reduced to a set of rules, which only require mechanical application. If one is bombarded year after year with one 'innovation' (set of instructions) after another, with barely time to take breath between one 'big idea' and the next, is it any wonder that you embrace seemingly attractive ideas without sufficient critical reflection – especially when those ideas, such as 'emotional intelligence', seem to come with government backing?

We have been fortunate in assembling a stellar cast of authors, each an international expert in their field, who seem to have enjoyed the chance to put the record straight about their own *bête noir* of a myth. In turn, they shine a sceptical light on some of the more pernicious myths in education, but they also point the way forward to a more realistic, if more complex, educational scenario. Myths of King Arthur's court, or of unicorns, had their genesis in some sort of reality, and these educational myths also often (not always) have a kernel of truth; however, this has been exaggerated or distorted. That kernel is worth seeking for the same reason as a traveller who gets lost is well advised to retrace his steps to the last junction where he went wrong, and explore from a position of relative certainty in which direction the true path lies. Reality usually proves to be more complex and messy than the mythical version. This may not suit the headline writers (or some policy-makers) but education is too important to be reduced to a set of 'two legs bad, four legs good' rules.

The book has been loosely divided into three sections of increasing specificity to the individual student. At the level of school organization, Dylan Wiliam shows how the supposed difference between 'good schools' and 'bad schools' is far less than commonly supposed, Guy Claxton and Bill Lucas show that physical capability is at least as 'intelligent' as mental gymnastics, Ed Baines presents the evidence that grouping students by their supposed ability does them no favours, Peter Blatchford nails the common misconception that students in small classes must learn better than those in large classes, and Rob

Webster and Peter Blatchford question the claims made for the effectiveness of teaching assistants. Turning to teaching methods, Margaret Brown shows the vacuity of the simple dichotomy of 'traditional' versus 'progressive' teaching, Bethan Marshall explores the dogmatic attachment to one 'best' way of teaching reading, Justin Dillon questions the uncritical approbation often given to informal and out-of-school educational experiences, Neil Humphrey critiques the government's social and emotional aspects of learning (SEAL) programme, and Jeremy Hodgen shows that calculators and computers are not 'good' or 'bad' in themselves; it is how they are used that matters. In the last section, we look at various supposed characteristics of learners: Mike Anderson and Corinne Reid expose some common myths about the application of brain science to education, Philip Adey takes to task both the idea that intelligence is largely fixed, and the alternative that there are a number of independent intelligences. Frank Coffield debunks the idea that children have distinct learning styles, Annette Karmiloff-Smith rejects simple notions of the evils of television for small children, and Julian Elliott and Simon Gibbs question the myths that have been built around dyslexia.

We would like to thank several Open University Press colleagues, particularly Fiona Richman who opened the door for us and encouraged us to put together a team of writers that we could only have dreamed of when we embarked on the task of editing this book. The strength of the book lies in the ideas of the authors and the rigorous and timely manner in which they have produced their contributions. They have made our job easier and more pleasurable than is normally the case with such books. We and they have done our best. Over to you.

Philip Adey and Justin Dillon
King's College London
October 2012

PART 1

School organization

CHAPTER 1

Are there 'good' schools and 'bad' schools?

Dylan Wiliam

All parents want their children to do well at school, and it is natural to assume that a child will do better at a 'good' school. This is presumably why politicians of all complexions make such a big thing of giving parents choices over the schools their children attend, and why parents spend so much time choosing schools, and at first sight, it certainly seems that there are huge differences in schools.

In 2010, in one particular school in England, only 29 per cent of the students achieved five good grades at GCSE, and for only two-thirds of these students did the five good grades include English and mathematics. At the other end of the spectrum, there were 287 schools in England where every single student achieved five good grades at GCSE, and there were 111 schools where every student achieved five good grades at GCSE with at least a grade C in English and mathematics.[1] It would be tempting to conclude that any school in which every student gets five good GCSE grades must be a very good school indeed, and any school where four out of five students fail to do so must be a very bad school, but as we shall see, things are not quite so simple. To see why, it may be helpful to consider an analogy with hospital care.

Evaluating hospitals

Suppose for a moment that someone needs to select a hospital for a serious operation, such as a coronary bypass. How should this individual choose the hospital? One, perhaps obvious, way would be to choose the hospital with the lowest mortality rate, but this would be likely to lead to a bad choice – no one would choose to have open-heart surgery at a cottage hospital just because no one had died there recently. Because it is widely accepted that raw mortality statistics do not give individuals the information they need, the NHS instead makes available what is called the Hospital Standardized Mortality Ratio. This is done by comparing the actual numbers of deaths in the hospital over a given time period with the numbers that might be expected, given the nature of their illness. One method of doing this, used by the 'Dr. Foster' research group, first takes into account the initial diagnosis by placing each individual into one of 56 different diagnostic categories which between them cover 80 per cent of the hospital deaths in England. They then make a series of further adjustments that take into account the fact that even within each of the 56 diagnostic categories, there will be a range of outcomes. For example, younger patients are likely to do better than older ones; for some conditions, the outcomes for males and females are likely to be different, and obviously outcomes are likely to be less good for patients suffering from more than a single condition. The actual number of deaths each year is then divided by the number of deaths that might be expected, and the answer is multiplied by 100, which gives the Hospital Standardized Mortality Ratio or HSMR. The average is approximately 100 (because across all hospitals, the actual mortality rate and the expected mortality rate will average out) and the values for English hospitals in 2010 ranged from just over 70 to 120.

As might be expected, most hospitals are reasonably close to the average. Around two-thirds of the hospitals in England had a HSMR between 90 and 110 in 2010, which means that the average mortality rate for the patients at these hospitals range from 10 per cent below to 10 per cent above what might be expected, given the patients attending those hospitals. However, for a couple of hospitals, the HSMR was around 70, which means that on average a patient's chance of dying at this hospital would be 30 per cent less than might be expected, given what was known about the patients admitted. Now of course, the reason for these low mortality rates could be due to factors unrelated to the quality of care provided by the hospitals, and that for some reason, many of the patients were not as seriously ill as they might appear to be given what was known about them. Similarly, while the mortality rates for some hospitals were 20 per cent higher than expected, we cannot be sure whether this is due to lower-quality care, or due to some other factors that were not taken into account. However, the calculation of HSMR does take into account the level of socio-economic deprivation, the ethnicity of the patients, and a range of other factors. For this reason, a HSMR of 120 does present a strong prima facie case for lower-quality care than is provided in other hospitals, and at least merits further investigation.

For the purpose of this chapter, there are three important features about the way that hospital mortality rates are calculated. First, the calculations are complex. The actual statistical technique used to calculate the expected mortality rate is called logistic regression, and while I have not surveyed the whole population of the UK, my experience of teaching statistics in schools and universities suggests that less than 1 per cent of the population knows what it is, let alone understands how to do it. We could use less sophisticated techniques, or even just use raw mortality statistics, but if we did so, we would make bad decisions. General hospitals that refer seriously ill patients to more specialized hospitals would look better than they should, because they effectively export all their serious cases, while the national centres of excellence that take these seriously ill patients would look worse than they should, because they are the hospitals of 'last resort' taking, and often saving the lives of, patients that less specialized hospitals could not, or would not, treat. The sophistication of the techniques used to estimate hospitality statistics is not done for the sake of complexity. The sophistication is needed to help people find out which hospitals are better, untainted by irrelevant factors such as how sick the people were when they went to the hospital.

The second is that it is very difficult, if not impossible, to get hold of the raw data on which the standardized mortality statistics are based. What is made widely available is the standardized mortality ratio for each hospital, which takes into account differences in hospital intakes. This could, of course, be regarded as a form of paternalism: denying the public information because non-specialist users might be confused, or might put greater faith in the data than is warranted. However, in this aspect of government policy, it seems to be accepted that the most useful data to give the public are statistics that take into account differences in the intakes of different hospitals. The third is that the differences in standardized mortality statistics between hospitals is large. Consider, for example, an illness with a 30 per cent survival rate (in other words, a 70 per cent mortality rate). Assuming that the treatment of this illness conforms to hospital averages, the chance of surviving this in the best hospital is over 50 per cent, but in the worst, less than 1 in 6.[2] These are large and important differences in outcomes.

Evaluating schools

In the same way that patients need meaningful information about the quality of care provided in different hospitals, parents need meaningful information about the quality of education provided in different schools. Without such information, it is impossible for patients, or parents, to make informed choices about hospitals and schools. But others also have a legitimate interest in the quality of services provided through taxation income. Ultimately, all those who pay taxes, or benefit from the services purchased with government income derived from taxes, have a right to know about whether this money is being spent wisely. So how should we hold teachers, schools, and local authorities accountable for the quality of state schools?

We saw that for hospitals, the raw 'outcome' measure for hospitals – mortality rate – is not used. Instead, the published statistics are standardized, to take into account the differences in intake, and the same thing is possible for schools. The remainder of this chapter focuses on secondary schools, and specifically the performance of students between the ages of 11 and 16, for two reasons. The first is that the issue of school choice appears to be more significant at secondary than primary level. Certainly efforts by successive governments to change the variety of kinds of school (City Technology Colleges, grant-maintained schools, specialist schools, academies and free schools) have focused almost exclusively on secondary schools. The second reason for focusing on secondary schools is that the quality of data is better. There is a hard-edged, high-stakes measure of educational achievement for almost all students in the country at the age of 16, and just as importantly, national tests for 11-year-olds give us a good measure of student achievement upon entry to secondary schools.[3] Of course national tests for 11-year-olds do give us an 'output' measure for primary schools, but the data on the achievement of children when they arrive at primary school comes from assessments by the teachers of those children, and currently, there is not in place any mechanism for ensuring that different teachers, in different parts of the country, are using the same standards to evaluate the achievement of their children.

As noted in the introduction to this chapter, the achievement of students varies greatly from school to school. Across the whole of England, 2,905 secondary schools had students from the age of 11 to 16 or 18[4] who took GCSEs or equivalents in 2010. As we saw earlier, in one school, only 29 per cent of the students achieved five good grades at GCSE and in 287 schools every single student did so. But what about the others? In half the schools, the success rate for five good GCSEs was 78 per cent or better, and in half it was 78 per cent or lower (in statistical jargon, we say that the median success rate for schools on this measure was 78 per cent in 2010), and many schools are quite closely grouped around this figure. The success rate for the middle half of all schools ranges from 69 per cent to 87 per cent. However, when we take as our measure the proportion of students getting five good GCSEs including English and mathematics, the success rate is much lower: the median value is 54 per cent, and the middle half of all secondary schools range from 44 per cent to 64 per cent. The fact that around one-fifth of all students in the country get five good grades at GCSE, but do not do so in English and mathematics means that comparing results between schools is far from straightforward. In one school, for example, every student managed to get five good GCSEs, but for only 45 per cent of these students did the five good GCSE grades include English and mathematics. In others, the proportion getting five good grades at GCSE is almost exactly the same whether we include English and mathematics or not. Now while we might agree that students should be able to pursue their interests and aptitudes in choosing the subjects they study at GCSE, it does highlight the difficulties of comparing schools on the basis of examination results. Where students are studying subjects they have chosen, their interest and motivation is likely to be higher, and therefore, presumably, they will get better results than if they studied subjects in which they had less interest. Allowing students choice in their GCSEs makes comparing results from school to school difficult for a different reason as well. Schools that are anxious to improve their results may persuade students to opt for subjects that are perceived to be easier, or channel them into courses that are regarded as equivalent to GCSE, but where the demands are less, or where the examination allows for a larger amount of coursework. In some cases, the interests of the school and the students may be well aligned – what is good for the student is good for the school. However, in other cases, the school may be able to improve its standing in so-called 'league tables' of examination results by channelling students into courses that are easier, but which do not do much to help the student in the long term.

However, a much more significant issue in comparing educational achievement across schools is that students are not allocated randomly to schools. If they were, then we could be pretty sure that differences in achievement were due to differences in the quality of education received. Some schools, such as the 164 remaining grammar schools in England, are explicit about the fact that they select students on the basis of either current achievement, or some prediction about how well they are likely to do in the future. But there are also less overt forms of selection. For example, one study found that only 17 of the 100 most socially selective schools – that is schools that have an intake that is much more socio-economically advantaged than the areas from which they draw students – were grammar schools. In fact at least, 50 non-grammar schools were more academically selective than at least one grammar school in England (of these 50 non-grammar schools, approximately half were faith schools).[5] Even when schools are labelled as 'comprehensive', therefore, we cannot be certain that this is an accurate description of their intake. To get a good understanding of how good schools really are, we need to look how much students are actually learning in schools.

What kinds of school are best?

A school in which all students get five good grades at GCSE may be a good school, but for the most selective of schools, this would be a rather modest, if not disappointing, achievement. Indeed, in many grammar schools, the majority of students get A and A* grades. But even this may be a modest performance if the school is highly selective, taking, as some grammar schools do, only the highest-performing 5 per cent of students in their catchment area. So one obvious way of understanding how students are doing at a school is to look at the level of achievement of students at the age of 11, and compare this with their achievement at age 16 to get the so-called 'value-added' by the school – how much the students actually learned. In other words, just as is done for hospitals, we calculate the expected achievements of 16-year-olds at the school based on their achievement at the age of 11, and compare it with the actual achievement at GCSE. Because students at different schools take different numbers of GCSEs, the grades that students gain on the best eight GCSE subjects are used as the measure of achievement. The result is multiplied by 1,000 to give an index of school 'value-added'.

As is done for hospitals, the value-added calculation takes into account not just the achievement of the students starting at the school, but also a number of what might be called 'contextual' factors. For example, girls make more progress than boys in secondary school, so in calculating the expected achievement for a girl, we would compare her progress with other girls starting at the same level rather than with the progress made by boys and girls combined. This may seem unfair on girls' schools. They have to get their students to a higher level of achievement to show greater than average value-added. However, the reason for doing this is simple. If the reason that the students at a particular school are doing well is because they are girls, the school should not get the credit for that. Just as importantly, parents choosing a school for their daughter need to know how well other girls did at that school. In addition, just as is done with hospitals, a range of other contextual factors, such as ethnicity, the level of deprivation in the areas where the students live, and whether the child has special needs, are taken into account. The resulting measure of student achievement is often called the 'contextualized value added' or CVA for a school.

The CVA measure for schools is not quite as neat as the Hospital Standardized Mortality Ratio because the final outcome measure – GCSE results – is not as clear-cut as whether a patient lives or dies. Obviously we can look at the grades that students get on GCSEs, but some students take other examinations that are counted as equivalent to GCSEs. For example, many schools enter less academic students for the BTEC[6] Applied Science examination rather than GCSE. While the standards of the BTEC Applied Science are meant to be equivalent to GCSE Science, the BTEC course offers more continuous assessment so it is very difficult to be sure that these so-called 'equivalents' really are equivalent. The fact that a number of different examination boards offer GCSEs also allow schools to 'shop around' to find the courses that suit their students best. This might not mean finding easier courses, but obviously schools are unlikely to change from one exam system to another unless they think their students' results are going to improve. This said, various agencies do try to ensure that the different courses that are deemed equivalent (GCSEs offered by different boards, BTECs and so on) are equally demanding.

There is, however, one serious weakness in the calculation of CVA, and that is it takes into account whether a student has special educational needs. Obviously, it makes intuitive sense that we should not expect a student with special needs to make the same amount of progress as a student without special needs. But in the CVA calculation, allowance is made for students simply because the school says that the student in question has special needs. As might be expected, the proportion of students in a school who are regarded as having special needs varies greatly. In 2010 seven comprehensive schools identified more than half of their students as having special educational needs, and 246 schools identified more than a quarter of their students as having special educational needs. Of course, these students may indeed have genuine special needs, but since the proportion of students identified as having special needs by processes involving external agencies is far lower, it does raise the possibility that some schools were trying to 'game' the system.

Because of the possibility of choosing easier, or less exam-based qualifications, and because labelling students as having special needs lowers the bar for these students, CVA is far from a perfect measure of how much students are learning at schools. But it does give a good indication of how much progress students are making, and when we look at this in detail, we uncover some rather counter-intuitive findings.

How much difference is there between schools?

As noted above, the average CVA is set to 1,000 each year. The CVA scale is arranged so that a score of 1,048 represents a school where each student in the school got one grade higher per subject in GCSE than they would have achieved had they gone to the average school. In 2010, the lowest value added was just over 900, and the best was just below 1,100. These two schools are clearly very bad and very good respectively. In the worst school, a student who would have got eight grade Cs in the average school would have ended up with eight grade Es instead. And in the best school, the same student would have got eight grade As. However, most schools are quite close to the 1,000 average. In fact, for almost half of all secondary schools in England, the value-added was so close to 1,000 that the difference was not statistically significant.[7] In other words, around half of all secondary schools in England are no different from average. Moreover, even when schools are significantly better or worse, for the vast majority, the differences are small.

In 2010, around 80 per cent of English secondary schools had a CVA between 976 and 1,024. What this means is that for four out of every five secondary schools in England, the choice between going to one school rather than another makes less than one grade difference per subject at GCSE. Another way to think about this is to group the schools into five equal-sized groups based on their performance: very low, low, average, high and very high. The difference between going to a very low-performing school and a very high-performing school is less than one grade per subject. Most people find these results surprising, counter-intuitive, and even implausible. While CVA is not a perfect measure of school quality, the 'headline result' here – that the vast majority of schools are pretty similar in how much progress students make – is supported by range of studies using other data.

For example, every three years, the Organisation for Economic Co-operation and Development (OECD) tests a random sample of 15-year-olds in English, mathematics and science in the OECD countries via the Programme for International Student Assessment (PISA). In some countries, there are great differences in scores between schools, but in most OECD countries (including the UK) the differences between students in the same school are far greater than the differences between schools. Even when there are differences between schools, much of those are caused by differences in intake. When differences in the social composition of schools is taken into account, we find that only 7 per cent of the variation in students' test scores can be attributed to the school. The other 93 per cent is outside the school's control. However implausible it seems, the fact remains therefore that as long as you go to school, which school you go to does not matter very much.[8]

So far, we have looked at the national variation in schools, and while looking at the best and worst schools in the country gives some sense of the variation within the system, this is not particularly relevant to parents. What they want to know is how to choose among the schools within reasonable travelling distance of their home. Rebecca Allen and Simon Burgess looked at the impact that the choice of school had on a student's GCSE grades. What they did was to look at students who took their GCSEs in 2009, and then looked at what grades they would have got had they gone to other schools in the area by looking at how well similar students who had gone to the other schools fared.

They found that if the parent had chosen, in 2004, the school that in 2009 turned out to be the best school for their child in terms of academic attainment, the increase, compared with the average for schools in the area, was around one-third of a grade per subject at GCSE.[9] Another way to think about this is in terms of reaching a 'threshold' such as getting five good grades at GCSE. It turns out that only 10 per cent of students are close enough to the threshold for the choice of school to make any difference. For the other 90 per cent, they are either so far above the threshold that even if they went to the average school, they would still get five good grades, or so far below the threshold that even if they went to the best school, they would still fall short. Another choice that some parents can afford to make is whether to send students to private schools or to use the state system, and here again, the differences are smaller than many people imagine. Private school students are included in PISA, and in the UK students in private schools are about two years ahead of state school students – a bigger margin than any other country. However, controlling for the social class of the students, students in state schools and private schools in the UK perform about the same – in fact there is not a single OECD country in which, after controlling for social class, students in private schools do better than in state schools.

This does not mean that parents are wasting their money sending their children to private schools. The presence of high-achieving students improves the achievement of other students in the class, so the same student will do better in a selective private school than a state school, but the reason is because of the peer group, rather than the quality of teaching. Indeed, the PISA data suggest that the average quality of teaching in private schools is actually slightly worse than in the state schools, since, as we saw, controlling for the social class of the students, the performance is about the same, and the class sizes are much smaller in private schools (in the UK, the average class size is 25 in state schools and 13 in private schools). See Chapter 4 for effects of class size.

Conclusion

Schools differ in many ways. Some are very active in the performing arts, while others have exceptional facilities for sports. Some students are likely to do better within a highly structured environment, while others would find such a school constraining, and would do better when there is more personal freedom. It is also important that students feel safe at school, and for some students it may also be important that at least some of their friends are going to the same school. All these are important things to take into account in choosing a school.

However, the policies of successive governments, across the political spectrum, appear to assume that the academic performance of schools is the most, and even perhaps the only, important thing. Schools where less than 35 per cent of students achieve five good grades are excoriated as unacceptably bad, even though in many cases, the students at those schools make more progress than the students attending the 164 remaining grammar schools.

Some, including Michael Gove, currently Secretary of State for Education, have argued that using value-added to assess the performance of schools is 'immoral' since it removes the incentives for schools serving disadvantaged communities to expect the highest standards. And yet, the same arguments are never made against risk-adjusted statistics for hospitals.

The raw mortality rate for hospitals like Great Ormond Street Hospital for Children will be higher than for the generality of hospitals because they take on patients that other hospitals cannot help. No one has ever suggested that using Hospital Standardized Mortality Ratios to compare hospitals is somehow immoral because it removes the incentives for doctors to do everything they can to save gravely ill children.

It does, however, seem to me to be rather immoral to hold some schools to a higher standard than others simply because they are situated in an area of socio-economic disadvantage. There are some schools where students make very little progress, but fortunately they are extremely rare. We must, of course, do everything we can to tackle the problem of low-performing schools, and, in some cases, it may be that the best thing to do is to close the school, and to open a new one – after all, schools exist to serve the interest of students, not to create jobs for teachers.

But it is a fundamental principle of natural justice that teachers and schools should be accountable for the things they can influence. Schools and teachers should be accountable for developing the whole person, and part of that should be how much academic progress students make at school. But it is just as wrong to blame schools serving disadvantaged areas for the low examination scores as it would be to blame a hospital that took only the most gravely ill patients for its high mortality rate. Contextualized value-added or CVA is far from perfect but it is, by some margin, the best measure we have with which to hold schools accountable. There are some problems with CVA, notably with some questionable equivalences between different qualifications, and some features that allow schools to 'game' the system; for example, by designating a large proportion of their students as having special needs, but these are reasonably easy to fix.

Schools do differ in their academic performance, but what is rather extraordinary is how small these differences are. For the vast majority of children, the choice of school will make very little difference to how much academic progress they make at the school, and other factors are likely to be far more significant. Of course parents need to make sure that the school is not one of those very rare schools where children make little progress but, this done, parents should focus on non-academic factors. Bad schools are extremely rare.

Notes

1. Source: Department for Education (2011) *Performance Tables 2010: Secondary Schools (GCSE and Equivalent)*. Available online at www.education.gov.uk/performancetables/schools_10.shtml (accessed 27 December 2011).
2. An average survival rate of 30 per cent is equivalent to an average mortality rate of 70 per cent. If the outcomes for this condition are in line with hospital averages, then the mortality rate would be 49 per cent (i.e., 30 per cent lower)

at the best hospital, and 84 per cent (i.e., 20 per cent higher) at the worst hospital. These rates are equivalent to survival rates of 51 per cent and 16 per cent and the best and worst hospitals respectively.

3. Of course, this does not work well in local authorities that have middle schools, but these are in the minority, and appear to be decreasing.
4. This figure excludes schools that changed status and name (e.g., by being converted into academies) during this time.
5. Sutton Trust (2008) *Social Selectivity of State Schools and the Impact of Grammars: A Summary and Discussion of Findings from 'Evidence on the Effects of Selective Educational Systems'*. Available online at www.suttontrust.com/research/summary-impact-of-grammars/GrammarsReviewSummary.pdf (accessed 31 December 2011).
6. In 1984, the Business Education Council, and the Technician Education Council, each of which had offered vocational awards in their respective areas, merged to form the BTEC. In 1996, this organization merged with the University of London Examinations and Assessment Council to form Edexcel, which is now wholly owned by Pearson plc.
7. Wilson, D. and Piebalga, A. (2008) *Accurate Performance Measure but Meaningless Ranking Exercise? An Analysis of the English School League Tables* (Vol. 07/176). Bristol, UK: University of Bristol Institute of Public Affairs.
8. Organisation for Economic Co-operation and Development (2007) *Science Competencies for Tomorrow's World, Volume 1: Analysis*. Paris, France: Organisation for Economic Co-operation and Development.
9. Allen, R. and Burgess, S. (2010) *Evaluating the Provision of School Performance Information for School Choice* (Vol. 10/241). Bristol, UK: University of Bristol Centre for Market and Public Organisation.

CHAPTER

Is vocational education for the less able?

Guy Claxton and Bill Lucas

> *Given the intrinsic richness of manual work – cognitively, socially, and in its broader psychic appeal – the question becomes why it has suffered such a devaluation as a component of education . . . Paradoxically, educators who would steer students toward cognitively rich work might do this best by rehabilitating the manual trades, based on a firmer grasp of what such work is really like.*
>
> (Matthew Crawford, *The Case of Working with Your Hands*, pp. 27, 32)

When, a few years ago, it was reported that a bright young woman had turned down the offer of a place at Oxford in order to take up an apprenticeship in hairdressing, there was outrage in the press. The general opinion was that she must be mad, perverse or subject to extremely bad advice or influence. Why would someone with the world at their feet throw away their lives, people asked in despair. It is true that this decision will, statistically, have a significant impact on her life choices and her income (though there are, of course, hair stylists who are wealthy, highly articulate and well-respected). But behind the outpourings of opinion one could hear the rumblings of a very deeply entrenched set of social attitudes about the relative merits of the academic and the vocational. These have profoundly influenced educational discourse, and the lives of millions of young people, in the UK for the last 100 years. In this chapter we want to unearth this collection of attitudes and assumptions, and submit them to the scrutiny of contemporary science.

Before we embark, a word about terminology. We are concerned about the status of, and practical arrangements for, learning that aims primarily at the development of physical skill and sensibility. Though we will focus on what goes on in schools, we are, as our opening paragraph suggests, also concerned about the way education both reflects and reinforces a wider set of social attitudes. This kind of learning has gone by a number of names: practical, physical, manual, technical, vocational and so on. In the USA this educational stream used to be called 'shop class', while in the UK it is now often associated with the subject of 'design technology' (DT). Vocational education has been traditionally associated with the crafts and trades – with a preparation for largely manual occupations such as carpentry, cookery, plumbing, caring, horticulture, mechanics – and 'hair and beauty'. Where academic students study 'subjects' and passed written 'examinations', vocational students followed 'apprenticeships' and gained 'diplomas' and 'qualifications'. In this chapter we most often use the terms 'vocational' or 'practical' to refer to the kinds of learning and accomplishment that have a lot of 'body' in them: skilled occupations that involve manual dexterity (and sometimes physical strength), practical 'gumption' (rather than abstract reasoning and erudition) and sensory acuity.[1]

The status of vocational learning

Walk into any school and it will be immediately obvious that practical accomplishment and physical learning are valued less than study that is more intellectual and scholarly. High-status subjects stay compulsory for longer, have more time on the curriculum allocated to them, and result (all being well) in examination grades that are valued more highly. On these three criteria, English, mathematics and science emerge as the highest status. These subjects centre most relentlessly on the disciplined use of symbols and arguments, and the expression of comprehension through explicit reasoning and written argumentation and computation. As high-stakes examinations get nearer, so even the non-cerebral aspects of these subjects get lost: English becomes more analytical and less imaginative, while science loses it technical and experiential aspect and becomes more frequently a kind of applied mathematics.

Below these three in the hierarchy come the classic subjects of history, geography and modern languages. Then may come more 'modern' subjects such as psychology, sociology, media studies or business studies. And finally come those that you cannot do just sitting at a desk, staring at a screen, or writing on a piece of paper: art, music and drama; sport and physical education; and DT. To mitigate the general neglect of art, craft and sport, schools typically make a fuss about some specific kinds of achievement in these areas – the unbeaten first XI, the school play well reviewed in the local paper, the success in a national 'art for schools' project. But in educational terms, there is little doubt where the centre of gravity of a school's concerns lie, and it is not in the craft workshops or the gym.

In England we are currently witnessing an intensification of this hierarchy of esteem.[2] A few years ago, schools were judged on the percentage of students who got good grades in five GCSE subjects, and these could include commensurate vocational qualifications such as GNVQs, or more recently BTECs. Then the metric by which schools were judged was narrowed to include only those students whose five good passes included English and mathematics. Now, the vocational equivalents are being excluded from this key performance indicator, so only the traditional academic subjects will 'count'. The three 'championship' subjects of history, geography and languages are being 'promoted' to the 'premiership' at upper secondary level by being heavily encouraged in the so-called 'English Baccalaureate'.

Seven myths arising from bad science

The lowly status of vocational, practical and physical education rests on a number of beliefs. We will describe these briefly, and then examine them in more detail in the light of contemporary research, especially cognitive and social neuroscience.

Practical *activities* are cognitively less demanding than intellectual ones

The chief executive officer (CEO) of a major UK learning and development company recently described trades such as plumbing and hairdressing as 'menial', implying that they do not require much in the way of intelligence. Such attitudes are very common. The application of these skills in the service of unblocking toilets or layering hair is assumed to be routine and rather mindless. Intellectual activities, on the other hand, such as writing précis or analysing arguments, are presumed to demand higher levels of cognition and more sophisticated intelligence.

Practical *learning* is cognitively less demanding than intellectual learning

Not only are practical trades easier and less demanding to carry out; they are seen as simpler to learn. There may be skills and techniques to be mastered, but any kind of learning that is of a more reflective or articulate nature is presumed to be largely unnecessary. Manual skills are thought to be learned largely through observation, imitation and practice, and these learning methods are presumed to be less cognitively sophisticated or demanding than those that underpin more intellectual kinds of performance.

Educational progress involves growing away from practical and embodied activities and towards those that involve reasoning, disembodied knowledge and symbol manipulation

This belief has scientific roots. The massively influential work of Jean Piaget has left a strong presumption in education that 'cognitive development' necessarily involves leaving behind concrete and 'sensori-motor' ways of learning, and progressing to modes of thinking that are 'post-formal', requiring logical reasoning about hypothetical situations that may have few personal, historical or motivational referents. From this, it has come to be seen as the educators' role to help young people make this progression as rapidly and easily as possible. By the end of primary school, for example, physical and imaginative 'play' – the very word is often contrasted with the *serious* business of 'learning' – has largely disappeared to be replaced by the more 'grown-up' activities of reading, writing and calculating. Dressing up and performing are still valued – but increasingly as light relief from the high-stakes business of 'literacy' and 'numeracy'. (Even the Latinate abstract nouns seem to add gravitas to the disembodied.)

Academic learning is a better preparation for life than practical learning

Learning to be abstractly rational, analytical and argumentative is assumed to be a better preparation for life than learning to solve practical problems in immediate, concrete situations. The ability to argue, analyse and discuss – to be explicit and discursive – in the absence of urgent need or practical context is seen as being of greater benefit to young people, as they get ready for life in the twenty-first century, than, say, the ability to observe a complex situation with patience and perspicacity. It is assumed that studying abstract, impersonal or historically remote subject matter leads to a better cultivation of these dispassionate, intellectual qualities than does engagement with the messy realities of everyday life. Latin and mathematics are often thought to provide the best 'training of the mind' – specifically, the most useful preparation for adulthood in the twenty-first century – that education can offer, precisely because they are remote from these messy contemporary uncertainties and predicaments.

Those young people who do not follow a traditional academic pathway are generally 'less able' than those that do

They are assumed to lack the 'mental capacity' that is required to study these harder, more abstract subjects, and their education therefore has to centre increasingly on activities that they do seem 'able' to engage with – by default, the lower-status subjects with their lower-value qualifications. If there is evidence that particular underachieving students are *not* lacking in the requisite 'brain power' (they are not 'less able' but they are not 'fulfilling their potential') then ancillary explanations for their lack of success in the scholarly domains must be sought: poor home background or emotional issues, having 'got in with a bad crowd' or being 'disaffected', or having a clinical condition such as 'attention deficit disorder' or 'dyslexia'. Whatever the specific diagnosis, the physical and practical areas of the curriculum become indelibly associated with those who are deficient in some way – intellectually, motivationally, or in their social and cultural milieu.

The only way the esteem of lower-status practical subjects can be (somewhat) repaired is by making them more academic

Given the previous 'myths', it can look as if the only way the esteem of lower-status practical subjects can be (somewhat) repaired is by making them more academic. If theoretical thinking and understanding is 'truly intelligent', and physical ingenuity and dexterity is not, then the only way to raise the status of the vocational subjects and qualifications is to add academic components to them, whether they genuinely contribute to the development of vocational expertise or not. So diplomas and apprenticeships have frequently been bulked up with watered-down theory, to make them look 'weightier' (just as supermarket chickens get injected with water to make them heavier, and therefore pricier). This of course runs the risk that such courses come to look and feel to students more like exactly the kind of school that they were trying to avoid – and so, as the statistics show, levels of attendance, engagement and completion tend to suffer.

Teaching of practical and vocational subjects is less intellectually demanding than teaching science or history

As a consequence vocational teachers are less esteemed, and often less well paid. Teaching hours are higher and remuneration lower in 'colleges' of further education than they are in 'universities' (and differences in nomenclature between further education and higher education mark these differences in value). One of the most common signifiers is the opposition between 'training' and 'education'. Those who merely *train* students to be able to change an oil filter or take old people to the toilet are doing a less demanding, less intricate, job than those who *educate* students about differential calculus or the causes of the First World War.

Each of these seven prevailing assumptions has grown up as a result of folklore, superstition and outdated scientific understanding. They are perpetuated by the cultural practices of schools and colleges, the values embedded in public examinations, and the repeated unthinking utterances of politicians and many curriculum planners and developers. And they seem very hard to shift. Despite widespread concern about these assumptions, expressed time and again over the last one hundred years, they stay, for the most part, stubbornly in place. Their resilience, in the face of repeated challenges, makes one suspect that they have deep cultural roots. To be effective in challenging and changing this particular kind of 'bad education', the first step has to be to dig around these roots and see where they run.

Descartes' error

To anyone looking inside a body, before about 100 years ago, it would have been just plain obvious that consciousness, reason and imagination could not arise from the machinations of any kind of meat, let alone the particularly dull-looking lump called the brain. Mind stuff was clearly different from body stuff. Minds were clever, conscious and sophisticated, while mere flesh was mechanical and simple. The 'housekeeping' processes with which bodies seemed mainly to concern themselves – breathing, digesting, contracting muscles and so on – did not warrant being called 'intelligent'. And minds were also capable of 'knowing God'; they had the capacity for purity and sanctity, while bodies were corruptible and unreliable. So minds were not only much more complex and intelligent than bodies, they were also 'higher'. The schism was both cognitive and moral – and unbridgeable. Descartes declared, for example: 'There is nothing included in the concept of the body that belongs to the mind; and nothing in that of the mind that belongs to the body'.[3]

This powerful attitude towards minds and bodies – 'Descartes' error', as neuroscientist Antonio Damasio has recently dubbed it – was born in classical Greece, strongly endorsed by the early Christian church, and turned into irrefutable 'common sense' by the learned philosophers of the Enlightenment, that period in our history when rationality was finally enthroned as the highest manifestation of our humanity.[4] 'Mind over matter', and especially over the physical matter of which we are composed, became the watchword. This disparity of esteem between the physiological and the intellectual became enshrined in the core social institutions of the Western world. Orthodox Christianity revolves around a struggle between our baser bodily impulses and our 'higher nature'. God gave us reason and 'free will' so we could overcome the sinful dispositions of the body, and be bettered by the struggle. The law's attitude to crime hinges on whether the accused is judged to have 'been in his right mind' – and therefore had the capacity (but not, evidently, the inclination) to override his antisocial impulse – at the critical moment. Medicine increasingly relies on measurement and machinery, while 'clinical judgement' born of experience is thought untrustworthy.

And for 100 years, schools value intellectual over physical gymnastics, and the mental over the manual. It was not always thus, as Sir Christopher Frayling reminds us:

> The original meaning of [the 3Rs] was completely different in Regency times, at the beginning of the 19th century. The three Rs were reading, wroughting and arithmetic – in other words, literacy, making things and numeracy... And then, in the era of Mr. Gradgrind and the Great Exhibition of the 1850s, the wroughting got dropped in favour of writing.[5]

Perhaps unsurprisingly, the middle classes who were to become the enthusiastic supporters and beneficiaries of grammar schools did not want their sons and daughters 'wroughting' when they could be practising the intellectual skills seen as the gateway to a more highly regarded and remunerated profession.

Of particular relevance is the way in which this image gives rise to a view of conscious understanding as senior to physical effectiveness. Comprehension is seen as prior to, and necessary for, competence. Not just 'doing', but being able to *explain* what you are doing, becomes a hallmark of intelligence. So arithmetic is not just a matter of being able to get the right answer, but of being able to 'show your working', and of having '*grasped the concept* of subtraction'. Indeed, it is sometimes assumed that you have to 'understand' something before you can put it into practice: that learning must proceed, as one model puts it, from 'conscious incompetence' to 'conscious competence' and only then to 'unconscious competence'.[6] Forty years ago, teacher trainers naturally assumed that lectures on the philosophy, psychology, sociology and history of education would somehow seep into the being of a training teacher, and then naturally manifest in enhanced competence in the classroom. The fact that they routinely did no such thing was ignored for decades.

While those deep-seated assumptions about both the *separation* of mind and body and the *primacy* of mind over body remain in place, attempts to generate 'parity of esteem' between so-called academic and practical learning are doomed to fail. For years, governments have tinkered with the structure, rhetoric and assessment of practical and vocational education. New diplomas try to blur the disparity of esteem, and courses in practical subjects are bulked up with gratuitous wodges of science or sociology. This attempt to raise the esteem of practical learning by trying to make it look more 'academic' rests on the very premise that needs to be questioned – that the more scholarly-looking the subject, the better it will be for getting on in life.

Examining the myths

Current cognitive science and neuroscience, however, are giving us quite a new image of the relationship between mind and body, and a vastly greater respect for the intelligent capacities of the meat of which we are made – especially that spongy kilo and a half between our ears called the brain. We are beginning to understand how 'mind' can indeed arise from matter; and how smart biological matter can be on its own, without any supervision, or even accompaniment, by conscious or rational thought. Let us briefly revisit the main 'myths' that contribute to the devaluing of practical learning, and see how they stand up in the light of current knowledge. (In the space available, we can do little more than offer tantalizing summaries and a few pointers towards further reading.)[7]

Is comprehension 'senior' to competence?

Antonio Damasio and his colleagues have shown that practical expertise is regularly distilled out of experience without any conscious understanding of the situation and its parameters. The ability to articulate what it is you have learned often arrives *after* you have learned to control and manipulate the situation, if at all. Indeed, the attempt to use conscious knowledge to guide learning frequently turns out to be counter-productive. The effort to apply what you *think* is going on, or what you have been told is going on, can actively interfere with the ability of your brain to pick up useful but subtle aspects of the situation just through attentive trial and error. In many complex arts and crafts, intuitive expertise and sensibility are often orders of magnitude more subtle than one is able to articulate – and necessarily so.[8]

There have been many experimental demonstrations of how 'thinking about what you are doing' is actually counter-productive. People who are actively prevented from conceptualizing what they are doing – golfers, in one study – actually perform better (under stress, for example) than those who have an articulate theory about what is going on. In many kinds of everyday problem-solving, people who have been *prevented* from thinking about information they have been given make better decisions than those who have been encouraged to think carefully. The relationship between conscious thought and intelligent action is much more complex and double-edged than is suggested by the out-of-date folk psychology on which much of education depends. Sometimes conscious thinking makes us more intelligent, sometimes less, and sometimes it is irrelevant.

Are practical trades and crafts undemanding of intelligence?

Of course occupations and activities differ in complexity, variability and unpredictability. Some 'assembly line' jobs are routine, repetitive and do indeed demand little cognitive resource. Some (like driving an underground tube train) are mostly routine, but require a constant vigilance for the non-routine, and a depth of flexibility and understanding to respond appropriately when necessary. Some afford a great deal of leeway in the degree of subtlety that a practitioner may apply. Working in a hotel kitchen may allow you to move between the freezer, the microwave and the serving area quite mindlessly, or to bring a good deal of skill and ingenuity to what you do. A politician being interviewed by a radio journalist may keep repeating today's party line, regardless of the questions they are asked, or may engage with what they are being asked in a much more fluid and thoughtful way. And some jobs absolutely demand a high level of knowledge, skill and flexibility, much of the time. The radio presenter has to keep thinking on her feet, just as the premiership footballer and the primary school teacher do.

However, it is also true that the *belief* that physical jobs are broadly 'menial' may stop us seeing, or looking for, such intricate intelligence as may be there. The assumption acts as a filter that makes us see what we expect to see. Examples of such 'top-down' perceptual bias are commonplace in psychology. So if we want to give ourselves the chance of seeing what intelligence is actually needed by a waitress or a mechanic, or what scope there is for individuals to serve or weld with greater sensitivity and imagination, we need to drop these filters and look afresh at what people actually do, rather than what we expect them to do.

In his book, *The Mind at Work,* American educational researcher Mike Rose has carried out such meticulous ethnographic observations in a range of vocational and professional settings, including a busy restaurant, a hairdressing salon, a carpentry shop and an operating theatre. He finds that such 'real-world intelligence' may be differently structured from more purely intellectual intelligence, but is certainly complex and intricate. Where an academic may be able to focus her mind on a single intellectual task – writing a paper or preparing a lecture, say – the intelligence in vocational settings commonly blends cognitive challenges such as planning, prioritizing and calculating with physical, emotional, social and moral challenges as well – and often in real time, under pressure. The waitress learns to walk and stand in a way that lessens physical strain, deploys mnemonic strategies to help her remember complex orders, uses imagery to tag the different dishes to the people round the table, notes (out of the corner of her eye) customers whose orders are overdue and are getting restless, and plans an economical route through the restaurant that enables her to have a friendly word with them, while also filling up water glasses and replacing items of cutlery. The apprentice carpenter has to carry out mathematical computations that, in a classroom, would have been quite straightforward, but which, in the workshop, are enmeshed in a complicated design process, being developed in real time, that makes the whole operation more intricate and demanding. There are people who got 'As' in their Mathematics exams who flounder in such a setting, just as there are people who did poorly on school tests, but quickly learn to cope well with the multidimensional pressures and tangible resources of the workshop.[9]

Is practical learning unsophisticated?

If the elegant problem-solving of the experienced tradesman or woman is worthy of respect, what about the processes of learning that delivered that package of physical, cognitive, social and emotional expertise? Is it defensible to see vocational learning as relatively simple and academic learning as more complex? Sometimes yes – but, if again we look with a clear eye, not by any means always. If we observe with a lens that is designed only to recognize academic kinds of learning – studying 'off-the-job', decontextualized discussion, written argumentation – then by definition the scholar will look a more powerful learner. The lens brings her learning activities into focus, while rendering other kinds of learning invisible or indistinct. Learning by imitation, by trial-and-error tinkering, or by careful attention to the present physical reality – this head of hair, this mass of pipework or this anxious old gentleman – may look crude when seen through the lens of scholarly learning, but on closer inspection they are nothing of the kind.

In his book, *The Craftsman*, Richard Sennett describes in detail the learning processes of a glass-blower trying to create a new kind of goblet. The dynamic interplay of heightened attention, specific experimentation, careful thoughtfulness and active imagination is clearly as complex, intricate and intelligent as the learning process of a lawyer preparing a detailed brief. For the latter, the medium of learning involves words, concepts and arguments; for the other it draws on a fluid orchestration of perception, action and reflection that includes, but is not limited to, conscious deliberate thinking. Indeed, in some ways the learning of the artisan is more sophisticated than that of the author or lawyer, for the latter has clear control of the medium, and can impose her will on the developing script, while the 'maker' may have to engage in a subtle negotiation with the refractory nature of the medium – this piece of wood has knots and whirls that must be treated in a particular way;

the condition of this head of hair tells the experienced stylist that certain treatments will work and others will not. (In fact, the author too has to learn how to bend and shape her use of words to convey a new argument or understanding.) This subtle integration of what needs to be done (or said) with the diverse affordances and constraints of this material and this situation is surely the stuff of real intelligence – whether the 'stuff' is words or welds, or the context is a seminar room or a car body repair shop.[10]

Do we (need to) grow out of physical and imaginative learning?

Actually, academics and professionals learn by observation, imitation, tinkering and imagination just as much as plumbers and beauticians do. The junior lecturer teaches in a way that is a complex distillation – partly conscious, largely unconscious – of the styles she observed as a student.[11] The philosopher tinkers and crafts as he shapes a paper for a journal, just as the sculptor or the electrician adjust their designs as they go along. Surgeons think – but they also rely on highly developed powers of imagination, as this quotation makes clear:

> [Before the operation] you just go out into the scrub sink where you are by yourself. You've got five minutes there. And all you're doing is just scrubbing your hands . . . and that's the time I'll try to piece together the anatomy with what I am about to do . . . I try to picture what I am going to see when I get there, because the x-rays are taken straight on or from the side, and we are coming in at a 20 degree angle to that. I try to combine those two views in my mind to make a three-dimensional image and rotate it into the view that you'll be looking at when you do the operation. And that is helpful . . .[12]

In the real world, surgeons make use of their imagination just as much as architects and plumbers do. Business executives draw on their intuition when making decisions, just as much as fire-fighters and chefs do. Research chemists tinker and tune their equipment and their theories, just as jewellers, interior decorators and gardeners do. Of course, as we have said, some jobs afford or require greater intricacy of learning than others do – but this dimension of cognitive complexity does not map at all neatly onto the vocational-academic spectrum that runs from the plumber at one end to the professor at the other. To suppose they do is merely a matter of prejudice or intellectual laziness.

Is academic learning a better preparation for real-world learning?

Academic study develops skills that equip you to be a better student – just as a BTec in 'health and social care' should equip you to learn more quickly how to manage a new group of young people with moderate learning difficulties. Learning to do something helps you learn how to do it better; but it does not necessarily help you to do anything else. There is scant evidence that academic study acts, in any way, as a better generic preparation than practical or vocational learning for coping with difficulty or lifelong learning. Scholarship is a specialized craft, just as caring is. Indeed, the amount of academic study pursued at school and college seems to have little or no beneficial effect on the clarity and rigour with which people think as they argue in the pub or discuss next summer's holiday round the kitchen table. Medical students' exam results do not correlate with their skill as clinicians, and air traffic controllers with higher academic qualifications do the job less well than those who are less academically accomplished.[13] The idea that studying History, Mathematics or Latin provides a powerful, generic training of the mind is an article of faith, not a proven fact. If anything, there are indications that the discipline of practical, physical learning and problem-solving may be a better incubator of useful, transferable habits of mind than academic study.[14]

Are 'vocational students' less able than their academic counterparts?

On the old view of the mind, vocational education is always second best. Students decide to follow the vocational route (typically at age 14) because they are not 'bright enough' to follow the academic. If they were, they would – so the story goes. However, there are at least two other common reasons why students choose a vocational path. They might enjoy practical, hands-on activities more than those that centre on reading, writing, thinking and talking; and they might have discovered that they derive greater satisfaction and pride from an object well made than an A grade essay. Or, they might be more impatient to leave school and take on the rights and responsibilities of adulthood, and the vocational route seems to offer them that opportunity more quickly. William Richardson sums up this third option:

> “Large numbers of young people want to leave school at the earliest opportunity. They hate the uniform; they feel infantilised; they are aware of the adult world out there, beyond school, and are eager to join it. It's not just a matter of their interests or their mentality; the vocational route is the one that seems to respond best to that urgency.[15]”

Unfortunately, there is no research that tells us the proportions of each of these three factors that contribute to the vocational choice. It is a sure bet, however, that the confusion between scholarly craft and aptitude on the one hand, and intelligence on the other, has caused a good many young people to be wrongly labelled 'low ability'. People who like to work with their hands, and are impatient to be treated as grown-ups, are unjustly stigmatized as 'unintelligent' as a result. Thus this aspect of 'bad education' is not just scientifically and pedagogically bad; it is morally bad too.

Conclusion: changing images of intelligence

These different kinds of research are leading us towards an expanded view of intelligence.[16]

Intellectual 'cleverness' – a mixture of abstract rationality, verbal dexterity, general knowledge and 'interesting opinions' – turns out not to be the be-all and end-all of intelligence; it is one specialized *kind* of intelligence that like all the other kinds has its uses and its limitations. The accusation that someone may be 'too clever by half' can now be scientifically underpinned.

Some researchers are returning to a deeper view of intelligence – one that is more like the old Scottish idea of 'gumption'. The *Cambridge Advanced Learner's Dictionary* defines 'gumption' as 'the ability to decide what is the best thing to do in a situation, and to do it with energy and determination'. Robert Sternberg, for example, now argues that intelligence is not, at root, for reasoning and arguing; it is for getting things done that matter, in specific situations. Intelligence is the process that enables us, in the heat of the moment, to reconcile what we would like or need to do with what we can do, especially when normal routines and habits do not apply. Intelligence is what integrates our concerns, our capabilities and the opportunities that are open to us.[17]

In the jargon of the cognitive sciences, real-world intelligence is *embodied* and *embedded*. It is about reading situations and bringing to bear our skills and experience in a way that enables us to pursue our goals and interests with clarity and vigour. We think as we go along, and our thinking is intimately bound up with what we are seeing, feeling and doing, a process that some scientists have dubbed 'thinkering'.[18] Thinking is part and parcel of shaping a head of hair or tracing a blockage in a fuel line or a waste pipe. Chefs and carers need to think all the time, and the thinking they do is intricate, subtle and appropriate. Matthew Crawford, author of *The Case for Working with Your Hands*, has been both a policy wonk and a motorcycle repairman, and his book is a meditation on the intelligence of manual work. He says: 'There was more thinking going on in the bike shop than in my previous job at the think tank' – and he means more good, intelligent, sophisticated thinking.[19] Much of what passes for brainwork in writing position papers, contributing to meetings or giving lectures, for example, is merely describing and defending received opinions. A living made by talking and writing does not necessarily demand much intelligence – though those who suffer from what we have called 'anti-manualism', of course, will find Crawford's claim absurd.[20]

Only rarely in the real world do we need to stop and reason in the way that IQ tests demand, yet educators usually fail to tell their students *when* they will need to think like this, and when not. It has been shown, for example, that rational thinking only works well when there are a small number of clearly defined factors to be considered.[21] When we are doing something real and messy, like designing a garden or deciding which flat to make an offer on, it is more intelligent to heed our intuition than to rely solely on logical analysis because, for logic to work, it has first to cut the problem down to a size that it can manage, and in doing so, it runs the serious risk of distorting and oversimplifying the predicament.

It is also intelligent to take our time, to allow our brains to weave all the factors together in a way that does justice to the situation – yet IQ tests and final examinations only measure how well you can think *under pressure*, which is quite a different kind of skill.[22] That is why someone's IQ is no indication of how intelligently they will behave in practical situations.[23] We all know very clever people who are conspicuously lacking in horse sense. And unfortunately there is no test of horse sense in the civil service exams. The word 'gumption', incidentally, comes from the Middle English *gome*, which meant 'to pay attention, to heed, to have presence of mind' (and which also leads to the antithesis of 'gumptious' which is 'gormless'.

Overall, therefore, there seems no good reason not to treat 'being good with your hands' as a legitimate form of real intelligence. And when we do so, a whole set of traditional stereotypes and assumptions begin to look a good deal less secure than we had thought. For a number of reasons, practical and vocational education should begin to be given the genuine esteem it undoubtedly deserves.

Notes

1. For the purposes of this short chapter we are ignoring the 'in-between' cases of engineering, medicine, architecture and so on. They have a strong physical/practical component, but high status by virtue of the cultural value placed on their professions, and of the academic bodies of knowledge and research with which they are associated.
2. Department for Education (DfE) (2011) *A Framework for the Curriculum: A Report by the Expert Panel of the Curriculum Review*. London: HMSO.
3. Sommers, F. (1978) Dualism in Descartes, in M. Hooker (ed.) *Descartes*. Baltimore, MD: Johns Hopkins Press.
4. Damasio, A. (1995) *Descartes' Error*. New Cork: Quill. For the history, see Dodds, E.R. (1951) *The Greeks and the Irrational*. Berkeley: University of California Press; Claxton, G. (2007) *The Wayward Mind*. London: Little Brown.
5. Sir Christopher Frayling, Rector of the Royal College of Arts, interviewed in *The Guardian*, 29 June 2004.

6. This theory is widely taught and quoted in the commercial 'learning and development' business, though its exact provenance is uncertain.
7. See, for example, Damasio, A. (2011) *Self Comes to Mind: Constructing the Conscious Brain*. New York: Pantheon; Tucker, D. (2007) *Mind from Body: Experience from Neural Structure*. Oxford: Oxford University Press; Pfeifer, R. and Bongard, J. (2007) *How the Body Shapes the Way We Think*. Cambridge, MA: MIT Press.
8. The studies referred to in this and the following paragraph are described in more detail in Claxton, G. (1997) *Hare Brain, Tortoise Mind: Why Intelligence Increases When You Think Less*. London: Fourth Estate.
9. Mike Rose (2004) *The Mind at Work: Valuing the Intelligence of the American Worker*. New York: Penguin.
10. Sennett, R. (2008) *The Craftsman*. London: Allen Lane.
11. Molyneux-Hodgson, S. (1999) Is authentic appropriate? In J.T Leach and J. Paulson (eds) *Practical Work in Science Education*. Amsterdam: Kluwer.
12. Brown, C. (2001) *The cutting edge: performance psychology with surgeons*. Paper presented at the American Psychological Association Annual Convention, San Francisco, 17–20 August.
13. Perkins, D.N. (1985) Post-primary education has little impact on informal reasoning, *Journal of Educational Psychology*, 77(5), 562–71; Wingard, J.R. and Williamson, J.W. (1973) Grades as predictors of physicians' career performance: an evaluative literature review, *Journal of Medical Education*, 48(4), 311–22; Berg, I. (1970) *Education and Jobs: The Great Training Robbery*. New York: Praeger.
14. See Sennett, op. cit.; Rose, op. cit.
15. Williamson, R. (2010) Quoted in B. Lucas, G. Claxton and R. Webster (eds), *Mind the Gap: Research and Reality in Practical and Vocational Education*. London: Edge Foundation.
16. See Lucas, B. and Claxton, G. (2010) *New Kinds of Smart: How the Science of Learnable Intelligence Is Changing Education*. Maidenhead: Open University Press.
17. See, for example, Sternberg, R. (2000) (ed.) *Practical Intelligence in Everyday Life*. Cambridge: Cambridge University Press.
18. *Urban Dictionary* (www.urbandictionary.com/define.php?term=Thinkering): 'to think about something by tinkering with objects related to the problem under consideration . . . often a very good way to explore aspects of difficult problems or to find solutions where none are obvious'. The word thinkering was coined by Ondaatje, M. (2004) *The English Patient*. London: Bloomsbury.
19. Crawford, op. cit., p. 27.
20. Claxton, G. and Lucas, B. (2011) Anti-manualism, in J. Mullen and C. Hall (eds) *Open to Ideas: Essays on Education and Skills*. London: Policy Connect.

21. Dijksterhuis, A. and Nordgren, L. (2006) A theory of unconscious thought, in *Perspectives on Psychological Science*, 1(2): 95–109.
22. Stanovich, K. (2009) *What Intelligence Tests Miss*. New Haven, CT: Yale University Press.
23. Scribner, S. (1984) Studying working intelligence, in B. Rogoff and J. Lave (eds) (2000) *Everyday Cognition*. Cambridge, MA: Harvard University Press.

CHAPTER

Grouping pupils by ability in schools

Ed Baines

Introduction

Debates about how pupils should be organized in school often provoke strong responses from parents, educators and politicians. The organization of children into mixed age classes or single sex classes often draws comment in favour or against from many. But the debate that draws the most attention concerns whether or not children should be grouped according to some judgement of their ability. It is important to note from the outset that 'ability' is not easily assessed and is unlikely to be the basis for the allocation of pupils into ability groups. Instead they are usually formed on the basis of performance on attainment tests or on 'perceived' ability in one or more curriculum areas. Because 'ability grouping' is the term most commonly used within education we will continue to use it in this chapter, though 'attainment grouping' is probably a better descriptor.

This chapter considers the thinking underpinning the practice of ability grouping in schools and arguments for and against it. It summarizes research findings that evaluate the effects of different forms of ability grouping relative to pupil academic performance and other pupil characteristics. It considers how teachers, teaching and teacher expectations vary across ability groups, and presents some conclusions on the practice of ability grouping.

The rationale for ability grouping

In the run-up to most UK parliamentary elections over the past 20 years and at frequent points in between, politicians raise the issue of grouping students by ability in a bid to be seen to be advocating driving up educational standards. This stance is perhaps based on a belief that such a perspective resonates with the electorate.[1] Similarly, the right-wing press often blames progressive mixed ability teaching for current dissatisfactions with the education system and low standards. Ability grouping is regularly presented as the silver bullet that will enable schools and teachers to 'get back to basics'. Writing in *The Sunday Times*, Minette Marrin[2] suggested that 'All the evidence shows that, contrary to 40 years of dogma, careful setting and streaming are best for every child . . . . It is high time that it was forced on all schools.' As we shall see throughout the rest of this chapter the research evidence suggests a rather different view.

But why not group pupils by ability? There is an intuitive and practical sense to the idea of allocating children to classes on the basis of ability. If we target resources, teaching expertise, learning support and so on, to classes according to pupils' level of ability and need, surely pupils of all attainment levels will benefit? Moreover, ability grouping, so the argument goes, makes teaching easier: it enables adaptation of the teaching approach and style to the needs of the students; it reduces the possibility of boredom and makes it easier to sustain motivation; it encourages the participation and engagement of the less able since they are not intimidated; and the more able benefit since they are not held back by the slower children.

There are however many arguments against the use of ability grouping and these are most notably rehearsed in Jeannie Oakes' second edition of her book, *Keeping Track*.[3] In essence, concerns about ability grouping focus on the inequalities that arise. This concern relates, in particular, to variable opportunities to access the curriculum, learning resources and educator expertise; concerns about the stigma associated with being in a low ability group (and in some cases being in a high ability group) and most importantly the likelihood that ability grouping also tends to inadvertently organize students by social class, race and gender. That is, lower ability groups contain higher concentrations of children from some ethnic minority groups and/or lower socio-economic backgrounds and of boys. Ability grouping may function to sustain or raise inequality and intensify existing societal divisions.

Types of ability grouping

Grouping by attainment is a form of selection that can be implemented at different organizational levels within the school system. At the level of school admissions, some schools are allowed to be a little selective. When combined together with the socio-economic mix of the school catchment area this can mean a more homogeneous range in ability and socio-economic status within a school even before students are allocated to classes.[4,5] But in this chapter we focus more on ability grouping within schools.

In the UK, 'setting' and 'within-class ability grouping', and to a lesser extent 'streaming', are the predominant forms of ability grouping used in schools.[6] But there is much confusion about the meanings of the different terms used. 'Streaming' (or 'tracking' as it is called in the USA) involves allocating students to classes for most or all curriculum subjects based on general assessments or combined attainment results. In the USA, tracking may involve students undertaking a markedly different curriculum to those in other tracks. In the UK, students usually undertake approximately the same curriculum but high ability classes are taken through it at a faster pace and/or greater depth.

'Setting', a form of ability grouping that is very common in the UK (sometimes referred to as 'regrouping' in the USA), involves children being allocated to classes on the basis of similar attainment levels for a particular curriculum area. In contrast to streaming, allocation to sets is carried out on the basis of some form of assessment in the particular curriculum area rather than a general measure of attainment. Setting allows students to be in different ability groups for different subject domains but also means that they can be taught in mixed ability classes in other parts of the curriculum.

'Within-class ability grouping' involves the formation of ability groups within classes and students may receive instruction, work and learning tasks that are appropriate for their particular level of perceived ability. Finally, there is 'mixed ability grouping' (sometimes referred to as 'heterogeneous grouping') where the class or group tends to reflect the academic variability of the school intake.

These forms of grouping are by no means mutually exclusive and some may be combined. For example, within-class ability grouping may take place within streams, sets or mixed ability classes. In fact, one criticism of early studies that compared homogeneous with heterogeneous ability grouping is that so-called mixed ability classes often involved ability grouping within the class, and thus were rarely taught as mixed ability classes.

Ability grouping and pupil academic performance

So what does the research evidence tell us about ability grouping relative to academic achievement and progress? Over the past 40 years or so there have been many research studies and systematic reviews synthesizing the results. Recently, there have been a number of international studies that have investigated the impact of ability grouping on academic achievement in schools across an array of countries. The ongoing Programme for International Student Assessment (PISA) studies take place every three years and involve assessments in Reading or Mathematics or Science of 15-year-olds across a large number of Organization for Economic Co-operation and Development (OECD) and non-OECD countries. These studies have repeatedly found that the more schools group by ability, the lower the pupil performance overall.[7] In contrast to the view of many politicians, ability grouping in schools seems to depress academic performance. This research also strongly suggests, consistent with the view presented by Jeannie Oakes, that ability grouping can exacerbate inequalities due to differences in socio-economic status (SES) already in the system.

The PISA studies have found that the earlier that children experience ability grouping within an educational system, the more likely the gap in attainment between those from high and low SES backgrounds without any benefit on overall achievement. That is, the gains that are made, for example, by the more able are offset by losses experienced by the less able. This gap occurs because there is likely to be a higher concentration of pupils from low SES backgrounds in low ability groups and an equivalent concentration of pupils from high SES backgrounds in higher ability groups. Similar findings were reported when studies examined inter-school tracking systems (these are systems where schools select children by ability, as in the previous UK system of grammar and secondary modern schools).[8] The authors of the most recent PISA study conclude that:

> in general, school systems that seek to cater to different students' needs through a high level of differentiation in the institutions, grade levels and classes have not succeeded in producing superior overall results, and in some respects they have lower-than-average and more socially unequal performance (p. 13).

The PISA studies are large scale and sophisticated, and a raft of potentially confounding factors were controlled for when the data were analysed. Nevertheless, they are limited in a number of ways. First, these studies involve the collection of data at one time point. This means that they cannot examine the effects of ability grouping on progress over time, nor can they establish causal relationships between ability grouping and achievement. A further limitation is that they can only make broad statements about major forms of ability grouping and are not sensitive to subtle differences in systems and practices. In examining the effect on attainment, the PISA study compared the performance of students that were ability grouped for *all* curriculum areas with students that experienced some ability grouping or none at all. These findings may therefore have limited relevance to a UK system where the number of schools that group by ability for all curriculum areas is unlikely to be substantial. A further shortcoming is that the great variety of systems and approaches used across countries prevents the identification of factors that explain these effects. The above limitations mean it is also important to examine studies that are more tightly controlled, examine progress over time and specifically focus on evaluating the effects of ability grouping within a country. There have been many such studies, the majority of which have been carried out in the USA and the UK and a number of meta-analyses and best-evidence syntheses were undertaken during the 1980s and early 1990s. In the following sections, findings from these analyses, organized by type of ability grouping, are considered alongside more recent research.

Streaming

Recent research in the UK has suggested a much greater use of streaming in primary schools than had previously been thought, with just over 16 per cent of students experiencing streaming.[9] Bob Slavin undertook a synthesis of 'best' evidence, which included 14 studies that examined streaming/tracking in comparison to heterogeneous classes at primary school level. He concluded that the effects on achievement were non-existent.[10]

At secondary school level, streaming was prevalent in the UK prior to the 1970s but declined in the 1980s. Estimates in the 1990s suggested it was in evidence in about 11 per cent of schools. More recent estimates suggest that this proportion has increased again, though it is unclear by exactly how much.[11] In his synthesis of 29 studies of ability grouping in secondary schools, Slavin similarly concluded that there were no consistent effects of homogeneous ability grouping, as opposed to mixed ability classes, on achievement in any curriculum area and actually slightly negative effects in social studies.[12] Similarly, when data were separated by ability group, no one ability level was found to benefit more than any other. An earlier meta-analysis of 51 studies by Kulik and Kulik[13] also found little consistent effect of streaming on academic performance and the overall average effect was negligible. There were some positive effects, however, for fairly specific programmes of study for gifted students but these seem to be due to the markedly enriched curriculum experiences these students encountered, rather than anything to do with the composition of the class. Consistent with this interpretation were the results of a later meta-analysis of a range of different forms of ability grouping in which Kulik and Kulik[14] reported little effect of ability grouping (streaming and setting) on achievement but only when there was little variation in instructional experience. When the instructional experience varied by ability group, the effects were more marked in favour of ability grouping, particularly for high ability students.

Since these meta-analyses were undertaken, there have been a number of naturalistic studies (a technique that involves observing people in their natural environment) that have examined tracking where the classes also undertake a different curriculum matched to the students' ability. Under these circumstances, students in high ability classes benefit from ability grouping but low ability students do much worse and actually fare better in mixed ability classrooms.[15,16] These results are similar to those found by the PISA studies. The effects can almost entirely be attributed to differential access to an enriched or accelerated curriculum combined with the ability grouping of the class.

Setting

Relatively few studies have examined the effect of setting or 'regrouping' on pupils' academic performance, largely because tracking and streaming are most widely used in the USA and previously within the UK (up until the early 1970s). Setting offers the advantage of greater accuracy in group placement, a match with the level of instruction offered and some flexibility in reassignment, especially when the curriculum and pace of instruction are similar across groups.

Studies undertaken since the publication of the 1997 *Excellence in Schools* White Paper suggest that, in England, setting in primary school is most likely for mathematics followed by literacy and then science.[17] A recent study suggests that 37 per cent of primary schoolchildren experience setting in either mathematics or literacy or in both subjects.[18]

In his 'best-evidence' synthesis, Slavin reported inconclusive findings relative to the use of 'regrouping' (setting) at primary level, largely because of the absence of studies that met the strict methodological requirements of the review. However, of the seven studies he examined, five showed positive effects in favour of ability grouping in reading and/or mathematics and one study found in favour of mixed ability classes. Slavin concluded that regrouping can be successful when instruction is substantially adjusted to match the ability level but has little impact when this procedure is not undertaken. Further evidence in favour of this conclusion comes from his analysis of 14 studies evaluating the impact of the 'Joplin Plan'. This is a form of grouping by achievement for reading but which is regardless of age and thus involves pupils potentially working in mixed age classes. Slavin reports an overall effect markedly in favour of this form of ability grouping with a moderate effect size of +.45. Studies were of good quality and all were in place for at least one year and some for three years, thus removing the possibility that the effects were due to the novelty of the arrangement.

Few impact studies have been carried out on setting in UK primary schools. One large scale study of over 14 000 pupils aged between seven and nine suggested that performance in mathematics was greater for pupils of all ability levels that had experienced mixed ability classes than those pupils who had experienced some form of setting by ability.[19]

Setting is the most prevalent form of ability grouping used in UK secondary schools. Its use increased during the 1980s with estimates suggesting that by the early 1990s over 80 per cent of schools used setting for at least two curriculum areas at the end of Key Stage 3 and 63 per cent for at least four. A more recent survey suggests that 94 per cent of students aged between 11 and 16 reported that they are set by ability for one curriculum area and 64 per cent reported setting for all core curriculum subjects.[20] Despite its prevalence, there are only a few studies of setting at secondary level, largely because this arrangement is not widely used in the USA.

In a substantial longitudinal study of setting in 45 comprehensive schools in England involving some 6,000 students, Judy Ireson and Susan Hallam compared pupils who experienced mixed ability classes with those who experienced different levels of setting (from setting in a few subjects to setting for most subjects). The authors found few effects of setting on student performance in national tests of mathematics, English and science at age 13–14 and later at age 15–16 years when SES and attainment at the end of primary school were controlled for.[21,22] However, low ability students made slightly less progress in mathematics by the end of Key Stage 3 (aged 13–14) when put in ability groups compared with students in mixed ability classes and high ability students made slightly more progress when they were in sets. Similarly, Dylan Wiliam and Hannah Bartholomew in a study of six secondary schools reported a similar divergence between students in high and low ability mathematics sets. Those in the high ability sets made greater progress while those in the low ability sets dropped further and further behind.[23]

Within-class ability grouping

With much of researchers' attention focused on the effects of streaming and setting, it is only relatively recently that an interest in within-class grouping has surfaced. Ability grouping within classes is a main form of differentiation used in British primary schools, especially since the introduction of the literacy and numeracy strategies in the late 1990s.

Grouping practices within classes hold a number of advantages over the other forms of ability grouping discussed so far. The main advantage is that within-class grouping can be more closely connected to learning and teaching objectives. They also offer greater flexibility in reassignment of students and greater opportunity for sustained interaction with teachers and peers. There is increasing interest in studying the nature and use of grouping practices for different teaching and learning objectives.[24]

Estimates on the use of within-class ability grouping in English primary schools suggest that around 60 per cent of pupils sit with other pupils of a similar ability. Within-class ability grouping was more likely in core curriculum areas but even in the non-core subjects, approximately 50 per cent of students were ability grouped. In secondary schools, the prevalence of within-class ability grouping was less clear.[25]

Within-class grouping has been considered by a number of meta-analyses of effects at primary school level and these tend to indicate that ability grouping within classes may have moderate effects on attainment when compared to no grouping or mixed ability grouping. This is especially the case when used with an enhanced curriculum (e.g. for use with gifted students). Slavin reported that within-class ability grouping in primary school mathematics was related to higher performance in all eight studies considered with an effect size of +.34, as well as in other subject areas. However, the number of studies considered overall was small and thus it is difficult to generalize from such findings. In another analysis, Yipping Lou and colleagues reported that students in mathematics and science benefited equally from homogeneous and heterogeneous within-class ability grouping but found moderately in favour of ability grouping for reading instruction.[26] Similar to other findings for ability grouping, low ability students appear to benefit more from mixed ability grouping while high ability students benefit equally from both approaches. Unfortunately, the evidence in favour of ability grouping within classrooms is variable with some studies reporting marked effects while others report weaker effects. These variable findings might be explained by the possible different purposes for which these groups can be used. For example, in some instances, students in ability groups may have been given work to do independently; in other scenarios, students may be instructed by teachers/adults. Within-class grouping can also be used for peer co-learning (including peer tutoring, cooperative and collaborative learning). These infrequently used strategies involve pupils tutoring, helping and supporting each other or working collaboratively as part of a team and independently of adults. Under these circumstances, mixed ability groups are preferred for academic and social reasons, though even here there are suggestions that some effort to reduce the variability in attainment within the group can be helpful. Noreen Webb at the University of California suggests that mixing low and middle ability students and middle and high ability students can help overcome some of the problems associated with using strict ability grouping or very wide mixed ability grouping for cooperative or collaborative learning activities.[27] Such an approach can mean that the more able students do not get frustrated by having to work with very low ability peers and that the context is less intimidating for the less able. But, most importantly, this approach can ensure that a range of perspectives and conceptual understandings remain present within the group and thus enabling children to learn from each other.

Mixed ability groups promote the use of elaboration, explanation and collaborative discussion between peers – all essential ingredients for developing high level understanding and high level thinking skills.[28] Homogeneous ability groups are less likely to facilitate these forms of talk possibly because all participants have similar understandings or assume that others already have these understandings.

Summary of effects on attainment

Evidence so far, therefore, suggests that setting or streaming alone tend not to have a greater impact on academic performance than heterogeneous grouping. It is only when educators begin to combine ability grouping with a differentiated curriculum and/or instructional methods that they begin to have an effect. Importantly, the overall average effect (for all students) seems to be negligible or against ability grouping. Focusing on particular groups of students, however, indicates that high ability groups benefit from the enriched or accelerated curriculum. More worryingly, lower ability students are negatively affected by an adjusted curriculum. But why is this the case when schools and teachers try so hard to meet the needs of students of all abilities? We explore some of the suggested reasons in the next section.

Other effects of ability grouping

A number of studies have found that other factors can change when an ability grouped system is in place, and these may explain some of the different findings associated with pupils' academic attainment and progress. Given the above conclusions and in an effort to seek explanations for some of the varied effects on performance, it is useful to consider how ability grouping may affect other factors in the school and the classroom environment.

Teaching and learning

The nature of teaching and learning within classes can vary quite dramatically between groups of high, middle and low ability students. This, of course, is part of the point of homogeneous ability grouping and is arguably part and parcel of trying to deploy resources strategically and to adapt practices to maximize the benefit for students of differing ability. However, some studies suggest that these good intentions result in teaching and learning practices of variable quality.

Much research highlights the low level, conceptually weak and fragmented nature of teaching and learning in low ability groups. Work is more structured, slow and repetitive and thus is tedious for those who may need to be inspired by education. Jo Boaler and colleagues undertook research into ability grouping practices in mathematics across six schools. They found that in low ability groups activities rarely involved the use of analytical skills or fostered creativity or independence. In contrast, students in high ability classes experienced sustained, responsive and interactive teaching, and challenging activities that encouraged analytical thinking.[29] That said, the pace of curriculum coverage in high ability classes was found to be too fast, so that students had difficulty developing a detailed or long-lasting understanding of the material.

One main appeal of the use of streaming or setting is that it allows more whole class teaching and thus makes the planning of lessons easier for teachers. But it is rare that students in a class are at the exact same level and a 'one-size-fits-all' approach to teaching will hold back some students and be too advanced for others. Such an approach can lead to a greater disparity in the academic performance across sets when students are taught in a primarily traditional way as opposed to an approach involving individualized teaching and within-class ability grouping.[30] A disparity between sets can make it even harder for students to move between them as they have so much to catch up.

Another issue is that schools may tend to allocate the most knowledgeable and experienced teachers to the high ability groups and the less knowledgeable or experienced teachers to the low ability and difficult classes.[31,32] On the face of it, this approach seems like common sense; there is no point in putting the least knowledgeable teachers with the most able students. But lower ability groups will be better served by teachers who are experienced and knowledgeable and who can provide rich learning experiences that are creative and inspiring. Such teachers may also have a better grasp of strategies for behaviour management and will be better placed to handle the concentration of pupils with behaviour problems that often exist in lower ability classes.[33]

Teacher expectations

Another factor that can explain the different experiences pupils have in high, middle and low ability groups are school and teacher expectations.[34] School expectations are reflected in curriculum and examination demands; for example, in the UK it is common for high ability streams and sets to be entered for GCSE examinations in some core subjects a year early. Similarly, schools implicitly convey greater value to students in the higher sets or streams and it is little wonder that students in these higher ability groups are more engaged in school and potentially feel a greater sense of school belonging.

Teacher expectations are more focused and context specific and are communicated through teacher–student interactions within the classroom and these may have a significant impact on student effort and motivation. Some students thrive in the high stakes and competitive environments fostered in high ability sets, while others do not enjoy the pressure and increased attention. Similarly, some students become dispirited by the low expectations evident in the middle and lower sets and eventually switch off.

Teacher expectations are also reflected in the teaching and learning practices adopted by teachers. Lower expectations may lead to less inspired and engaging approaches to teaching and learning. Of particular importance to this discussion is the compelling research finding that students placed in sets above their assessed level of achievement make more progress than students of equivalent ability that are in ability groups at approximately the 'right' level.[35] On the other hand, placing students in groups below their level of ability tends to reduce their progress, irrespective of their attainment level. There may be multiple explanations for these effects including teacher expectations but also the student's own expectations, motivation and self-concept. Nevertheless, these findings illustrate the effects that inappropriate placement can have.

Pupils' friendships, self-concept and attitudes

Ability grouping can affect students in other ways beyond academic performance including their self-concept and beliefs about their abilities, their expectations and career aspirations but also their relationships with peers and friendships, their values, attitudes and behaviours.[36]

A controversial aspect of ability grouping is that it can affect who children make friends with. In secondary school, adolescents often look to their immediate peers to help them think about how they should see themselves, how they should behave, how they should think about learning and school. One theory, suggested over 40 years ago, proposes that ability grouping can provoke a polarization in peer cultural attitudes to school among consistently high and low ability students.[37] Although there is a tendency, even within mixed ability classrooms, for students to seek out peers that are like-minded and from similar social and economic backgrounds, ability grouping between classes, and especially streaming, makes this polarization even more likely. Polarization is particularly problematic for the lower ability classes since it can result in a counterproductive, anti-learning peer culture that can exacerbate poor behaviour and eventual alienation from school.

By way of contrast, one of the main advantages advocated by supporters of the comprehensive school system involving mixed ability classes is that it allows students from a range of different social, economic and ethnic backgrounds to mix. A number of studies have suggested that the less able and those that are disruptive are less likely to hold negative attitudes and display poor behaviour when in the presence of more able peers within mixed ability classroom structures.[38]

Conclusions

Ability grouping has been the subject of much research both in the USA and the UK and, more recently, through international comparison studies. Highly controlled studies suggest that ability grouping alone and without other adjustments, for example, in curriculum or instructional approach, has little overall effect on students' academic performance. On the other hand, naturalistic and international comparison studies suggest that ability grouping can lead to a range of other differences between ability groups and these can come together to create a detrimental overall average effect on student performance. Ability grouping has a differential effect on achievement and progress for different ability groups.

We have seen how adjustments to the curriculum and form of instruction, school and teacher expectations, teacher expertise and the influence of peers can combine to ensure that the more able pupils benefit from ability grouping, while the less able are disadvantaged by this approach. One problem, in particular, is that ability grouping fails to provide the opportunity to conquer, and arguably exacerbates, societal divisions because it also unintentionally groups students by social class, ethnicity and gender. Ability grouping can compromise the positive effects schools can potentially have on students from low SES backgrounds, particularly if introduced too early in a school career. The system of ability grouping can create an educational rut that is difficult for pupils to get out of. It is important to note that there is much variation between schools with some ensuring a fairer and more flexible approach to ability grouping than others. Nevertheless, the overall trend is against the use of ability grouping between classes.

Of the different forms of grouping, streaming and tracking are particularly problematic given their over general approach to student allocation for all subjects, the immediate constraints put on progress and the lack of flexibility in moving from one stream to another. Setting is more sensitive to a student's level but even this strategy may not be enough to avoid constraining progress, powerful expectation effects and a tendency for teachers to teach to the average level. Movement up or down a stream or set usually only takes place at particular transition points, such as the end of a school year, by which time there may be a substantial gap between the classes creating additional difficulties. Use of within-class ability grouping and individualized/differentiated instruction, whether within mixed ability classes or within sets, enables greater flexibility and adaptability in approach. It also enables the use of alternative approaches to instruction such as peer co-learning that are enhanced by a certain level of mixed ability grouping. Pupil collaborative learning has a strong research base highlighting its value for the learning of all pupils, particularly when used strategically with other forms of teaching.[39]

These conclusions are not new. Many of the studies on ability grouping were completed more than 10 years ago and the international comparison studies are also not that recent. So why do politicians of successive governments persist in advocating selection, streaming and setting as the solution to many of the problems with education? According to the current Prime Minister, David Cameron, it is because this policy is popular with parents, though surely this is not sufficient justification for its use. More importantly, why do schools persist in the practice of ability grouping when the research evidence strongly suggests that it can constrain progress, increase inequality and alienate pupils from learning? Aside from its 'common sense' appeal, one reason is that it may actually make teaching and lesson preparation easier for teachers since they only have to teach to one particular level rather than prepare teaching at multiple levels. Furthermore, schools want to be seen to be working hard for all children and are likely to be pressed by middle-class, educated parents of more able and/or talented students to make a special effort to support their children's learning. Yet it is important to remember that some of the most educationally successful countries in the world (such as Finland and Japan) avoid grouping students by ability until around 14 years of age. These countries go to great lengths to encourage students to work to the best of their abilities (discouraging the view that there is such a thing as inherent ability – see Chapter 12) but also go to great lengths to help students keep up with their more able peers. It is notable that many of these countries also experience greater levels of equality within their societies.

So where should we go from here? Particularly important issues to understand and address, especially if ability grouping is here to stay, are the reasons why low-attaining students struggle to make progress under an ability grouped system. There is a need for new and creative ways for instructing children in the low ability sets. Expectations about what low-attaining pupils can achieve need to be greater and instructional strategies need to be motivating and engaging. To address these matters sensibly there is a need for highly experienced and well-trained teachers to teach low ability groups.

In considering alternatives to ability grouping, there is a need for an approach that is flexible, that does not create conditions that hamper or limit academic progress, but that is sensitive to, and supportive of, the changing learning needs of all pupils. Such an approach should also not be overly demanding of teachers. An important change might be to increase flexibility and sensitivity to students' level of understanding through the greater use of within-class ability grouping and differentiating work to meet the individual needs of pupils. Greater use should be made of peer co-learning since these approaches can enhance the learning of all pupils while allowing peers to act as models of behaviour, motivation and attitudes. Creating classes that preserve a mixed ability composition but also allow a reduced range in pupil attainment for a given subject may offer another solution. Forming classes for a particular subject consisting of low and middle ability students and other classes of middle and high ability students would be one approach. This might not be too dissimilar to current practices of setting in some schools. Either way, an important change would be to move away from an ability-based class organization, to avoid the labelling and expectations that go with it, and to support teachers (possibly through training) in adopting teaching approaches and expectations that do not constrain but rather support the learning needs of all pupils.

Notes

1. Mulholland, H. (2007) Cameron promises 'grammar streaming' in schools, *The Guardian Newspaper*, 18 June. Available online at www.guardian.co.uk.

2. Marrin, M. (2005) Improving schools is as easy as c-a-t, *The Sunday Times*, 23 October. Available online at www.timesonline.co.uk.
3. Oakes, J. (2005) *Keeping Track: How Schools Structure Inequality* (2nd edn). New Haven, CT: Yale University Press.
4. Organization for Economic Co-operation and Development (OECD) (2010) *PISA 2009 Results: What Makes a School Successful? – Resources, Policies and Practices* (Vol. IV). Available online at www.dx.doi.org/10.1787/9789264091559-en (accessed 12 January 2012).
5. Schoffield, J.W. (2010) International evidence on ability grouping with curriculum differentiation and the achievement gap in secondary schools, *Teachers College Record*, 112: 1492–528.
6. Benn, C. and Chitty, C. (1996) *Thirty Years On: Is Comprehensive Education Alive and Well or Struggling to Survive*? London: David Fulton Publishers.
7. OECD (2010) *PISA 2009 Results: What Makes a School Successful? – Resources, Policies and Practices* (Vol. IV). Available online at www.dx.doi.org/10.1787/9789264091559-en (accessed 12 January 2012).
8. Hanushek, E.A. and Woessmann, L. (2006) Does educational tracking affect performance and inequality? Differences-in-differences evidence across countries, *Economic Journal*, 116(510): C63–C76.
9. Parson, S. and Hallam, S. (2011) The practice of streaming and setting in UK primary schools: evidence from the Millennium Cohort Study, *Kohort*, Summer, pp. 1–2. Available online at www.cls.ioe.ac.uk/downloads/FINAL%20(web)%20Kohort%20summer%202011.pdf (accessed 12 January 2012).
10. Slavin, R. (1987) Ability grouping and student achievement in the elementary schools: a best-evidence synthesis, *Review of Educational Research*, 57: 293–336.
11. Ipsos Mori (2010) *Young People Omnibus 2010 (Wave 16): A Research Study Among 11–16 Year Olds.* Research report produced on behalf of the Sutton Trust January–April. Available online at www.suttontrust.com/research/young-people-omnibus-2010-wave-16/ (accessed 10 January 2012).
12. Slavin, R. (1990) Ability grouping in secondary schools: a best-evidence synthesis, *Review of Educational Research*, 60: 471–99.
13. Kulik, C.-L. and Kulik, J. (1982) Effects of ability grouping on secondary school students: a meta-analysis of evaluation findings, *American Educational Research Journal*, 19: 415–28.
14. Kulik, J.A. and Kulik, C.-L. (1992) Meta-analytic findings on grouping programs, *Gifted Child Quarterly*, 36: 73–77.
15. Hallinan, M.T. and Kubitschek, W.N. (1999) Curriculum differentiation and high school achievement, *Social Psychology of Education*, 2: 1–22.
16. Callahan, A.M. (2005) Tracking and high school English learners: limiting opportunity to learn, *American Educational Research Journal*, 42: 305–28.

17. Baines, E., Blatchford, P. and Kutnick, P. (2003) Grouping practices in classrooms: changing patterns over primary and secondary schooling, *International Journal of Educational Research*, 39: 9–34.
18. Parson, S. and Hallam, S. (2011) The practice of streaming and setting in UK primary schools: evidence from the Millennium Cohort Study, *Kohort*, Summer, pp. 1–2. Available online at www.cls.ioe.ac.uk/downloads/FINAL%20(web)%20Kohort%20summer%202011.pdf (accessed 12 January 2012).
19. Whitburn, J. (2001) Effective classroom organisation in primary schools: mathematics, *Oxford Review of Education*, 27: 411–28.
20. Ipsos Mori (2010) *Young People Omnibus 2010 (Wave 16): A Research Study Among 11–16 Year Olds*. Research report produced on behalf of the Sutton Trust January–April. Available online at www.suttontrust.com/research/young-people-omnibus-2010-wave-16/ (accessed 10 January 2012).
21. Ireson, J. and Hallam, S. (2001) *Ability Grouping in Education*. London: Chapman.
22. Ireson, J., Hallam, S. and Hurley, C. (2005) What are the effects of ability grouping on GCSE attainment? *British Educational Research Journal*, 31: 443–58.
23. Wiliam, D. and Bartholomew, H. (2004) It's not which school but which set you're in that matters: the influence of ability grouping practices on student progress in mathematics, *British Educational Research Journal*, 30: 279–95.
24. Blatchford, P., Kutnick, P., Baines, E. and Galton, M. (2003) Toward a social pedagogy of classroom group work, *International Journal of Educational Research*, 39: 153–72.
25. Baines, E., Blatchford, P. and Kutnick, P. (2003) Grouping practices in classrooms: changing patterns over primary and secondary schooling, *International Journal of Educational Research*, 39: 9–34.
26. Lou, Y., Abrami, P., Spence, J., Chambers, B., Poulsen, C. and d'Apollonia, S. (1996) Within-class grouping: a meta-analysis, *Review of Educational Research*, 66: 423–58.
27. Webb, N.M. and Palincsar, A.S. (1996) Group processes in the classroom, in D.C. Berliner and R.C. Calfee (eds) *Handbook of Educational Psychology*, pp. 841–73. New York: Macmillan.
28. Baines, E., Rubie-Davies, C. and Blatchford, P. (2009) Improving pupil group work interaction and dialogue in primary classrooms: results from a year-long intervention study, *Cambridge Journal of Education*, 39(1): 95–117.
29. Boaler, J., Wiliam, D. and Brown, M. (2000) Students' experiences of ability grouping: disaffection, polarisation and the construction of failure, *British Educational Research Journal*, 26: 631–48.

30. Wiliam, D. and Bartholomew, H. (2004) It's not which school but which set you're in that matters: the influence of ability grouping practices on student progress in mathematics, *British Educational Research Journal*, 30: 279–95.
31. Boaler, J., Wiliam, D. and Brown, M. (2000) Students' experiences of ability grouping: disaffection, polarisation and the construction of failure, *British Educational Research Journal*, 26: 631–48.
32. Oakes, J. (2005) *Keeping Track: How Schools Structure Inequality* (2nd edn). New Haven, CT: Yale University Press.
33. Hargreaves, D. (1967) *Social Relations in a Secondary School.* London: Routledge & Kegan Paul.
34. Boaler, J., Wiliam, D. and Brown, M. (2000) Students' experiences of ability grouping: disaffection, polarisation and the construction of failure, *British Educational Research Journal*, 26: 631–48.
35. Ireson, J., Hallam, S. and Hurley, C. (2005) What are the effects of ability grouping on GCSE attainment? *British Educational Research Journal*, 31: 443–58.
36. Hallam, S. (2002) *Ability Grouping in Schools.* London: Institute of Education, University of London.
37. Kelly, S. and Covay, E. (2008) Curriculum tracking: reviewing the evidence on a controversial but resilient educational policy, in T. Good (ed.) *21st Century Education: A Reference Handbook*. Thousand Oaks, CA: Sage Publications.
38. Hallam, S. (2002) *Ability Grouping in Schools.* London: Institute of Education, University of London.
39. Baines, E., Blatchford, P. and Chowne, A. (2007) Improving the effectiveness of collaborative group work in primary schools: effects on science attainment. ESRC Teaching and Learning Research Programme, special issue of the *British Educational Research Journal*, 33: 663–80.

CHAPTER 4

Class size: is small better?

Peter Blatchford

The class size issue has been the subject of a huge amount of debate and coverage. The debate rears its head at regular intervals, and has been intense and at times aggressive. There are two opposed views. The first view seems the most in line with common sense. What could be more obvious: fewer pupils in a class is surely better for the pupils and for the teacher? One of the main reasons parents give for spending money on private education is that class sizes are smaller. The expectation is that small classes allow a better quality of teaching, more individual attention to pupils' individual characteristics, and a higher level of performance. Teachers are also often strongly of the view that small classes make their job easier. A survey of teachers conducted in 2009 by the Association of Teachers and Lecturers (ATL) found that almost all felt that there should be a maximum number of pupils in a class, a quarter believed that current pupil to teacher ratios were unacceptable, and the majority felt that large class sizes adversely affected pupil concentration and participation and teachers' stress levels. Christine Blower, the head of the National Union of Teachers (NUT) said in a BBC Radio 4 *Today* item on the class size topic in January 2012 that class size does matter because every extra pupil adds to the burden of a teacher.

This kind of view about the benefits of small classes has influenced policy-makers and politicians. Some educationalists, such as Chuck Achilles in the USA,[1] have argued that small classes are so important that they should be the cornerstone of education policy. In Hong Kong, as a result of mounting political pressure, the Government implemented a programme of class size reduction (CSR) in primary schools starting from 2009/10. There have been class size reduction programmes in other countries in East Asia (e.g. in mainland China, Singapore, South Korea and Japan), as well as in the USA, the Netherlands and Canada. In the UK, the Labour Government was sufficiently persuaded about the effect of class sizes that it introduced a cap of 30 in a class for children aged up to 7. The Scottish Government went even further and introduced a cap of 25 pupils in the class.

But there are powerful voices lined up against smaller classes. There is a good deal at stake for politicians and policy-makers because teachers usually represent the main element of education funding and even small reductions in class size can be extremely expensive. In the 1980s, in response to lobbying by teacher associations and local authorities to reduce class sizes, Conservative education ministers were keen to say that there was no proven link between class size and pupil achievement (though one suspects they still sent their own children to independent schools with smaller class sizes). Some politicians and policy-makers worry that teachers' arguments in favour of small classes are more about making life easier for them and strengthening teacher numbers than raising pupil performance. Some economists such as Eric Hanushek[2] have been widely quoted for his claim that reducing class sizes is not a cost-effective use of public funds and that money would be better spent in other forms of investment, in particular improving teaching quality.

The debate over class size is intensely political. As someone who has researched the topic extensively, I am often approached by policy-makers, politicians, teacher representatives, journalists and parents for my comments. Parents are often concerned about their children being in what they feel is too large a class, and want to get academic support that they can then use in lobbying the school and its governors. (I have also had a few queries from parents worried about their children being in a class that is too small and possibly too cliquey and dominated by the teacher.) Politicians, policy-makers, teacher unions and the media commonly look to research findings on class size effect for answers. What do they show?

In this chapter, I provide a review of evidence on the effects of class size. I seek to answer the question: are small classes better for pupils and teachers? We shall see that there have been two main types of research: first, research on the effects of class size on pupils' academic performance and, second, research that investigates effects on classroom processes such as teaching and pupil attention. I draw out what I think are the main conclusions from this research. I also base my views on the extensive research experience of my colleagues and me at the Institute of Education in London. I argue that some of the popular views about the effects of class size are not born out by the research evidence, but that several general conclusions can be identified. I also argue that attention now needs to move to a new type of policy-related research, which I explain nearer the end of the chapter. Given word limits this chapter is inevitably selective and concentrates on pedagogical and educational implications of class size effects. It concentrates on school-based research at primary and secondary, and has little to say about further and higher education.

What is class size?

In order to study class size effects it is first important that we obtain reliable measures of class size itself. Although this process may appear straightforward, in practice there are a number of complications. The terms 'class size', 'pupil/teacher ratios (PTRs)' and 'class size reduction (CSR)' have been used interchangeably. Class size might seem to be the most obvious and easily available measure, but the number of children actually in the class at any time may be different to the number according to the class register. PTRs are usually calculated by dividing the full-time equivalent pupils on a school's roll by the full-time equivalent number of qualified teachers, and are different to class size because they take no account, for example, of non-contact time. Given the huge increase in teaching assistants (TAs) in schools in the UK it might appear more realistic to calculate an adult/child ratio (where adults would include teaching and non-teaching staff) but this would assume that non-teaching staff were equivalent to teaching staff – an assumption that many educators and research (see below) would challenge. Although class size figures are probably more helpful as a guide to what pupils experience in schools, figures on PTRs are commonly given, and for some purposes class sizes are not available. International comparisons are often only available in terms of PTRs.

These characteristics of class size and PTR measures are not trivial because the class size experienced by a pupil on a moment-by-moment basis is the unit most likely to be influential in affecting the learning and teaching in the classroom.

The effect of class size on educational outcomes

The first, and most common, type of research has addressed whether smaller classes lead to better educational performance in pupils. There have been a number of key research projects and research reviews[3] and this section reports some of their key findings and conclusions. I also draw on a large-scale research project, carried out by the Institute of Education, which I describe below. There have been four main approaches that have been used: correlational, meta-analysis, experimental and longitudinal approaches. I briefly describe the main results from each approach.

Correlational/cross-sectional designs

This is the most obvious approach. It examines associations between class size, on the one hand, and some measure of pupil academic performance on the other. This kind of approach was used by early studies in the UK, and it also characterizes studies from an economist's perspective. Interestingly, and counter-intuitively, these studies often found that pupils in larger classes outperformed pupils in small classes. However, this type of research is potentially misleading because we often do not know whether the relationship between the 'independent variable' (in this case class size) and the 'outcome' (pupil achievement) can be explained by another, confounding factor. To list three: the results could be explained by relatively poor attaining pupils tending to be in smaller classes; teachers being forced to change their style of teaching in larger classes; or experienced (and possibly better) teachers being assigned to larger classes.

Another way of approaching associations between class size and pupil performance is to compare the educational performances of countries with different class sizes. In recent international comparisons countries with the largest class sizes – Japan and South Korea – have the highest levels of performance while countries with the smallest class sizes – for example, Italy – have the lowest levels of educational performance.[4] (Paradoxically, Asian countries with the highest performance have recently been pushing for small class sizes – partly fuelled by evidence from Western countries where results are far less impressive!) Though intriguing, global international comparisons of this sort are fraught with many methodological caveats (e.g. not controlling for other potentially influential factors in pupil achievement levels), and the, often counter-intuitive, results might be attributable to a host of cultural, educational and economic differences.

Meta-analyses and other reviews

One of the main efforts to arrive at coherent evidence on the effects of class size on pupil outcomes has been through reviews of the research literature. There have several different types of reviews: general narrative,[5] meta-analyses,[6] and 'best evidence'[7]. Glass et al.'s meta-analysis was influential at the time it was published in the 1970s. It involved taking the results from 77 studies and calculating overall effects using a common metric for each study. Results showed that effects on attainment increased as class size decreased, with the largest effects for classes smaller than 20. However, results are difficult to interpret because conclusions will inevitably depend on the quality of the studies included, and some of these are suspect as Bob Slavin's review[8] points out.

Another frequently used method of evaluating the effects of class size and CSR is to compare them with other initiatives in terms of their effects on pupils' attainments. A number of authors conclude that class reductions are less effective than other and less costly alternative reforms.[9] A recent review conducted for the Department for Education (DfE)[10] makes this one of its main conclusions about the effects of class size, and this is one of the main arguments of those who argue that small classes are not important. However, one needs to be careful with this kind of comparison. It is not a fair test in the sense that educational initiatives, with which CSR is often compared – such as one-to-one tutoring, peer tutoring and computer-assisted learning – are distinctive *methods* of teaching, while CSR merely sets limits on the numbers of pupils in a class involved. To be a fair test we would need to also take into account what teaching and instruction would be appropriate in classes of different sizes. I return to this point at the end of the chapter.

Experimental studies

The difficulty with simple correlational research, as we have seen, is that it cannot overcome the problem that an extraneous factor might explain the results. In other words, it could be something about the kinds of pupils (or teachers) in small or large classes, which might explain any differences found. Another way of expressing this point is to say that the allocation of pupils and teachers to classes of different sizes may be non-random, and, therefore, biased.

To overcome this important problem, it is often argued that experimental designs should be used in which pupils and teachers are randomly assigned to classes of different sizes. If this allocation is done properly, then any relationships between class size and later differences in pupils' academic performance in classes of a different size must be attributable to class size and not to any other factor. It should be no surprise that studies of this sort are so rare in educational research because they are fraught with ethical problems (imagine having to explain to parents that their child will this year be in a larger class than others) and financial problems (a few years ago, Peter Mortimore and I designed a possible UK experimental study but because smaller classes inevitably involve hiring more teachers and possibly creating more classrooms, it was prohibitively expensive). This is one reason for the high profile achieved by the STAR research in Tennessee. The principal investigators, who included Chuck Achilles and Jeremy Finn, and state politicians and teacher representatives, set up a study with a bold experimental design involving the random allocation of pupils and teachers to three types of classes in the same school: 'small' classes (13–17), 'regular' classes (22–25) and 'regular' with full-time teacher aide. The project involved over 7,000 pupils in 79 schools and students who were followed from kindergarten (aged 5) to third grade (aged 8). Pupils in small classes performed significantly better than pupils in regular classes and gains were still evident after Grade 4, when pupils returned to normal class sizes.

The STAR project was an important and timely study and results have provided the basis for a number of educational initiatives and policies in the USA and other countries. There have been criticisms; for example, student attrition from the study, the lack of pupil baseline data, and the possible effect of the allocation to experimental conditions on the validity of conclusions, but later reanalyses tend to support the main findings.

There have also been several other research projects in the USA (the main ones are SAGE, Primetime, California – see reviews in footnote 3). The strongest of these – SAGE – produced positive effects on pupil academic outcomes, but results are difficult to interpret because the study involved changes to pupil/teacher ratios rather than class size reductions, and this was only one of several educational interventions, so it is not clear what caused any effects on pupil outcomes. Overall, results from these studies are not conclusive.[11]

Longitudinal correlational studies

Despite the common view that they provide the gold standard of evidence in the social sciences, experimental designs can have some often overlooked limitations (e.g. not covering the full range of class sizes, and unintended effects of assignment to small or larger classes on the attitudes and behaviour of participants). An alternative, and possibly more valid, approach is to examine relationships between class size and pupil academic outcomes, as they occur in the real world, and to make adjustments for potentially confounding factors such as pupils' prior attainment, level of poverty, teacher characteristics and so on. This was the approach adopted by a large-scale study in the UK (the Class Size and Pupil Adult Ratio (CSPAR) project), which I directed. This study used a longitudinal, naturalistic design and studied the effect of class size on pupils' academic attainment, and also classroom processes such as teaching and pupil attention.[12] We tracked over 10 000 pupils in over 300 schools from school entry (at 4/5 years) to the end of the primary school stage (11 years). There was a clear effect of class size on children's academic attainment over the first year of school (4/5 years), in both literacy and mathematics, even after adjusting for other possible confounding factors. The effect sizes were comparable to that reported by the STAR project. The relationship between class size and first (reception) year progress in literacy varied for pupils of differing baseline attainment (bottom 25 per cent, middle 50 per cent and top 25 per cent). As class size got smaller, there was a statistically significant increase in attainment for all three groups, though the effect was larger for pupils with lower baseline attainment. Effects were still evident on literacy progress at the end of the second year of school (Year 1), though by the end of the third year the effects were not clear. There were no clear longer-term effects of class size differences on mathematics achievement. Though this finding indicates that the early benefits 'wash out' after two years in school, there were no restrictions in terms of which size of class they moved to from year to year. In other results it was also found that moving to a class of a different size, especially a larger class, had a negative 'disruption' effect on students' academic progress.

Although sophisticated, the CSPAR was still essentially correlational in design and so one cannot be exactly sure about causal direction. However, key potentially confounding variables were controlled for and one can be fairly confident that results reveal an *independent* effect of class size on pupil attainment – that is, that smaller classes lead to higher academic attainment – over and above other variables.

Some conclusions about class size effects on attainment

As a way of summarizing research on the effects of class size on student academic outcomes, several general conclusions can be identified.

Who benefits most?

One of the clearest findings, as seen in both the experimental STAR project and the longitudinal CSPAR study (probably the best designed studies in this field), is that the effects of class size on academic outcomes are clearest with the youngest students. This finding offers support for policies involving CSR in the first years of school. There is little or no evidence that class size reduction by itself benefits students later in their school careers.

Benefits for how long?

There is debate about the long-term benefits of CSR, which mirrors similar debates about the long-term effects of pre-school education. In the STAR project, effects lasted after the four-year intervention, once students had re-entered normal class sizes (i.e. after Grade 3). But some re-analyses of the STAR data suggest that the main effects were actually in the first year of the study and effects thereafter were minimal.[13] In the CSPAR study, as we have seen, effects were evident in the first and second years only, and this suggests effects 'wash out' after two years in school, though, as described above, children in this study (in contrast with the STAR project) were not restricted in terms of which size of class they moved to from year to year.

Threshold effects?

One issue that often comes up when considering the effects of class size is whether there is an optimal number in a class in terms of pupil attainment. A common interpretation of the research evidence is that class size only has an impact when there are fewer than 20 pupils in a class. This view was repeated in January 2012 in the Radio 4 *Today* programme discussion referred to earlier. I do not think this view is justified by the research evidence. The selection of 20 as the threshold seems to have its origins in the Glass review, which we have seen is widely questioned, and in the STAR project where small classes, of around 17 pupils on average, were compared with a larger comparison group, of around 23 on average. Small wonder that 20 in the class comes out as a significant tipping point because this happens to be the midpoint between 17 and 23! Class sizes of 17 are uncommon in many countries, even in the USA, and an alternative approach, as has been seen, is to examine the effects of class size as they occur naturally across the full range of class sizes, rather than presuppose class sizes likely to be important. This was the approach adopted in the CSPAR study and we found the relationship between class size and pupil progress to be fairly linear, that is, across the full distribution of classes, pupil performance tended to increase as class size decreased. The conclusion seems clear: for the youngest children in school, the smaller the class the better, and there is not an optimal class size below which effects are more marked. I have not seen any good psychological reasons advanced for a tipping point below or above which class size effects change in intensity or character. It is also likely that effects will vary between different countries, educational systems and teaching approaches. In general I think it is probably oversimplistic to talk about optimal class sizes in an exact way.

Class size and extra adults

These days, in many countries, there are many paraprofessionals in addition to teachers working in classrooms. In the UK, TAs now make up a quarter of the entire school workforce, and they spend much of their time in predominantly instructional activities with students.[14] We need therefore to consider the possible effects of adults other than the teacher in a classroom. Although positive findings have come from studies of the effectiveness of specific curriculum interventions given by TAs,[15] the largest study yet conducted on the effect of TA support on pupil academic outcomes found negative results; that is, those pupils with most support from TAs made less progress than similar pupils with less or no support, even controlling for the reasons why pupils were allocated more support in the first place (usually reflected in low initial attainment or classification of special educational need.[16] This conclusion is supported by findings from other research. It therefore seems that additional (non-teacher) staff in classes are not an adequate alternative to CSR. (See also Chapter 5.)

Measures of student 'outcomes'

Most studies of the effect of class size have looked at pupil outcomes in the main curriculum areas of literacy and mathematics. This pattern is understandable given the importance of these areas in any consideration of academic progress, but it can provide a narrow picture of class size effects. Some have noted that small classes seem to promote more positive pupil attitudes, enthusiasm, confidence and ability to learn independently, rather than narrowly defined subject domain performance, but these kinds of pupil 'outcomes' have rarely been studied in research.

It seems to me that this lack of attention to non-academic outcomes might help explain the disparity between teachers' confidence in small class effects (which is based on a wide perception of pupil functioning) and more modest results from research (which has mostly focused on academic test results).

Effects of class size in relation to classroom processes

Information on classroom processes affected by class size differences is important because without it there are difficulties in explaining effects on pupils' academic performance, and it is also difficult to offer practical guidance on how to maximize the opportunities provided by classes of different sizes. Knowledge about mediating processes might also help explain why previous research has not always found a link between class size differences and outcomes. It may be, for example, that when faced with a large class, teachers alter their style of teaching; for example, using more whole-class teaching and concentrating on a narrower range of basic topics. As a result, children's progress in these areas might not be different to children taught in smaller classes. Another possibility is that some teachers do not alter their teaching to take advantage of smaller classes and it is this reluctance that might explain why class size differences have little effect. Knowledge about mediating classroom processes is still relatively limited and this lack of clear research evidence is not helped by methodological weaknesses in much research in this area.[17]

Once again, I draw on the main reviews of research evidence, as described above. The evidence suggests that there are two main classroom processes affected by class size differences: effects on teachers and effects on pupils.

The most consistently identified classroom process affected by reduced class size is individualization of teaching and individual attention. Glass and Smith concluded that smaller classes resulted in greater teacher knowledge of pupils and frequency of one-to-one contacts between teachers and pupils. Other studies also report more individual teaching and attention in smaller classes,[18] more feedback,[19] better relationships with and knowledge of pupils[20] and more differentiation.[21]

Systematic observation techniques allow a direct and reliable method of measuring teacher attention to pupils.[22] In a Canadian study,[23] one of the few observation measures on which there were differences was the proportion of pupils addressed as individuals. This proportion increased in a linear way as class sizes decreased from 37, 30, 23 to 16. In the CSPAR, large-scale systematic observation studies conducted when pupils were aged 4/5[24] and 10/11[25] showed that at both ages, though there was a heavy reliance on whole class teaching and individual work, pupils in small classes were more likely to experience one-to-one teaching and were more often the focus of a teacher's attention. Elsewhere my colleagues and I have concluded that in smaller classes there was more likelihood of what we call 'Teacher support for learning', a main feature of which was individualized teaching in small classes.[26] In a further UK observation study, this finding was replicated, and, moreover, it was found to continue into secondary schools.[27] The connection between class size and individualization therefore seems a robust finding. There is also an indication from research, though less strong, that small classes have benefits in terms of easier classroom control and management, lower teacher stress and higher morale.

There is a good deal of evidence that pupil inattentiveness in class has negative effects on pupils' achievement[28] and studies of class size effects show that pupils in smaller classes attend more and spend more time on task, participate more, and are more absorbed in what they are doing. Finn and Achilles[29] (1999:103) argue that:

> “When class sizes are reduced, the pressure is increased for each student to participate in learning, and every student becomes more salient to the teacher. As a result, there is more instructional contact, and student learning behaviours are improved.”

Jeremy Finn and his colleagues take this argument further and claim that student classroom engagement is the key process that explains why smaller classes lead to better attainment and conclude that class size affects student engagement more than teaching.[30] More recent research in the UK[31] allowed a more complete examination of class size and pupil attentiveness across both primary and secondary years. Interestingly, there was a statistical interaction between class size and pupil attainment group (i.e. whether the pupil is from high, medium or low attainment groups) on pupil behaviour, in the sense that low-attaining pupils were far more likely to be off task in larger classes, and, conversely, more likely to benefit from smaller classes, in comparison to middle and high-attaining pupils. The research literature, therefore, suggests that class size affects individual attention and pupil engagement.

Effective teaching in small classes

The two main types of research on class size effects have, as we have seen, addressed relationships with academic outcomes and classroom processes. If class size reduction is going to be used as an educational initiative then it is important to ensure that the education provided for students is as effective as possible. First, we need to look at what might constitute effective teaching in small classes.

One view is that no special forms of teaching are required. Chuck Achilles is adamant that teachers do not need special training to teach in small classes because the benefits for teaching are an automatic consequence of reducing class size. In a phrase, small classes allow teachers to teach better.[32]

However, consistent evidence that teachers do not always change their teaching in small classes leads me to the conclusion that there is a need for teachers to carefully consider ways in which they should change their practice to make the most of having fewer pupils. In general, there are two different schools of thought about effective teaching in small classes. The first view bases its strategy on views on effective teaching more generally. Maurice Galton is clear that '[t]he "principles of effective teaching are the same in classes of all sizes"'[33] (pp.6 7). In a similar vein, another experienced classroom researcher, Caroline Evertson, has argued that CSR programmes should heed research that supports calls for the teaching of problem-solving, independent learning strategies, learner-centred classrooms and higher-order thinking skills.[34]

The second view, however, is that specific guidance about changes to teaching practices in small classes is warranted. This position is supported by evidence, as we have seen, of consistent relationships between class size and classroom processes, and evidence of the way that teachers can be resistant to change when faced with small classes. Readers will find ideas on effective teaching in small classes in a number of places.[35] My colleagues and I have argued that it would be particularly valuable to concentrate on strategies for increased personalized, appropriate instruction, in line with the research literature, but to ensure also that we do not see all the benefits of smaller classes in terms of increased opportunities for individualized teaching rather than other pedagogical approaches.[36] Worryingly, for example, we have found *less* collaborative groupwork in smaller classes, probably because teachers feel they want to concentrate on maximizing their teaching with individual pupils. This practice is unfortunate because research evidence supports the use of collaborative groupwork as part of an everyday pedagogical approach[37] and it is likely to be most effectively introduced with fewer pupils in a class (though this suggestion requires more research).

What kind of research is needed?

Despite the importance of creating an evidence base of effective teaching in small classes it has been possible to find next to no research that helps. This is a serious omission given the enormous policy and resource implications of class size. But what kind of research would be appropriate? Conclusions about the efficacy of CSR, as we have seen, are often made on the basis of comparisons with other interventions; for example, one-to-one tutoring, but this is not a fair test in the sense that CSR is not an intervention like tutoring but simply involves changing the number of people in a room, with no control over what happens in the room. We therefore need to evaluate the effect of CSR along with (though separable from) pedagogical changes that are expected to work well. To undertake this task, careful, controlled experiments would be valuable. Such studies should be based on random allocation if possible, though high-quality quasi-experimental designs would also be valuable.

Conclusion

Perhaps the most interesting feature of the class size debate is the often wide gap between professional experience – which is usually that smaller classes will tend to result in more effective teaching and pupil learning – and research evidence which, as we have seen, has been less clear about the effects of class size differences. My feeling is that this disparity is likely to have much to do with the fact that teachers have in mind a wide range of pupil attributes, covering academic achievement but also pupil attitudes to learning and behaviour, while research on the effects of class size has been mostly directed at test scores of pupil attainment in mathematics and literacy.

Nevertheless, in this chapter I have concluded on the basis of a careful review of the research evidence that class size does matter, but that it has to be seen in relation to pupils' age. The beneficial effects of smaller classes are most obvious with the youngest pupils in schools (up to about age 7 years). This conclusion is strongly suggested by perhaps the two best-designed projects, one experimental (STAR) and one naturalistic longitudinal (CSPAR). One conclusion, therefore, is that this is the age group for whom policy initiatives involving CSR should be directed. At the time of writing (January 2012) a council leader in London is seeking to encourage the raising of the legal maximum limit of 30 pupils at reception and Key Stage 1 in England. In the face of rising birth rates, and evidence from high performing Asian countries, there have also been favourable voices in the media for the setting up of very large class sizes. In my view these positions are opposed by the research evidence, and would be a retrograde step. We have also seen that extra adults in the class are not as effective as CSR and that there is little support for the idea of an optimal class size (e.g. 20 in a class).

Interestingly, research on relationships between class size and classroom processes has probably been clearer overall than that on academic outcomes. It indicates that effects are most likely on teacher individual attention towards students and student engagement in class. There is some support for the view that these effects tend to follow naturally from having fewer pupils in a class, that they extend across primary and secondary years (unlike effects on academic outcomes), and seem most marked in the case of lower-attaining pupils. Nevertheless, there is also evidence that teachers do not always change their style of teaching in small classes, and do not make the most of opportunities that small classes provide, which might explain the relatively modest effects on pupil performance found in some research.

The main point I want to end with is that the benefits of class size reduction, should they be introduced, are not likely to be maximized without attention to effective teaching in small classes. The commonly voiced argument that class size does not matter but teacher quality does is too simplistic. Posing the policy implications as being a choice between either investment in CSR or investment in teacher quality is, in my view, no more sensible than saying we should either invest in teacher training or school buildings: both are clearly important.

But just reducing class sizes and hoping for the best is not likely to be effective, and it is little surprise if some class size reduction efforts have led to little discernible impact on pupils. The main effort, now, should be in developing informed pedagogical changes in small classes. It is suggested that now is the time to invest in high-quality, adequately funded research that would systematically develop and evaluate the effectiveness of these pedagogical approaches along with CSR so that separate and combined effects can be judged. Work on this aspect has begun in earnest in East Asian countries but is lacking in Western countries. Given the enormous financial and staffing stakes involved in decisions about class size, it is vital that we move towards an evidence base that can help.

Notes

1. Achilles, C.A. (1999) *Let's Put Kids First, Finally: Getting Class Size Right.* Thousand Oaks, CA: Corwin Press; Achilles, C.A. (2000) Should class size be a cornerstone for educational policy, *The National Center on Education in the Inner Cities (CEIC) Review*, 9(2): 15, 23.
2. Hanushek, E. (2011) The economic value of higher teacher quality, *Economics of Education Review*, 30: 466–79.
3. Anderson, L. (2000) Why should reduced class size lead to increased student achievement? In M.C. Wang and J.D. Finn (eds) *How Small Classes Help Teachers Do Their Best* (pp. 3–24). Philadelphia, PA: Temple University Center for Research in Human Development and Education. Biddle, B.J. and Berliner, D.C. (2002) Small class size and its effects, *Educational Leadership*, 5(5): 12–23. (Longer review in: Biddle, B.J. and Berliner, D.C. (2002) What research says about small classes and their effects. Part of series *In pursuit of Better Schools: What Research Says.* Available online at www.WestEd.org/policyperspectives or www.edpolicyreports.org) Blatchford, P. (forthcoming) Three generations of research on class size effects, in Karen R. Harris, Steven Graham and Timothy Urdan (eds), *The American Psychological Association (APA) Educational Psychology Handbook.* Washington, DC: APA. Blatchford, P. and Mortimore, P. (1994) The issue of class size in schools: what can we learn from research? *Oxford Review of Education*, 20(4): 411–28; Blatchford, P., Goldstein, H. and Mortimore, P. (1998) Research on class size effects: a critique of methods and a way

forward, *International Journal of Educational Research*, 29: 691–710; Day, C., Tolley, H., Hadfield, M., Parkin, E. and Watling, G.R. (1996) *Class Size Research and the Quality of Education: A Critical Survey of the Literature Related to Class Size and the Quality of Teaching and Learning.* Haywards Heath: National Association of Head Teachers; Ehrenberg, R.G., Brewer, D.J., Gamoran, A. and Willms, J.D. (2001) Class size and student achievement, *Psychological Science in the Public Interest*, 2(1): 1–30; Finn, J.D., Pannozzo, G.M. and Achilles, C.M. (2003) The 'why's' of class size: student behaviour in small classes, *Review of Educational Research*, 73(3):321–68; Galton, M. (1998) Class size: a critical comment on the research, *International Journal of Educational Research*, 29: 809–18; Grissmer, D. (1999) Class size effects: Assessing the evidence, its policy implications, and future research agenda, *Educational Evaluation and Policy Analysis*, 21(2): 231–48; Hattie, J. (2005) The paradox of reducing class size and improving learning outcomes, *International Journal of Educational Research*, 43: 387–425; Wilson, V. (2006) *Does Small Really Make a Difference? An Update. A Review of the Literature on the Effects of Class Size on Teaching Practice and Pupils' Behavior and Attainment.* Scottish Council for Research in Education (SCRE) Centre: University of Glasgow.

4. Department for Education (DfE) (2011) Class size and education in England evidence report. Research Report DFE-RR169.
5. Biddle, B.J. and Berliner, D.C. (2002) Small class size and its effects, *Educational Leadership* 5(5): 12–23.
6. Glass, G.V. and Smith, M.L. (1978) *Meta-analysis of Research on the Relationship of Class Size and Achievement.* San Francisco: Far West Laboratory for Educational Research and Development.
7. Slavin, R.E. (1989) Class size and student achievement: small effects of small classes, *Educational Psychologist*, 24(1): 99–110.
8. Slavin, R.E. (1989) Class size and student achievement: small effects of small classes, *Educational Psychologist*, 24(1): 99–110.
9. Hattie, J. (2005) The paradox of reducing class size and improving learning outcomes, *International Journal of Educational Research*, 43: 387–425; Robinson, G.E. (1990) Synthesis of research on the effects of class size, *Educational Leadership*, 47(7): 80–90; Slavin, R.E. (1989) Class size and student achievement: small effects of small classes, *Educational Psychologist*, 24(1): 99–110.
10. Department for Education (DfE) (2011) Class size and education in England evidence report. Research Report DFE-RR169.
11. Ehrenberg, R.G., Brewer, D.J., Gamoran, A. and Willms, J.D. (2001) Class size and student achievement, *Psychological Science in the Public Interest*, 2(1): 1–30.
12. Blatchford, P. (2003) *The Class Size Debate: Is Small Better?* Maidenhead: Open University Press; Blatchford, P., Bassett, P., Goldstein, H. and Martin,

C. (2003) Are class size differences related to pupils' educational progress and classroom processes? Findings from the Institute of Education Class Size Study of children aged 5–7 Years, *British Educational Research Journal*, 29(5): 709–30. Special Issue 'In Praise of Educational Research', Guest editors: S. Gorrard, C. Taylor and K. Roberts.

13. Ehrenberg, R.G., Brewer, D.J., Gamoran, A. and Willms, J.D. (2001) Class size and student achievement, *Psychological Science in the Public Interest*, 2(1): 1–30.
14. Blatchford, P., Russell, A. and Webster, R. (2012) *Reassessing the Impact of Teaching Assistants: How Research Challenges Practice and Policy.* Abingdon, UK: Routledge.
15. Alborz, A., Pearson, D., Farrell, P. and Howes, A. (2009) *The Impact of Adult Support Staff on Pupils and Mainstream Schools.* London: Department for Children, Schools and Families and Institute of Education.
16. Blatchford, P., Russell, A. and Webster, R. (2012) *Reassessing the Impact of Teaching Assistants: How Research Challenges Practice and Policy.* Abingdon, UK: Routledge.
17. Finn, J.D., Pannozzo, G.M. and Achilles, C.M. (2003) The 'why's' of class size: student behaviour in small classes, *Review of Educational Research*, 73(3): 321–68.
18. Bain, H. and Achilles, C.M. (1986) Interesting developments on class size, *Phi Delta Kappan*, 67(9): 662–5; Harder, H. (1990) A critical look at reduced class size, *Contemporary Education*, 62(1): 28–30; Turner, C.M. (1990) Prime time: a reflection, *Contemporary Education*, 62(1): 24–27.
19. Bain, H. and Achilles, C.M. (1986) Interesting developments on class size, *Phi Delta Kappan*, 67(9): 662–5; Cooper, H. M. (1989) Does reducing student-to-teacher ratios affect achievement? *Educational Psychologist*, 24(1): 79–98.
20. Finn, J.D., Pannozzo, G.M. and Achilles, C.M. (2003) The 'why's' of class size: student behaviour in small classes, *Review of Educational Research*, 73(3): 321–68.
21. Anderson, L. (2000) Why should reduced class size lead to increased student achievement? In M.C. Wang and J.D. Finn (eds) *How Small Classes Help Teachers Do Their Best* (pp. 3–24). Philadelphia, PA: Temple University Center for Research in Human Development and Education.
22. Finn, J.D., Pannozzo, G.M. and Achilles, C.M. (2003) The 'why's' of class size: student behaviour in small classes, *Review of Educational Research*, 73(3): 321–68.
23. Shapson, S.M., Wright, E.N., Eason, G. and Fitzgerald, J. (1980) An experimental study of the effects of class size, *American Educational Research Journal*, 17: 144–52.
24. Blatchford, P. (2003a) *The Class Size Debate: Is Small Better?* Maidenhead: Open University Press.

25. Blatchford, P., Bassett, P. and Brown, P. (2005) Teachers' and pupils' behaviour in large and small classes: a systematic observation study of pupils aged 10/11 years, *Journal of Educational Psychology*, 97(3): 454–67.
26. Blatchford, P., Moriarty, V., Edmonds, S. and Martin, C. (2002) Relationships between class size and teaching: a multi-method analysis of English infant schools, *American Educational Research Journal*, 39(1): 101–32.
27. Blatchford, P., Bassett, P. and Brown, P. (2011) Examining the effect of class size on classroom engagement and teacher-pupil interaction: differences in relation to prior pupil attainment and primary vs. secondary schools, *Learning and Instruction*, 21: 715–30.
28. Creemers, B. (1994) *The Effective Classroom*. London: Cassell; Lan, X., Cameron Ponitz, C., Miller, K.F., Li, S., Cortina, K., Perry, M. and Fang, G. (2009) Keeping their attention: classroom practices associated with behavioural engagement in first grade mathematics classes in China and the United States, *Early Childhood Research Quarterly*, 24: 198–211; Rowe, K.J. (1995) Factors affecting students' progress in reading: key findings from a longitudinal study, *Literacy, Teaching and Learning*, 1(2): 57–110.
29. Finn, J.D. and Achilles, C.M. (1999) Tennessee's class size study: findings, implications, misconceptions, *Educational Evaluation and Policy Analysis*, 21(2): 97–109.
30. Finn, J.D., Pannozzo, G.M. and Achilles, C.M. (2003) The 'why's' of class size: student behaviour in small classes, *Review of Educational Research*, 73(3): 321–68.
31. Blatchford, P., Bassett, P. and Brown, P. (2011) Examining the effect of class size on classroom engagement and teacher-pupil interaction: differences in relation to prior pupil attainment and primary vs. secondary schools, *Learning and Instruction*, 21: 715–30.
32. Achilles, C.A. (1999) *Let's Put Kids First, Finally: Getting Class Size Right*. Thousand Oaks, CA: Corwin Press.
33. Galton, M. and Pell, T. (2010) Study on class teaching in primary schools In Hong Kong: Final Report, University of Cambridge.
34. Evertson, C.M. (2000) Professional development and implementation of class size reduction, *The National Center on Education in the Inner Cities (CEIC) Review*, 9(2): 8.
35. Wang, M.C. and Finn, J.D. (eds) (2002) *How Small Classes Help Teachers Do Their Best*. Philadelphia, PA: Temple University Center for Research in Human Development and Education; Finn, J.D. and Wang, M.C. (2002) *Taking Small Classes One Step Further*. Information Age Publishing, Greenwich, Connecticut and Laboratory for Student Success; *National Center on Education in the Inner Cities (CEIC) Review* (2000). Temple University Center for Research in Human Development and Education, Temple University, Cecil B. Moore Avenue, Philadelphia, PA.

36. Blatchford, P., Russell, A., Bassett, P., Brown, P. and Martin, C. (2007) The effect of class size on the teaching of pupils aged 7–11 years, *School Effectiveness and Improvement*, 18(2): 147–72.
37. Baines, E., Blatchford, P. and Chowne, A. (2007) Improving the effectiveness of collaborative group work in primary schools: effects on science attainment, *British Educational Research Journal*, 33(5): 663–80.

CHAPTER 5 Supporting learning?: How effective are teaching assistants?

Rob Webster and Peter Blatchford

Introduction

The huge and unprecedented increase in teaching assistants (TAs) is one of the most profound changes to have taken place in UK schools over the past two decades. This rise in numbers of TAs can be seen as part of a general increase in education paraprofessionals with similar roles worldwide. Schools in Australia, Italy, Sweden, Canada, Finland, Germany, Hong Kong, Iceland, Ireland, Malta, South Africa, as well as the USA, have experienced similar increases in paraprofessionals.[1] Yet no other education system in the world has expanded both the number and role of its paraprofessionals to quite the same extent as the systems in England and Wales. (They are also known as 'learning support assistants' and 'classroom assistants' in the UK and in the USA; the titles 'teacher aides' and 'paraeducators' are commonplace. In this chapter, we refer to all those with equivalent classroom-based support roles collectively as TAs.)

The number of full-time equivalent TAs in mainstream schools in England alone has more than trebled since 1997 to about 190 000 in 2011. In all, TAs comprise a quarter of the workforce in English and Welsh mainstream schools.[2] Around 6 per cent of TAs are 'higher level' TAs. The expansion of the TA workforce represents a considerable investment of public money. According to government data in 2008/09 £4.1 billion was spent on TAs and other education support staff.[3]

In this chapter we critically examine the evidence of the impact of TAs, drawing heavily on the results from the recent Deployment and Impact of Support Staff (DISS) project. First though, we look briefly at the two main drivers that have led to the huge growth in TA numbers in English and Welsh schools: (1) the drive to include greater numbers of pupils with Special Educational Needs (SEN) in mainstream education; and (2) policy aimed at remodelling the school workforce.

Inclusion

The idea that TAs could help schools meet the needs and demands of including pupils with SEN and disabilities can be traced back to the Plowden Report of 1967. But the idea really took off in 1994 with the introduction of the government's *SEN Code of Practice*, which promoted the idea of employing TAs to help pupils who had an individual education plan or a statement of SEN. These documents set out bespoke provisions such as curricular interventions and, where appropriate, remedial therapies. By 2000, the proportion of statemented pupils being educated in special schools in England had decreased from around half to around one third.[4]

Furthermore, since 2000, there has been a steady increase in the number of pupils with SEN who do *not* have a statement. These pupils are currently categorized as either School Action or School Action Plus. Government data show that in 2003, the proportion of pupils with SEN (with and without a statement) in mainstream schools in England was 16.6 per cent; the corresponding figure for 2010 was 20.7 per cent.[5] Given that TAs and the number of pupils with SEN have both increased, it is perhaps no surprise that they have – as we shall see – become interconnected.

School workforce remodelling

During the mid-to-late 1990s, the performance culture in education and the public sector at large, along with the heavily bureaucratic processes that accompanied it, were a major contributing factor to increased teacher workload and feelings of pressure. This strain inevitably affected teacher recruitment and retention, so much so that the government commissioned the consultancy firm Pricewaterhouse Cooper (PwC) to conduct an independent review to investigate.

PwC recommended that central to 'a programme of practical action to eliminate excessive workload and . . . raise standards of pupil achievement' was the 'extension of the support staff role'.[6] The then education secretary Estelle Morris developed this theme, envisioning TAs 'supervising classes that are undertaking work set by a teacher, or working with small groups of pupils on reading practice', as part of a remodelled school workforce.[7]

In its 2001 White Paper, *Schools: Achieving Success*, the government heralded TAs as 'central to what has been achieved so far in raising standards', in terms of 'provid[ing] high quality daily teaching in the basics', and set out formal proposals to greatly increase their number.

In January 2003, *The National Agreement: Raising Standards and Tackling Workload*, was signed by the government and all but one of the unions representing teachers and support staff. The agreement introduced a series of measures designed to 'tackle workload', such as employing and deploying TAs to take on teachers' routine, clerical tasks and cover short-term teacher absences, which in turn would allow teachers to 'raise standards' by allowing them to spend more time on planning and assessment.

Assumptions about the impact of teaching assistants

There are two main assumptions that flow from the ways in which schools deploy TAs in service of the inclusion and workforce remodelling agendas: (1) that support from TAs leads to positive outcomes for pupils, particularly lower-attaining pupils and those with SEN; and (2) that there are positive effects for teachers. There has until recently been very little research on the impact of TAs and the support they provide. We now look at the research evidence that does exist to help us determine the veracity of these assumptions.

Assumption 1: Support from TAs has a positive impact on pupil outcomes

Learning outcomes

The majority of what little evidence there is on TAs' impact on learning, reported in systematic reviews and syntheses of evidence,[8] tends to focus on curriculum intervention studies aimed at improving the academic progress of lower-attaining pupils and those with SEN. The broad conclusion we can draw from experimental studies that examined the effect of TAs who have a pedagogical role delivering specific curricular interventions (mostly for literacy) is that TAs tend to have a direct positive impact on pupil progress when they are prepared and trained, and have support and guidance from teachers and the school about practice. However, the data also shows that these kinds of curricular interventions (which are not always well-planned) account for only around 30–40 minutes of a TA's day,[9] and are not at all typical of how TAs are used for the majority of the day.

So what about the rest of the time? What effect does TA support have on pupil learning in normal, everyday circumstances; that is, the contexts within which they spend most of their time? The best data we have on this comes from the largest study of TAs even undertaken: the longitudinal Deployment and Impact of Support Staff (DISS) project. In contrast to much previous research on TAs, the DISS project was naturalistic in design. It did not involve a targeted intervention, nor did it examine what was possible under certain circumstances (e.g. the impact on pupil progress of TAs trained to deliver curricular interventions). Instead, it sought to capture the effects of TAs in normal everyday circumstances over the school year.

The DISS project studied effects of TA support (based on teacher estimates and measures from systematic observation) on 8,200 pupils' academic progress in English, mathematics and science. Two cohorts of pupils in seven age groups in mainstream schools were tracked over one year each. Multi-level regression methods controlled for potentially confounding factors known to affect progress (and TA support), such as pupils' SEN status, prior attainment, eligibility for free school meals, English as an additional language, deprivation, gender and ethnicity. The results were striking: for 16 of the 21 results (there were seven age groups and three subjects), support from TAs had a negative effect on progress; there were no positive effects of TA support on pupil progress over the school year in any subject or for any year group.[10] Those pupils receiving the most support from TAs made less progress than similar pupils who received little or no support from TAs. It is extremely unlikely that these results are explained by existing characteristics of pupils who received TA support, because the analysis controlled for pre-existing pupil characteristics that typically affect progress and the reason why pupils are allocated TA support, in particular SEN status and prior attainment. Furthermore, there is evidence from the DISS study that the negative effect of TA support on learning outcomes is most marked for pupils with the highest levels of need.[11]

An alternative way of conceptualizing the negative effects of TA support on pupil progress is to translate the results from the regression analyses into national curriculum levels – the commonly understood indicator of pupil attainment used in England and Wales. In general, pupils in Key Stage 2, for example, are expected to progress by three national curriculum sub-levels every two years (there are three sub-levels to one national curriculum level). Using this conversion, pupils who received the most TA support were behind their peers by just over one sub-level – which equates to about eight months – as a result of TA support. Great care should be taken over the accuracy of this kind of age equivalent calculation – not least because it depends on some questionable, general assumptions – but it does help obtain some measure of the scale of the difference in attainment between those with the most and least support from TAs.

Behavioural, emotional and social development

In addition to the effect of TAs on academic outcomes, the DISS project also assessed the effects of the amount of TA support in relation to the 'softer' types of pupil functioning in school, which we called 'positive approaches to learning'. These included distractibility, confidence, motivation, disruptiveness, independence and relationships with other pupils. The results showed little evidence that the amount of TA support pupils received over a school year improved their positive approaches to learning, except for those in Year 9 (13–14-year-olds), where there was a clear positive effect of TA support across all eight outcomes.[12] At that age, pupils with the most TA support had noticeably more positive approaches to learning.

Assumption 2: TAs have a positive impact on teachers and teaching

The DISS study found that there had been significant improvements in terms of teacher workloads, job satisfaction and levels of stress, largely as a result of TAs and other support staff taking on routine clerical tasks. As noted above, this was an anticipated outcome of the National Agreement and, as expected, helped free up teachers' time in order to concentrate on teaching and related activities. So, the contribution of TAs to meeting the first aim of the National Agreement – tackling workload – can be seen as successful.

In terms of the effects on teaching, the DISS project showed that the presence of TAs had two general beneficial effects. First, TA presence was associated with a greater amount of adult individual attention towards pupils. Second, there seemed to be benefits in terms of classroom control, with the presence of TAs leading to a reduction in the amount of talk from adults addressing negative behaviour. This is an important contribution by TAs and should not be underestimated.

Where do the assumptions about TA impact come from and why do they persist?

Largely as a result of the DISS project, a more rounded picture of TA impact on pupils' academic outcomes has begun to emerge. It is possible to offer some speculative suggestions on the origin and subsequent pervasiveness of the assumptions that underpinned the fairly rapid expansion of TAs in both number and role.

We described earlier how the drive to include greater numbers of pupils with SEN in mainstream settings led to an increase in TA recruitment. Building on the parent-helper model, many schools recruited mothers and carers to the TA positions that were created and connected to support for pupils with SEN. This 'discourse of care',[13] shows TAs' functional priorities as a predominantly nurturing role, in contrast to the educative one adopted foremost by teachers.

That schools should almost collectively arrive at the view that it should be TAs and not teachers who should work directly with lower-attaining pupils and those with SEN is itself a questionable notion, and one that seems to have grown out of convenient assumptions about impact and convenient resourcing arrangements (TAs are cheaper to employ than teachers).

When a statement of SEN is drawn up, it is frequently the case that it specifies that a TA or TAs will deliver most or all of the various provisions. This detail, we argue, has become conflated with the overall legal status of the statement itself. Secondary schools, in particular, describe being fettered by their 'legal obligation' to provide adult support for pupils with a statement in the form of TA support, despite the guidance in the 2001 *SEN Code of Practice* being quite unequivocal that such a model of support is advisory, not mandatory.[14]

The ubiquitous model of TAs working with lower-attaining pupils and those with SEN, it seems, partly informed the New Labour Government's policies on how the TAs' role could be extended as part of the school workforce remodelling reforms. It took as read that increasing the number of TAs to support such pupils would lead inexorably to improved outcomes for *all* pupils.

On the face of it, this is a common-sense view and is reflected in findings from two large-scale surveys on the *impressions* of TA impact (one being from the DISS project), which together surveyed over 7,000 teachers. Both surveys reported that teachers believed TAs (and some other support staff) had a strong effect on learning outcomes by allowing teachers more time for planning and preparation.[15] At the time, however, neither the PwC review nor the White Paper (among a number of government documents from the time) contained any systematic, clear research data to support this assumption. There was a reliance on case studies which, while they can have merit as a research tool, are not well suited to tell us anything about causality. In fact, at the time these policies, which would greatly extend the role of TAs, were being drawn up, rigorous empirical evidence on the impact of TA support on pupil attainment was so scant as to be non-existent.[16]

The assumption that support from TAs equals academic progress seems to have passed unchallenged into educational folklore via the mechanisms of practice, policy and statute. However, as we have seen, this assumption has not only turned out to be unfounded, but also, as the results from the DISS project in particular have shown, they have had a damaging effect on the learning of the most disadvantaged pupils. We can, however, explain *why* we think support from TAs has the impact it does, and in doing so, we can begin to highlight clear ways in which schools can rethink the main effects of TA deployment.

Alternative explanations for the impact of TAs on pupil outcomes

At a time when the UK education systems face closer scrutiny as expenditure is squeezed, it is perhaps not surprising that there have been strong views expressed about the appropriateness of retaining 'cost-ineffective' TAs.[17] This was no doubt fed by media headlines following the publication of the DISS project findings, such as, 'Teaching assistants blamed for poor results' (*The Daily Telegraph*) and 'Teaching assistants impair pupil performance' (*The Times Educational Supplement*). These partial views of the research represent another assumption about TA impact that we must address: that the relationship between TA support and pupils' academic progress is somehow the fault of TAs. This, as we shall now explain, is erroneous. It is far more likely that it is the organizational factors governing TAs' employment and deployment that explain the provocative impact findings.

The data collected as part of the multi-method DISS project facilitated the creation of the 'Wider Pedagogical Role' (WPR) model (presented in Figure 5.1), which summarizes and interprets other results from the study concerning the broader context within which TAs work, and factors which are likely to maximize or impede their effectiveness. The model summarizes results from the UK, but there are likely to be similarities with situations in other countries.

Characteristics of TAs, such as qualifications, are, in isolation, unlikely to account in any significant way for the negative effects of TA support. Similarly, the key finding from the DISS project relating to TAs' conditions of employment – that schools tend to rely on TAs' goodwill in

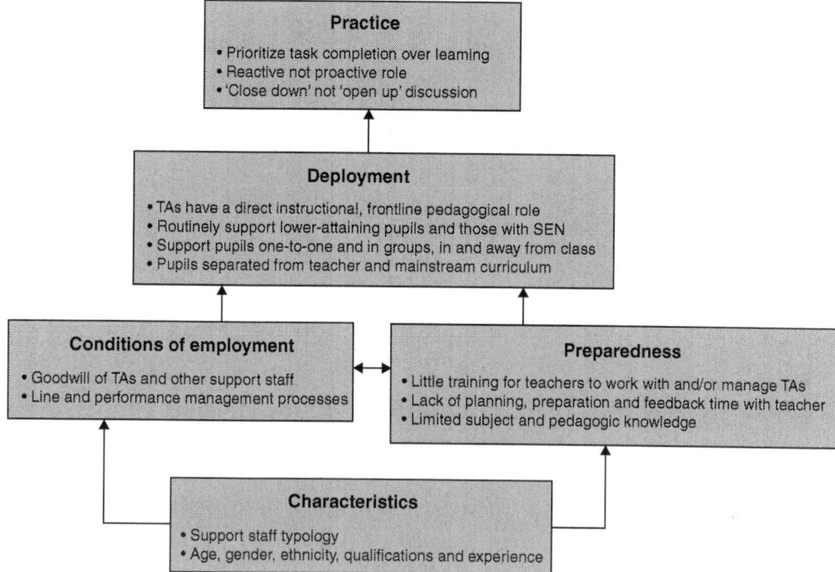

Figure 5.1 The wider pedagogical role model

order to have time to meet with teachers after school – contributes to, but does not fully explain, the impact results. We argue that it is the WPR model's core components – preparedness, deployment and practice – which have a greater bearing on TA effectiveness, and therefore provide the most fruitful explanations for their impact. We now expand on this, and begin to highlight the ways in which these components can be reconceptualized and modified, so that TAs might have a more positive impact on pupil outcomes in future.[18]

Preparedness

Preparedness concerns the DISS study's findings about the lack of training and professional development of TAs and teachers, and day-to-day aspects of planning and preparation before lessons, and feedback afterwards, which are likely to have a bearing on learning outcomes for pupils. For example, the DISS survey of over 4,000 teachers found that 75 per cent reported having had no training to help them work with TAs, and 75 per cent reported having no allocated planning or feedback time with TAs.

Deployment

The extent to which TAs have a teaching, or pedagogical, role was revealed through the analysis of over 1,600 work pattern diaries collected as part of the DISS project. These results showed that TAs spend over half their day (6.1 hours) in a direct pedagogical, instructional role, supporting and interacting with pupils (3.8 hours), and this exceeds time spent supporting the teacher and curriculum (1.4 hours) or performing other tasks (0.9 hours). This was confirmed by many hours of classroom observation made as part of the project. These observations also confirmed that the TA's role is routinely to support lower-attaining pupils and those with SEN in one-to-one and group contexts. Furthermore, findings from systematic observations revealed that such pupils were nine times more likely to have sustained (e.g. lasting longer than 10 seconds) interactions with TAs than with teachers, and that they were six times more likely to be actively involved (i.e. beginning, responding to or sustaining) an interaction with TAs than with teachers. In summary, the more severe a pupil's needs, the more interactions with a TA would increase, and interactions with a teacher decrease. These findings are in line with the unintended consequences of one-to-one paraprofessional support described by Professor Michael Giangreco[19] in the USA.

Using TAs to support pupils who have the greatest difficulty with learning and participation might seem pedagogically valuable, but it also means that TA-supported pupils become separated from the teacher and miss out on everyday teacher-to-pupil interactions and mainstream curriculum coverage (especially where TAs are given responsibility for leading curriculum interventions away from the classroom).

Practice

The DISS project showed that pupils' interactions with TAs are much lower in quality than those they have with teachers.[20] TAs are more concerned with task completion than learning, and inadequate preparation leads to TAs' interactions being reactive – or, as TAs themselves frequently described it in interviews – working 'on the hoof'. In addition, analysis of these data found that teachers generally 'open up' pupil talk, whereas TAs 'close down' talk, both linguistically and cognitively.[21]

TAs, therefore, do not at present know how to make the best use of the extended, more frequent interactions they have with pupils.

Ways forward: The Effective Deployment of Teaching Assistants project

As Michael Giangreco has succinctly argued, we would not accept a situation in which children without SEN are routinely taught by TAs instead of teachers.[22] Therefore, following the DISS project, there was a clear case for challenging the status quo regarding TA deployment in UK schools, and in particular, how, without action, the most disadvantaged children would continue to be let down by the current arrangements.

To address this situation, we worked in collaboration with 10 primary and secondary schools to set up an intervention study to address the main effects of the widespread and problematic models of TA employment and usage, by developing more effective models of deployment and preparedness. The key strength of the Effective Deployment of Teaching Assistants (EDTA) project was the way in which the WPR model provided a clear, credible and robust structuring framework for the intervention. The model is not only an explanatory framework, but also a useful organizing structure for reconfiguring the management and deployment of TAs in ways that we believe can release their huge potential. The introduction of fairer conditions of employment, improved day-to-day lesson planning, decision-making about the appropriate roles of adults in the classroom – especially with regard to meeting the needs of pupils with SEN – and a clearer purpose to TA–pupil interaction, we argue, can lead to improved educational outcomes.

The EDTA study employed an innovative methodology consisting of a developmental phase and an ongoing evaluation. The developmental phase consisted of an intervention over the school year in which participants worked through the key components of the WPR model in a series of three trials, each lasting a school term. The study adopted a within-school comparative approach, evaluating practice before and after the introduction of the trials. The evaluation sought to compare new models developed through the trials with existing models of TA deployment and teacher and TAs working together, as evidenced in pre-intervention visits. The main research question was whether involvement in the study led to more effective deployment, preparation and practice of TAs.

The evaluation of the study involved analyses of data from several sources: audits of participants' perceptions of the frequency and quality of TA preparation and training, and the ways in which teachers and TAs were deployed in the classroom; structured observations of the actions and roles of teachers and TAs in the classroom; and semi-structured interviews. The data collection tools were structured around the key components of the WPR model: preparedness, deployment and practice.

The evaluation showed that the trials conducted by each school had the overwhelming effect of improving the way school leaders and teachers thought about and deployed TAs. The prevailing refrain from the participants was one of 'no going back to the ways things were done before'. The EDTA study showed that when schools clearly understood and fully engaged with the main problems associated with the widespread and problematic models of TA preparation, deployment and practice, the true value of TAs became evident.

Not only did the project trials help to raise the status of TAs and greatly improve their confidence, but the process of developing alternative models of TA deployment prompted teachers to evaluate the impact of *their own* practice and develop a meaningful understanding of the TA role. Below, we summarize the key changes that occurred in schools and classrooms across the three WPR model dimensions.

Preparedness

Involvement in the intervention greatly improved TAs' pre-lesson preparation. The quality and clarity of teachers' lesson plans improved over the year, and reduced instances of TAs going into lessons 'blind' or relying on picking up information via teachers' whole class delivery. This also addressed TAs' sense of pressure associated with working 'on the hoof'. Teachers made more effort to meet with TAs before lessons, and some schools went further, adjusting TAs' hours of work in order to create meeting time. The creation of time to meet had a positive effect on both teachers' and TAs' perceptions of preparedness. Greater awareness of the specific issues relating to TAs' practice led to schools providing tightly focused training on pedagogical techniques.

Deployment

Having presented them with findings from observations in their own classrooms of how they deployed not only TAs, but also themselves, teachers changed their models of classroom organization. TAs worked more often with middle- and higher-attaining pupils, creating the opportunity for teachers to spend more time working with lower-attaining pupils and those with SEN. These alternative models of deployment not only reduced the occasions when TA-supported pupils were separated from the teacher, the curriculum and their peers, but also greatly improved and enriched teachers' understanding of the learning needs and progress of struggling pupils.

Involvement in the EDTA project prompted school leadership teams to think more strategically about the purpose of the TA role and the appropriateness of what is expected from them in terms of pupil outcomes. The process brought to the surface entrenched and unhelpful mindsets towards the use of TAs in general and in relation to the provision for pupils with SEN, which school leaders had begun to challenge. The positive experiences of participation in the project were used to develop and formalize new models of TA deployment, which were to be implemented across the school.

Practice

The fine-grained detail of TAs' interactions with pupils gathered in the DISS project helped teachers and TAs obtain a thorough understanding of the effects of ineffective types of talk (e.g. spoon-feeding). Following training, the quality of TAs' questioning techniques improved. Teachers also introduced strategies to support greater pupil independence and decrease dependency on adult support.

Conclusion: How effective are TAs and how effective could they be?

The EDTA study was formulated on the basis of findings from one of the most credible research studies on TA impact ever undertaken (the DISS project). While we must stop short of making any claims relating to academic progress, we are confident that the findings from this albeit small-scale study show that the type of innovative models, strategies and techniques schools developed to address the issues concerning TA preparation, deployment and practice are of the kind that are very likely to improve the efficiency and effectiveness of TAs.[23] A book of guidance for school leaders and teachers compiling the models, strategies and techniques developed in this project is currently in press.[24] That the schools involved in the study were able to make positive, and in some cases fundamental, changes to TA deployment without additional resources is also significant, given the austerity measures facing not only the UK education systems, but many more worldwide.

So, how effective are TAs? On the basis of the DISS study findings, we would have to conclude that under current arrangements, TAs are nowhere near as effective as they could be. But, as we have seen in the results of our recent developmental research, it is possible that by systematically addressing all the factors that comprise the WPR model – chiefly TAs' preparedness, deployment and practice – schools can put into place the type of systems and models of deployment that we believe can lead to a demonstrable positive impact on outcomes for all pupils.

Notes

1. Giangreco, M.F. and Doyle, M.B. (2007) Teacher assistants in inclusive schools, in L. Florian (ed.) *The SAGE Handbook of Special Education*, pp. 429–39, London: Sage Publications.
2. Department for Education (DfE) (2012) *School workforce in England (provisional) November 2011*. London: DfE.
3. Whitehorn, T. (2010) *School Support Staff Topic Paper*. London: DfE.
4. House of Commons Education and Skills Committee (2006) *Special Educational Needs Third Report of Session 2005–06* (Vol. I). London: The Stationery Office.
5. Department for Education and Skills (DfES) (2010) *Statistical First Release: Special Educational Needs in England, January 2010*. London: DfE; DfES (2005) *Statistical First Release: Special Educational Needs in England, January 2005*. London: DfES.
6. PricewaterhouseCooper (2001) *Teacher Workload Study: A Report of a Review Commissioned by the DfES*. London: PricewaterhouseCooper.
7. Morris, E. (2001) *Professionalism and Trust: The Future of Teachers and Teaching*. London: DfES/Social Market Foundation.

8. Alborz, A. et al. (2009) *The impact of adult support staff on pupils and mainstream schools*; Slavin, R.E. et al. (2009) *Effective Programs for Struggling Readers: A Best Evidence Synthesis*. London: Department for Children, Schools and Families (DCSF) and Institute of Education; Howes, A. et al. (2003) *The Impact of Paid Adult Support on the Participation and Learning of Pupils in Mainstream Schools*. London: Institute of Education, Evidence for Policy and Practice Information and Coordinating Centre.
9. Farrell, P. et al. (2010) The impact of teaching assistants on improving pupils' academic achievement in mainstream schools: a review of the literature, *Educational Review*, 62(4): 435–48; Webster, R. et al. (2011) The 'wider pedagogical role' of teaching assistants, *School Leadership and Management*, 31(1): 3–20.
10. The full results, by year group and subject, are presented in Blatchford, P., Russell, A. and Webster, R. (2012) *Reassessing the Impact of Teaching Assistants: How Research Challenges Practice and Policy*. Abingdon: Routledge; Blatchford, P. et al. (2011) The impact of support staff on pupil 'positive approaches to learning' and their academic progress, *British Educational Research Journal*, 37(3): 443–64.
11. Webster, R. et al. (2010) 'Double standards and first principles: framing teaching assistant support for pupils with special educational needs, *European Journal of Special Educational Needs*, 25(4): 319–36.
12. Blatchford, P., Russell, A. and Webster, R. (op. cit.); Blatchford, P. et al. (op. cit.).
13. Dunne, L., Goddard, G. and Woodhouse, C. (2008) Teaching assistants' perceptions of their professional role and their experiences of doing a foundation degree, *Improving Schools*, 11(3): 239–49.
14. Blatchford, P., Webster, R. and Russell, A. (2012) *Challenging the Role and Deployment of Teaching Assistants in Mainstream Schools: The Impact on Schools. Final Report on the Effective Deployment of Teaching Assistants (EDTA) project.* (Available online at: http://www.schoolsupportstaff.net/edtareport.pdf).
15. Blatchford, P., Russell, A. and Webster, R. (op. cit.); Hutchings, M. et al. (2009) *Aspects of School Workforce Remodelling Strategies Used and Impact on Workload and Standards*. London: DCSF.
16. Cook-Jones, A. (2006) The changing role of the teaching assistant in the primary school sector. Paper presented at the European Conference on Educational Research, Geneva, 13–16 September.
17. Bassett, D. et al. (2010) *Every Teacher Matters*. London: Reform.
18. The following findings from the DISS project are described in more detail in Blatchford, P., Russell, A. and Webster, R. (op. cit.).
19. Giangreco, M.F. (2010) One-to-one paraprofessionals for students with disabilities in inclusive classrooms: is conventional wisdom wrong?, *Intellectual and Developmental Disabilities*, 48(1): 1–13.

20. Rubie-Davies, C. et al. (2010). Enhancing student learning? A comparison of teaching and teaching assistant interaction with pupils, *School Effectiveness and School Improvement*, 21(4): 429–49.
21. Radford, J., Blatchford, P. and Webster, R. (2011) Opening up and closing down: comparing teacher and TA talk in mathematics lessons, *Learning and Instruction*, 21(5): 625–35.
22. Giangreco (op. cit.).
23. Blatchford, P., Webster, R. amd Russell, A. (op cit).
24. Russell, A., Webster, R. and Blatchford, P. (in press) *Maximising the Impact of Teaching Assistants: Guidance for School Leaders and Teachers.* Abingdon: Routledge.

PART

2

Teaching methods

CHAPTER

6

Traditional versus progressive education

Margaret Brown

Introduction

It has become conventional, at least in Anglo-Saxon countries, for aspiring or recently elected governments to claim, first, that educational standards are low in comparison to other countries, and, second, that this terrible state of affairs has been caused by capitulation of the previous administration to progressivism, probably arising from 'the educational establishment'. The obvious treatment for this condition is government insistence on measures that guarantee a return to traditional teaching and learning.

By the time that any changes are formulated and implemented, and a new round of disappointing international comparisons are available to evaluate them, the secretaries of state and ministers, and possibly even the governments, are likely to be long departed; even if they remain, teachers and educationists can once again be safely blamed for subverting the reforms.

Good education appears so simple and unproblematic from the ringside seat of the politician, and media-driven parental support can always be relied upon to encourage a return to tradition in our schools. But before we examine critically examples of this political rhetoric, we need to look at what is usually meant by the terms 'traditional' and 'progressive' in relation to education.

What distinguishes traditional and progressive education?

There are a variety of different characterizations of traditional and progressive education, with some authors using the words to describe only different teaching methods and others using them to describe different ideologies, encompassing different views as to the aims of education and the ways children learn, as well as different views of the content, methods and evaluation of education.[1]

In summary, a traditionalist:

- values the learning of facts, principles and procedures;
- prioritizes the basic skills of literacy and numeracy, and division of knowledge into traditional disciplines;
- believes that the teacher's key responsibility is to present knowledge clearly, to demonstrate procedures and to ensure that pupils memorize and practise until they can reproduce accurately;
- assesses learning through tests of memorization and skills.

In contrast, a progressivist:

- values the development of the whole person, emotional, artistic and social as well as intellectual;
- prioritizes processes ('soft skills') such as problem-solving, creative thinking, teamworking and integrating knowledge from different disciplines;
- believes that the teacher's key responsibility is to ensure pupils engage fully in motivating enquiry;
- assesses learning through holistic tasks.

These rather bald and simplistic descriptions read like caricatures; yet some policy-makers and even educationists seem surprisingly keen to argue strongly for one or other of these extreme positions. But before we examine examples of this phenomenon, we need to ask some deeper questions about the nature and desirability of this characterization.

What are the problems of a traditional/progressive dichotomy?

Many would argue that these descriptions of traditional and progressive represent not a dichotomous choice but two ideological poles of a single continuum. Unlike armchair pundits, classroom practitioners are much more likely to settle for an intermediate position between the extremes, although they may prefer their ideological balance point to be closer to one end than to the other.

But before going too far in pursuing this linear model, one should first ask whether a single line is perhaps too simple to describe the complexity of views on teaching and learning. For example when analysing views and practices of primary teachers in relation to numeracy, one set of researchers[2] felt that there were three distinguishable extreme orientations:

- transmissionist (broadly 'traditional' as defined earlier, valuing direct transmission of knowledge);
- discovery (broadly 'progressive' as defined earlier, valuing independent inquiry);
- connectionist (valuing the development of concepts and the linking of them together).

Generalizing from a linear representation, the three ideological poles can be represented by the vertices of an equilateral triangle; a teacher's individual ideology can then be described by some point inside the triangle, its position in relation to the vertices depending on the relative weightings of the three orientations.

Of course it is also possible to add other dimensions to the analysis, or to separate out different aspects,[3] although for practical use, as a way of describing and understanding different educational orientations, there will need to be a balance of simplicity and complexity in the model we choose; I will therefore not use anything more complicated than a three-dimensional model for the purposes of this chapter. Again the classroom reality is usually much more complex than any of the three extreme positions. For example, a history teacher teaching about the Congress of Vienna may well require students:

- to learn the dates, names of people and countries and the facts associated with the settlement;
- to take part in a simulation where students work in teams, each investigating the background and deciding the position to take for a participating country, and acting out the negotiation;
- to be able to relate the issues that arise to more abstract ideas such as military and economic power, occupation and nationalism, and linking with knowledge relating to geography, economics and statistics.

Traditionalists tend to argue that if pupils acquire fluency in the facts, principles and techniques then they will gradually come to understand and link the underlying concepts and be able to use them in solving problems. For example, a traditionalist may argue that the teacher's plan for the Congress of Vienna is inefficient in that it takes a lot more time than simply learning the facts about it, and moreover risks disorder in the classroom. It also takes more of the teacher's time to prepare, and requires more expertise in being able to react to unexpected queries and outcomes. They might suggest that pupils may easily get confused between what actually happened and what happened in their own simulation. A progressive might argue that, on the contrary, recalling the facts about the Congress of Vienna is of little importance for most pupils; it is the processes of analysing a position, synthesizing a strategy, working in a team and negotiating with others that are of use in adult life. The traditionalist might reply that these 'soft' skills are either innate, or can be learned later on the job, and anyway are dependent on a clear grasp of the underlying facts. A connectionist might respond that the facts are likely to be readily forgotten if presented and learned as a dry narrative with little obvious relevance for modern teenagers; they are much more likely to be understood and retained and capable of further application if pupils become personally involved with them and are forced to use them in solving a problem themselves, and are required to connect them with powerful abstract ideas. A pragmatist, of course, might argue that only a well-contrived balance of different types of activity is likely, in practice, to make school life bearable for most teachers *and* most pupils.

A later section will ask who is right: what does research evidence tell us about the effectiveness of, in particular, traditional and progressive learning? Before that, though, we need to investigate the stated positions of some politicians.

What do politicians say?

This section demonstrates the simplistic nature of some political messages about teaching and learning. For practicality, it is limited to the political context in England and focuses mainly, but not exclusively, on mathematics, to balance the next chapter that relates to the teaching of literacy. However, many of the views expressed are likely to be familiar to those in other Anglophone countries and those whose specialism is in other subjects.

Complaints about low standards, of course, are not a recent phenomenon; for example, in England there have been regular concerns about the lack of arithmetical competence at least since the middle of the nineteenth century.[4] These concerns resulted in the introduction of a national curriculum in 1862 (remarkably similar to what is being proposed in 2012), and the argument between progressive and traditional ideologies in primary mathematics has been going on at least as long.[5]

In more recent times, a second national curriculum was legally imposed in 1988 by the Thatcher Government justified partly as a reaction to mediocre results in the Second International Mathematics Survey (SIMS) as compared with those of our main industrial competitors.[6] In the words of a White Paper acting as a launch for this policy:

> The government believes that, not least in the light of what is being achieved in other countries, the standards now generally attained by our pupils are neither as good as they can be, nor as good as they need to be if young people are to be equipped for the world of the twenty-first century. By the time they leave school, pupils need to have acquired, far more than at present, the qualities and skills required for work in a technological age.[7]

The case is carefully phrased so that it is difficult to argue with. However, one should perhaps note that while England's performance in international mathematics tests was then, and remains, below that in Japan, perceived then as a major competitor, the evidence that it was below that of Germany was based on studies where the samples were not comparable. A more careful analysis of the data suggested that England's standards were probably higher than those in Germany; this finding was later confirmed by early PISA (Programme for International Student Assessment) data. Second, the previous Labour Government had invited Sir Wilfred Cockcroft to chair a 'Committee of Inquiry into the Teaching of Mathematics in Schools' to address concerns expressed about weak numeracy skills. But in its report to the Thatcher administration in 1982,[8] it found that there was no real evidence that low standards of numeracy were a problem for employers. Indeed, it was later demonstrated that there was a negative correlation between countries' economic performances and their positions in international league tables.[9]

Although in the quotation above the appeal is made to international comparisons, and emphasizes skills standards, the language in the White Paper falls somewhat short of what we have defined as the characteristics of traditionalism, partly because of the authorship of Her Majesty's Inspectorate (HMI) and civil servants, and partly because the Secretary of State at the time, Sir Keith Joseph, had a rather broader educational vision. However, the then Prime Minister, Margaret Thatcher, was clearly on the side of traditionalists, since she notes in her memoirs[10] that she was only interested in 'key subjects', and envisaged a 'basic syllabus' and 'simple tests' in basic literacy and numeracy skills. She further complained that her original intention was subverted by the educational establishment.

Interestingly, it was, in fact, under the generally more liberal regime of her successor as prime minister, John Major, and his first education minister, Kenneth Clarke, that a more traditional turn occurred. Major called for 'a return to basics in education' as part of an ill-fated 'back to basics' theme in his speech to the 1991 Conservative Party Conference. Right-wing pressure groups seized the educational agenda and the key positions of influence in educational quasi-non-governmental organizations (quangos), and national assessment was switched from mainly holistic tasks into short tests. Examinations taken at 16 (General Certificate of Secondary Education, GCSE) with a high proportion of coursework were outlawed, and a report was commissioned and published recommending a return to more didactic whole class teaching.[11]

Margaret Thatcher's traditionalist views were, strangely enough, closely related to those of David Blunkett, the first Secretary of State for Education under Tony Blair in the incoming New Labour Government in 1997. For example, a press release issued less than two weeks after the election relating to the planned introduction of National Literacy and Numeracy Strategies was headed: '*Blunkett sets tough new national targets to boost three R's*' (a reference to the Victorian primary regime of 'Reading,' Riting and 'Rithmetic'). In his speech to the North of England Education Conference that year, he noted that:

> Numeracy is a vital skill which each youngster must learn properly. Yet for perhaps thirty years we have not focused on what we know works. The new daily maths lesson will ensure that children know their tables, can do basic sums in their heads and are taught effectively in whole class settings.

Moving to the 2010 Coalition government, the first Secretary of State, Michael Gove, continued the earlier Conservative traditions by portraying a dire state in England in international comparisons and using this to justify a more traditional approach. For example in a recent speech to the Royal Society (29 June 2011) he says:

> ...In the last decade, we have plummeted down the international league tables: from 4th to 16th place in science; and from 8th to 28th in maths. ... One of the lessons from the international evidence is that in East Asia there is much greater focus on fundamental number concepts, fractions and the building blocks of algebra in primary school.....We should also bear in mind that in Shanghai, they have daily maths lessons and regular tests to make sure that all children are learning the basics....We want to reverse the devaluation of the exam system. We want a National Curriculum that acts as a foundation of core knowledge...

He further notes in a foreword to a paper by Tim Oates:[12]

> In recent years there has been a loss of stability and purpose with new subjects and topics added – more often in response to pressure groups than for sound pedagogical reasons. The most

> recent overhaul of the National Curriculum in 2007 was a serious backward step as concepts were replaced with vague generic statements of little value . . . . the decision to teach in a particular way may not be appropriate for all schools or teachers, but what is crucial is first identifying the crucial concepts and ideas that each year group should learn. ”

Similarly, Nick Gibb, the Schools Minister, in a speech to the 100 Group (10 February 2011) says:

> - . . . in maths' tests, Chinese 15-year-olds are now some two years ahead of students in this country
> - the reading level of our pupils is now nearly a year behind that of children in countries like Korea and Finland . . . .
>
> This is why we want to return the National Curriculum to its fundamental purpose of setting out the essential knowledge that all children should acquire, organised around subject disciplines. ”

There are several interesting features here. First, the international data quoted on mathematics is misleading[13] and the downwards trend is contradicted by data from the Trends in International Mathematics and Science Study (TIMSS surveys).[14]

Second, Nick Gibb suggests that Chinese students are on average two years ahead of British students. He fails to note that the Chinese sample includes only students from one, very economically advanced, city and not the whole country, and, moreover, that over 10 per cent of the city population was not available for testing as they were either not in any school or were held back in low grades.

It is also useful to note that Michael Gove, here and in other speeches, tends to talk about concepts as well as, or even instead of, factual knowledge as the focus of education; it is not very clear however what he means by this. Nick Gibb mentions only knowledge, and informal reports suggest that in private discussions he is focused mainly on knowledge of facts and procedures including phonics, multiplication tables and facility with pencil and paper algorithms such as long division or the solution of quadratic equations, all of which he favours teaching to younger age groups than at present. This use of PISA results to justify more routine skills is especially odd given that the PISA surveys focus on the ability to solve complex verbal problems; it is on TIMSS where the questions are more routine that we do comparatively well.

A further observation on these quotations from ministers is the reluctance to propose any teaching method that removes some of the possible charges of traditionalism. However one might surmise that in proposing a curriculum that is based in factual and procedural knowledge, it is assumed that an explanation-demonstration-practice-test model is expected. Nevertheless, this is by no means essential; for example, teachers might elect to use an investigation of number patterns as an opportunity also to practise multiplication procedures. This approach would be likely to be far more motivating than doing a repetitive exercise since it has some deeper purpose and is combined with the more challenging thinking in processes such as generalization. The political views quoted here have all been in favour of traditional education, although to varying extents. Since traditional education is widely viewed as popular with the electorate, quotations from political speeches recommending progressive education are difficult to find.

In contrast to traditional ideologies, the more extreme forms of progressivism are more likely to be found among educational theorists than politicians. Theorists such as Dewey and Montessori have had a deep effect on professional practice, especially at primary level, through teacher training and through official reports such as the 1931 Hadow Report[15] and the 1967 Plowden Report.[16] Both these reports backed theme-based enquiry rather than subject-based knowledge as the focus of primary education. But the 1988 English national curriculum, while not specifying any particular teaching method, was secondary-dominated in style and therefore subject-oriented. It was not until the tail end of the last Labour Government that progressivism started to edge its way back in, led less by the series of relatively ineffective Secretaries of State and more by senior staff at the Qualifications and Curriculum Development Agency (QCDA), who spearheaded interdisciplinary work at secondary level under a revised and slightly bizarre process-centred national curriculum. Secondary teachers seem to have found this approach difficult to understand and anyway, in practice, they were under pressure to allow GCSE examinations to dominate the Curriculum, with the effect that there is not much evidence of effective implementation. At primary level the government-commissioned Rose Review,[17] influenced by the privately financed Cambridge Primary Review,[18] struck a more moderate balance between the traditional and the progressive, but arrived too close to the 2010 election to be implemented.

Is traditional education more effective than progressive education?

A particular problem with convincing politicians and other successful people about educational change is that they have often themselves been educated at very traditional, selective, schools and feel that this has prepared them and their friends well for elite professions, so must be the best option for all. Certainly some people do come to understand and be able to apply knowledge even when the teaching is mainly related to the learning of facts and routine procedures. This success seems likely to be because they reflect and talk to others in trying to make sense of what they are taught, linking it with what they already understand. There is nothing special about this way of learning – most humans at least start with a natural desire to make sense of the world; but the availability of personal drive, social support and opportunity to reflect and discuss will increase the probability of success and also build confidence for future learning.

Alternatively, many people exposed to a traditional style of teaching find themselves bored and unmotivated, or frustrated at being unable to easily remember or understand, and they may well give up at some stage, especially in the absence of social support. Again, taking mathematics as an example, there are a number of research studies that demonstrate that people of all ages and classes have come to dislike, even hate, mathematics because an inability to understand parts of it makes them feel inadequate.[19] Lack of understanding leads to difficulty in remembering techniques since steps in arbitrary techniques are easily forgotten; missing steps can only be repaired through testing out possibilities, but this development needs a base of understanding that allows evaluation of what is 'reasonable'.[20] Lack of meaningfulness, therefore, in the long term, leads to faulty techniques and lack of confidence, negative attitudes and, for some, even an apparent willingness to deny the value of the subject in order to maintain self-image. ('I was never any good at maths but what use to you are quadratic equations?'.) Some students may appear to follow apparently irrational strategies as they have no expectation from teachers that mathematics should make sense, and be fundamentally consistent. But in the short term, unconfident students, and indeed unconfident teachers, may express a preference for the security of traditional methods that emphasize imitation and repetition and do not challenge an insecure understanding.

Unfortunately, primary teachers are often among those who lack confidence in mathematics.[21] The effect of this state of affairs can be positive in that it can encourage primary teachers to strongly support methods of teaching that do make mathematics meaningful for pupils. In the study of effective numeracy teaching, with comparative effectiveness measured by the gains in learning over a year, it was found that the most effective teachers were 'connectionists' who were keen to connect together mathematical ideas and to relate them to real life. Pupils of both traditional ('transmission') teachers, who focused on teaching procedures, and progressive ('discovery') teachers, who believed in building up facts and patterns through the use of apparatus, had lower average gains on numeracy tests.[22] Interestingly, there was no particular form of classroom organization that was adopted by these effective teachers – some chose to work predominantly with the whole class, some with groups and some almost always with individual children working through assignments on their own.

In fact, there are very few studies that show a strong 'process-product' correlation in the sense of suggesting that either traditional or progressive teaching methods are superior in terms of learning gains. Large-scale correlational studies cannot easily establish causation, and many actually show no significant differences between traditional and progressive teaching styles; for example, a review of Dutch studies[23] noted that the proportion of whole class teaching appeared to have a significant correlation with attainment in only 3 out of the 29 studies. Although in all these three the correlation was positive, there may be explanations other than teaching method alone as very few such studies have strictly comparable (i.e. randomly allocated) samples. And indeed the whole class teaching may have been more progressive than the small group teaching.

Large-scale studies certainly have the problem of characterizing teachers' styles accurately. For example, in a study in the UK in the 1970s, popularly thought to prove for all time that traditional teaching was superior,[24] self-reporting by teachers via questionnaires rather than independent observations were not a very reliable method of categorizing teachers, especially when many teachers occupy an intermediate position. And indeed when the data from this study was re-analysed using more rigorous statistical methods, the difference effectively disappeared.[25]

While older studies seem, if anything, to favour more traditional methods,[26] this is less true of some more recent meta-analyses of factors in interventions that seem to have the greatest effects on attainment. For example, in mathematics, when only rigorously controlled studies are included, those on the instructional process, in general, have only a small effect at secondary level, slightly more in primary level, and collaborative groupwork seems to have a slight advantage over other forms of organization.[27] (See also Chapter 4.)

However, there are also problems in the smaller-scale studies which allow more accurate observations and contrasts of teacher styles and which probably more often in their results favour progressive methods. For example, one much quoted example in secondary mathematics involved only one traditional and one progressive school;[28] although the children were comparable, the teachers in the progressive school were clearly of higher quality.

One problem, of course, of trying to compare traditional with progressive teacher orientations is that, as we have noted, people with different orientations will have different views about what it is important to teach and therefore to assess, and also about what assessment methods should be used. For example, in the USA, some studies have shown that traditional methods may be marginally better for teaching traditional knowledge in routine tests, but more progressive methods work better in achieving more abstract thinking, such as in creative problem-solving.[29]

As shown above, politicians tend to quote international studies as evidence that traditional teaching methods work best. But although the Pacific Rim countries that head the tables may use predominantly traditional teaching methods, so do many countries at the bottom of the table. There seem likely to be other reasons for the superior performance of East Asian countries.[30] In fact, close analysis of international comparative data suggests:

> All we can safely say (we hope) is that students do experience different types of instructional arrangements cross-nationally and that the influence of these arrangements generically appears to be weak relative to such matters as prior learning and the contents of learning opportunities during the course of study.[31]

Conclusions

Broadly, the previous section suggests that it is unlikely that swinging the country to very traditional, or indeed to extreme progressive, teaching methods will make any real difference to scores in international tests. Although there is not very much evidence, there is, however, some suggestion that the differential effects on student confidence and attitude are greater than those on attainment, and at least for some students these can be incapacitating. Since, for purposes of life and employment, students need both knowledge and generic skills, the teacher's problem is more of finding a rational intermediate balance point. And, if anything, the evidence suggests that another dimension entirely, concerned with fostering a complex network of conceptually connected knowledge and skills, is what makes the real difference.

Notes

1. For details of one way of distinguishing different ideologies of education, see, for example, Ernest (1991) *The Philosophy of Mathematics Education*. Basingstoke: Falmer Press.
2. Askew, M., Brown, M., Rhodes, V., Johnson, D. and Wiliam, D. (1997) *Effective Teachers of Numeracy*. London: King's College London.
3. Again, see Ernest (op. cit.), or Ball, S.J. (1990) *Politics and Policy-making in Education*. London: Routledge.
4. McIntosh, A. (1981) When will they ever learn? Article reprinted from *Forum*, 19(3), in A. Floyd (ed.), *Developing Mathematical Thinking*. London: Addison-Wesley, for the Open University.
5. Brown, M. (2010) Swings and roundabouts, in I. Thompson (ed.) *Issues in Teaching Numeracy in Primary Schools* (2nd edn). Maidenhead: Open University Press.

6. See, for example, Prais, S. and Wagner, K. (1985) *Schooling Standards in Britain and West Germany*. London: National Institute for Economic and Social Research.
7. Department of Education and Science/Welsh Office (1985) *Better Schools* (Cmnd 9469). London: Her Majesty's Stationery Office (HMSO) (Section 9).
8. Department of Education and Science/Welsh Office: Committee of Inquiry into the Teaching of Mathematics in Schools (1982) *Mathematics Counts*. London: HMSO.
9. Robinson, P. (1999) The tyranny of league tables: international comparisons on educational attainment and economic performance, in R. Alexander, P. Broadfoot and D. Phillips (eds) *Learning from Comparing: New directions in Comparative Educational Research, Vol. I: Contexts, Classrooms and Outcomes* (pp. 217–35). Oxford: Symposium Books.
10. Thatcher, M. (1993) *The Downing Street Years* (p. 593). London: Harper Collins.
11. Alexander, R., Rose, J. and Woodhead, C. (1992) *Curriculum Organisation and Classroom Practice in Primary Schools: A Discussion Paper*. London: Department of Education and Science.
12. Oates, T. (2010) *Could Do Better: Using International Comparisons to Refine the National Curriculum in England*. Cambridge: Cambridge Assessment.
13. Jerrim, J. (2011) England's 'plummeting' PISA test score between 2000 and 2009: is the performance of our secondary school pupils really in relative decline? DoQSS Working Paper No. 11.09. London: Institute of Education.
14. Brown, M. (2011) Going back or going forward? Tensions in the formulation of a new National Curriculum in mathematics, *The Curriculum Journal*, 22(2): 151–65.
15. Board of Education (1931) *Report of the Consultative Committee on the Primary School* (Hadow Report). London: HMSO.
16. Central Advisory Council for Education (1967) *Children and their Primary Schools* (Plowden Report). London: HMSO.
17. Department of Children, Schools and Families (DCSF) (2009) *Independent Review of the Primary Curriculum: Final report* ('The Rose Review'). Nottingham: DCSF.
18. Alexander, R. (ed.) (2009) *Children, their World, their Education: Final Report and Recommendations of the Cambridge Primary Review*. London: Routledge.
19. For example, with older middle class women, Buxton, L. (1981) *Do You Panic about Maths? Coping with Maths Anxiety*. London: Heinemann. With younger secondary students: Nardi, E. and Steward, S. (2003) Is mathematics T.I.R.E.D? A profile of quiet disaffection in the secondary mathematics classroom. *British Educational Research Journal* 29(3): 345–67. With older secondary students: Brown, M., Brown, P. and Bibby, T. (2008)

'I would rather die': reasons given by 16 year-olds for not continuing their study of mathematics, *Research in Mathematics Education*, 10(1): 3–18.

20. Brown, J.S. and Van Lehn, K. (1982) Towards a generative theory of 'bugs', in T.P. Carpenter, T.A. Romburg and J.M. Moser (eds) *Addition and Subtraction: A Cognitive Perspective* (pp. 117–35). Hillsdale, NJ: Lawrence Erlbaum; Brown, M. (1982) Rules without reasons? Some evidence relating to the teaching of routine skills to low attainers in mathematics, *International Journal of Mathematics Education in Science and Technology*, 13(4): 449–61.
21. Bibby, T. (2002) Shame: An emotional response to doing mathematics as an adult and a teacher, *British Educational Research Journal*, 28(5): 705–21.
22. Askew et al. (op. cit.)
23. Creemers, B. (1997) *Effective Schools and Effective Teachers: An International Perspective*. Warwick: Centre for Research in Elementary and Primary Education.
24. Bennett, N. (1976) *Teaching Styles and Pupil Progress*. London: Open Books.
25. Aitken, M., Bennett, N. and Hesketh, J. (1981) Teaching styles and pupil progress: a re-analysis, *British Journal of Educational Psychology*, 51: 170–86.
26. For example, Galton, M., Simon, B. and Croll, P. (1980) *Inside the Primary Classroom*. London: Routledge; Galton, M. and Simon, B. (eds) *Progress and Performance in the Primary Classroom*. London: Routledge; Good, T.L., Grouws, D.A. and Ebmeier, H. (1983) *Active Mathematics Teaching*. New York: Longman; Brophy, J.E. and Good, T.L. (1986) Teacher behavior and student achievement, in M. Wittrock (ed.) *Handbook of Research on Teaching* (pp. 328–75). New York: Macmillan.
27. Slavin, R. and Lake, C. (2008) Effective programs in elementary mathematics: a best-evidence synthesis, *Review of Educational Research* 78(3): 427–515; Slavin, R., Lake, C. and Goff, C. (2009) Effective programs in middle and high school mathematics: a best-evidence synthesis, *Review of Educational Research*, 79(2): 839–911.
28. Boaler, J. (1997) *Experiencing School Mathematics: Teaching Styles, Sex and Setting*. Maidenhead: Open University Press.
29. Peterson, P.L. (1988) Teaching for higher order thinking skills in mathematics: the challenge for the next decade, in D.A. Grouws and T.J. Cooney (eds) *Perspectives on Research on Effective Mathematics Teaching*, (pp.114–42). Reston, VA: NCTM/Lawrence Erlbaum.
30. Askew, M., Hodgen, J., Hossein, S. and Bretscher, N. (2010) *Values and Variables: Mathematics Education in High-performing Countries*. London: The Nuffield Foundation.
31. Burstein, L. (1992) *The IEA Study of Mathematics III: Student Growth and Classroom Processes* (p. 278). Oxford: Pergamon Press.

CHAPTER

Synthetic phonics: the route to reading?

Bethan Marshall

Introduction

In a speech made in Oxford in 2011, Tim Brighouse cites from a selection of over 300 HMI reports made on schools in the 1950s and says that in a third of the schools there were problems with English teaching and standards. The comments make stark reading.

> Reading ability is poor . . . by the end of their school careers few pupils can be considered established as readers
>
> *(Birmingham Secondary Modern, 1956)*
>
> There is a problem of illiteracy
>
> *(Birmingham Secondary Modern, 1958)*
>
> Problems of illiteracy persist into the fourth year
>
> *(Cheshire Secondary Modern, 1957)*
>
> A few boys in each form cannot read . . .
>
> *(Boys Secondary Modern Liverpool, 1956)*
>
> Many boys write with difficulty
>
> *(Cheshire grammar school, 1958)*
>
> Pupils show an insecure grasp of the fundamentals
>
> *(Derbyshire Secondary Modern, 1960)*[1]

He concludes: 'over half my generation have levels of competence similar to that expected of present day 9-year-olds'.[2]

If we look back to the turn of the twentieth century we find very similar anxieties. In 1912 the English Association wrote that, 'It is a plain fact that the average girl or boy is unable to write English with a clearness or fluency or any degree of grammatical accuracy'.[3] The Newbolt report in 1921, quoting Boots Pure Drug Company commented that, 'The teaching of English in present day schools produces a very limited command of the English language'.[4] In the same report all but a few employers complained that they had found difficulty in 'obtaining employees who can speak and write English clearly and correctly'.[5] Seven years later little had changed. The Spens Report of 1928 wrote, 'It is a common and grave criticism that many pupils pass through grammar school without acquiring the capacity to express themselves in English'.[6] The Norwood Report of 1943 claimed to have received 'strong evidence of the poor quality of English of Secondary School pupils [. . .] the evidence is such as to leave no doubt in our minds that we are confronted by a serious failure of secondary schools'.[7]

And it appears that nothing has changed. The *Evening Standard* ran a campaign on literacy in the capital from 2010–2011 and the results look equally disturbing. Headlines include '1 in 4 children leaves primary school unable to read or write properly' and '40 per cent of inner city primary schools have a reading age of between six and nine when they start secondary school'.[8] And as with the Newbolt Report, employers complain as well, '40 per cent of London firms say their employees have poor literacy skills – and report that it has a negative impact on their business'.[9]

It is, then, little wonder that Secretaries of State introduce measures to combat illiteracy. Michael Gove, for the Coalition Government, made himself clear at the Conservative Party Conference the year before he became Secretary of State for Education:

> Wanting to teach children to read properly isn't some sort of antique prejudice – it's an absolute necessity in a civilized society and I won't rest until we have eliminated illiteracy in modern Britain. The failure to teach millions to read is the greatest of betrayals. But I'll be taking on the education establishment because they've done more than just squander talent.[10]

Yet, 11 years earlier David Blunkett was saying almost exactly the same in a *Daily Mail* article:

> Yet there still remain the doubters to whom these [traditional] methods remain anathema. I still encounter those in the education world who would prefer the quiet life of the past, where education was 'progressive' and where the failure of half our pupils was taken for granted. There are even those who suggest that learning to read properly threatens creativity. Can they really be taken seriously? Are they actually claiming that to be illiterate helps you to become a better artist?[11]

So what is actually happening with literacy levels, as they always seem poor, or, more worrying – in a downward spiral. Brookes,[12] in a study of the last 30 years of literacy levels, claimed that there has been no change at all, but in the international league tables the results of children in England seem to be getting worse. In 2003, the international study Progress in International Reading Literacy Study[13] (PIRLS) found that 10-year-olds in England were the third best readers in the world with only Sweden and the Netherlands doing better. The success of England's standing in PIRLS was much vaunted by Labour who attributed it to the efficacy of the National Literacy Strategy (of which more later). But the validity of these findings has been queried[14] and the most recent PIRLS study (2010) shows a decline in our results from third in 2001, to seventh in 2005 and finally to seventeenth in 2010.[15] This, as we have seen, has caused Gove to pillory, rather than praise, the Labour Government.

Synthetic phonics

Both governments, however, have come to the same conclusion by way of addressing the problem of illiteracy by introducing synthetic phonics in the initial teaching of reading. Labour did this on the basis of two reports written by Sir Jim Rose, a former Office for Standards in Education (Ofsted) chief inspector, The Rose Report[16] and The Rose Review.[17] The Coalition Government agreed with its findings.

The Rose Report declared that:

> Despite uncertainties in research findings, the practice seen by the review shows that the systematic approach, which is generally understood as 'synthetic' phonics, offers the vast majority of young children the best and most direct route to becoming skilled readers and writers.[18]

Moreover, this method was to be exclusive:

> For beginner readers, learning the core principles of phonic work in discrete daily sessions reduces the risk, attendant with the so-called 'searchlights' model, of paying too little attention to securing word recognition skills. In consequence, the review suggests a reconstruction of the searchlights model for reading.[19]

This is because, according to the report:

> if beginner readers, for example, are encouraged to infer from pictures the word they have to decode this may lead to their not realising that they need to focus on the printed word. They may, therefore, not use their developing phonic knowledge. It may also lead to diluting the focused phonics teaching that is necessary for securing accurate word reading.[20]

The 'searchlights' model of learning to read was one advocated by the National Literacy Framework (NLS), which is now defunct. The NLS[21] was introduced in 1997 by the New Labour Government and sought to improve the literacy rates of primary children. Although it took a predominantly phonics approach to the teaching of reading, it did suggest other strategies as well; for example, looking at pictures to decipher a word or using grammatical knowledge to work out what was being said in a sentence. With The Rose Report this strategy ended and synthetic phonics was introduced across the board. Primary school teachers were retrained and beginner teachers are now only taught synthetic phonics as an aid to reading. The teaching of synthetic phonics in primary schools began in 2007.

So what exactly is synthetic phonics. Advocates of this method argue that there are 44 phonemes in the English language; in other words, the sounds that letters can make. If we take the letter A, for example, this has three phonemic sounds, å as in cat, ah as in bath (if you speak English with a southern or received pronounciation (RP) accent) and ae as in plate. Children need to learn each phonemic sound first and then they can learn to identify digraphs. Digraphs are when two letters are combined together as in 'sh', or 'th'. From here they progress to trigraphs where three letters are combined such as 'thr'. And so it continues. Children are only introduced to books when they have mastered all 44 phonemes. Special reading scheme books have to be written for the scheme as only words that can be decoded phonemically can at first be introduced.

Synthetic phonics differs from analytic phonics, the other main use of phonics in teaching children to read. Analytic phonics also identifies phonemic sounds but relies also on a pupil's propensity to make analogies. In particular, it depends on onset, the initial phonemic sound, and an analogous sound, usually rhyme. The Dr Seuss books, such as *The Cat In the Hat*, are a good example of analytic phonics. The title itself is an illustration of onset and rhyme in the words 'cat' and 'hat' but other reading schemes rely heavily on analytic phonics, too; *The Oxford Reading Tree* being one such example. The academic Usha Goswami, who sympathizes with analytic phonics, was involved in writing them when she was based at Oxford University.

Clackmannanshire

Both the Labour Government, and the current administration, favour synthetic phonics largely because of a report on the teaching of literacy in schools in Clackmannanshire.[22] Clackmannanshire is a small authority in Scotland, having 19 primary schools in total. The researchers, Johnson and Watson, originally began their work in 1997 but they reported on it seven years later as the study was intended to be longitudinal. The programme started off in just three primary schools but after 16 weeks it expanded to include all 19 primaries, as the results appeared so good. Seven years later they compared the results of the pupils in Clackmannanshire with comparable students elsewhere. What they found was that although the Clackmannanshire primary pupils, at the age of 11, were three-and-a-half years ahead in their ability to decode print, in comprehension they were only three months ahead. In the main, however, all that was reported was the first set of data not the second. Synthetic phonics was the apparent silver bullet politicians had been searching for in terms of improving literacy.

There were, however, several problems with the research. First and foremost, it was never intended to be an all-encompassing defence of synthetic phonics. Sue Ellis (2007), who submitted evidence to the Rose Report, claimed that:

> “The Clackmannan phonics research reported by Watson and Johnston (2005) was an experimental trial to compare different methods of teaching phonics. It wasn't designed (despite media reports) to investigate whether phonics instruction provides a more effective 'gateway' to reading than a mixed-methods approach. The researchers did not collect the range of data nor conduct the sorts of fidelity checks that would be required to address such a question.[23]”

And although the schools did use synthetic phonics, local authority money was put in as well so that 'These staff carried out home visits, ran story clubs and after-school homework clubs, worked with parent groups, set up library visits and borrowing schemes as well as working in classrooms'[24] as well as 'Schools [being] involved in a separate and concurrent initiative, the New Community Schools Initiative, [which] introduced personal learning planning. This included some, but not all, of the early intervention schools'.[25]

Nor was it a peer-researched project. Traditionally, when published, research projects are peer reviewed by fellow academics and they tend to have advisory committees during the research process that both guide and comment on the research as it progresses. The Clackmannanshire research had neither but research undertaken by the American Reading Panel[26] did. It looked at hundreds of peer-reviewed articles in its analysis of whether or not analytic or synthetic phonics was a better way of teaching reading and it found that there was no difference between the two approaches.

But this finding should be set beside, perhaps, a more fundamental difficulty with any phonics teaching of reading and that is that English is not a particularly consistent phonetic language. There are numerous exceptions to any phonic rule. Moreover, meaning can and does play an important part in teaching children to read. If we take the word 'read', we have to know the context and meaning of the phrase in which it occurs to know how it is pronounced – is it read as in reed or read as in red? Then again, in that sentence, it could be both or either. Take another example – tear and tear. Is it a word that makes us cry or one that rips us apart? Is it a verb or a noun? Only when we know what it means can we interpret it correctly. Or the start of so many children's tales and stories – 'Once upon a time there was'. How is one supposed to read that ever familiar phrase using synthetic phonics? The 'O' is pronounced as a 'w' and the verb 'was' is actually pronounced 'woz'. Teaching children to read based on phonemic sounds alone, without any heed to meaning, could be seen as flawed, as the results in Clackmannanshire seem to indicate.

Progressive approaches

Interestingly, the All-Party Parliamentary Group agrees. Unlike both the Labour and Coalition Governments it does not subscribe to a one approach fits all method of teaching reading. In a *Report of the Inquiry into Overcoming the Barriers to Literacy*[27] it says that 'There is no single panacea which guarantees that all children will become readers'.[28] They wrote also that 'There was a great concern that "phonics" and "reading" were being used interchangeably by policy makers when they were not the same thing at all: reading isolated words is not reading for meaning'.[29] And they concluded that 'We need to accept that children do not "learn in a straight line". There are many different ways to learn and different learning preferences: this is why the focus on only synthetic phonics is not appropriate'.[30]

In so doing, the All-Party Parliamentary Group sounds almost sympathetic to the other review of primary teaching undertaken during the Labour Government – *The Cambridge Review*.[31] This was a major research project that was coordinated by Professor Robin Alexander but, in that review, he extends his definition of literacy even further. In the Review he defines it thus:

> Literacy achieves our listed aim of empowerment by conferring the skill not just of learning to read and write but to make these processes genuinely transformative, exciting children's imaginations (another listed aim), extending their boundaries, and enabling them to contemplate lives and worlds possible as well as actual.[32]

The power of literacy moves beyond the printed words on the page to the very meaning of their lives within society. As Alexander put it in his pamphlet *Education as Dialogue: Moral and Pedagogical Choices for the Runaway World*.[33]

> In some countries education has been required to mould individuals into compliant subjects; in others it has attempted to develop active and questioning citizens . . . Thus, education may empower and liberate, or it may disempower and confuse.[34]

While he does not say so it could be said that imposing a system of synthetic phonics is an attempt to 'mould' pupils into 'compliant subjects' rather than to encourage 'questioning citizens'. And here Robin Alexander is like so many in education who take a more progressive approach. Possibly the best known, and the coiner of the term 'progressive' is the American pragmatist John Dewey. In defining the difference between the progressive approach and the one that he considered more traditional he talks of the traditionalists as preparing:

> The young for future responsibilities and for success in life, by means of acquisition of the organised bodies of information and prepared forms of skill which comprehend the material instruction. Since the subject matter as well as standards of proper conduct are handed down from the past, the attitude of the pupils must, upon the whole, be one of docility, receptivity, and obedience.[35]

This sounds like the kind of teaching, however expertly and enlivened it might be, that comes with teaching synthetic phonics. Learning to read is the acquisition of a set of rules and 'prepared form of skills'. But the language that Alexander has used is similar too. In his pamphlet pupils will be 'compliant'; in Dewey they will manifest 'docility' and 'obedience'.

It is those who advocate critical literacy, however, who make the link between this kind of 'docility' and traditional print literacy most explicit. For such writers the type of literacy, detailed in government documentation, is simply 'schooled literacy'[36] an ability to decode the print on the page but little else. Critical literacy, by contrast:

> becomes a meaningful construct to the degree that it is viewed as a set of practices and functions to either empower or disempower people. In the larger sense, literacy must be analysed according to whether it promotes democratic and emancipatory changes.[37]

And again:

> Critical literacy responds to the cultural capital of a specific group or class and looks to ways in which it can be confirmed, and also at the ways in which the dominant society disconfirms students by either ignoring or denigrating the knowledge and experiences that characterise their everyday lives. The unit of analysis is social and the key concern is not individual interests but with the individual and collective empowerment.[38]

Others, such as Shirley Bryce Heath, have problematized the issue still further by examining the literacy of different social groups and noting how children from certain communities are disadvantaged by narrow definitions of 'schooled literacy'.[39] As Gee notes, such a perception of what it means to be literate means that 'the ability to talk about school based sorts of tasks is one way in which Western-style schools empower elites: they sound like they know more than they do'.[40]

Even those with a less overtly radical agenda use the term 'critical literacy' to describe a form of literacy that goes well beyond the basics. Richard Hoggart, in his essay 'Critical literacy and creative reading', writes:

> The level of literacy we now accept for the bulk of the population, of literacy unrelated to the way language is misused in this kind of society, ensures that literacy becomes simply a way of further subordinating great numbers of people. We make them literate enough to be conned by the mass persuaders . . . The second

> slogan has to be 'Critical Literacy for All' Critical Literacy means . . . teaching about the difficulties, challenges and benefits of living in an open society which aims to be a true democracy.[41]

For all these writers, to varying degrees, literacy becomes a means of 'reading' the society in which we live. Integral to this task is a demand that we do not take 'authority' at face value but question and challenge it as part of the democratic process. They do not want passive subjects but active citizens.

Reading for meaning and pleasure

If we return once more to the way in which we teach early reading, we again find contrasts between those advocating synthetic phonics and those who advocate a completely different way of becoming literate. The academic, Margaret Meek, for example, believed that children would learn to read using 'real books' rather than reading schemes. She takes what she calls a social constructivist, or Vygotskian perspective on early reading (see, for example, Meek 1988 and 1991).[42] Implicit in her idea of what it means to be literate is the notion that language, the way we interact as well as read and write, is crucial. The idea that language is essential to the learning process gained currency in this country through the writing of, among others, James Britton, Douglas Barnes and Harold Rosen in books such as *Language, the Learner and the School*[43] and *Language and Learning*.[44] Their work built on the writing of the Russian psychologist Lev Vygotsky. Although Vygotsky's research was carried out in the 1930s it was not translated in the West for nearly 30 years. Vygotsky argued that language was an essential cognitive tool:

> [By] focusing attention on the interaction between speech and the child's social and cultural experiences, Vygotsky provides us with a model of learning which emphasises the role of talk and places social discourse at the centre. Most significant is the notion that children can learn effectively through interaction with a more knowledgeable other (which may be a peer or adult.[45]

This notion underpinned Vygotsky's pivotal learning theory of the zone of proximal development (ZPD).[46] In essence he argued that as each new learning situation arises we move from a state where we do not understand to a position where we can understand if supported through interaction with the more knowledgeable other (the ZPD) to a situation where we are independent. The aim of the teacher is to support the pupil through this process either through class or group discussion. The theory of ZPD has often been connected in practice with the work of Bruner. He coined the term 'scaffolding'[47] to describe the process by which children needed initial support on engaging in a new activity and then have that support gradually withdrawn as they become more independent and are able to work unaided.

Implementing Vygotsky and Bruner's theories effectively in the classroom demands what Dewey would call 'high organisation based upon ideas'[48] whereby teachers have 'the difficult task to work out the kinds of materials, of methods, and of social relationships that are appropriate'[49] to help pupils learn. In other words, they orchestrate classroom activities where dialogue and discussion become essential exploratory tools to extend and develop thinking.

Margaret Meek, then, sought to build on what young children already know, which includes their knowledge of how books work and how print conveys meaning. In this way reading and writing are always taught within a clearly defined context. They do not exclude phonics but do not wholly rely on it either. The work of the Centre for Language in Primary Education (CLPE) has built on this work. Research publications such as *The Reader in the Writer*[50] show how children use their readerly knowledge of how stories and texts work in their writing.

This is very different from the phonics approach to reading, either analytic or synthetic, and again it sees literacy as far more than simply decoding print. Moreover, and significantly, there is some indication that viewing literacy as simply decoding print can prevent children from taking pleasure in reading. In 2005, an Ofsted report on English teaching was published.[51] It was written before the Rose Report but after the first cohort of children to complete primary school using the NLS and it makes for interesting reading. While it never actually criticizes the literacy hour it does virtually everything but. Hints that all was not well with the framework were already to be found in the annual reports of the then Chief Inspector David Bell.[52] Six months before the review on the teaching of English, he bemoaned the lack of reading in schools, particularly in primaries. Children, he complained, were not encountering enough whole texts during lessons, being given instead extracts from novels. He worried, therefore, that they would lose out on the pleasure of reading. The previous year he had noted that the creative curriculum was being constrained by teachers teaching to the Key Stage 2 national test.

While, as has been said, the criticism is never overt, in the Ofsted review on English teaching,[53] what becomes increasingly evident is that if teachers actually use the framework as their guide in the classroom, their performance will be merely satisfactory or worse. Quoting from the HMCI's annual report, the review notes in its section on the quality of teaching that trainee teachers tend 'toward safe and unimaginative teaching . . . partly because [they] use the structure and content of the strategy too rigidly'.[54] And again, 'For too many primary and secondary teachers . . . objectives become a tick list to be checked off because they follow the frameworks for teaching too slavishly'.[55]

The effects of such approaches are made clear throughout the review. If we look, for example, at the comments on reading, the authors cite research evidence in support of its inspection findings. The Progress in International Reading Literacy Study found that while 10-year-olds in English schools had comparable reading standards to those in other countries, they were less interested in reading for pleasure. There was also a decline in whether or not they found reading enjoyable between 1998 and 2003. The National Foundation for Educational Research (NFER) also found in its 2003 survey that 'children's enjoyment of reading had declined significantly in recent years'.[56]

While reading for pleasure may seem an inessential but pleasant biproduct in the business of raising literacy standards, research evidence from the past 30 years suggests otherwise. As the Ofsted review notes, the Bullock Report of 1975 found that a major source of adult illiteracy was that, 'they did not learn from the process of learning to read that it was something other people did for pleasure'.[57] The Programme for International Student Assessment (PISA) also found that: 'Being more enthusiastic about reading, and a frequent reader, was more of an advantage on its own than having well educated parents in good jobs', concluding, 'finding a way to engage students in reading may be one of the most effective ways to leverage social change'.[58] Yet Ofsted's own report on the situation in England, *Reading for Purpose and Pleasure*, observed that reading was 'negatively associated with school',[59] particularly with boys and their parents. As we have seen, the latest PISA[60] report stated that England has not improved in literacy, and we have slipped to seventeenth place in their league table.

Conclusion

Debates about literacy have always been controversial. In terms that are eerily familiar, Katherine Bathurst, an Inspector for the Board of Education in 1905, describes the process of learning to read a from a new boy's point of view:

> A blackboard has been produced, and hieroglyphics are drawn upon it by the teacher. At a given signal every child in the class begins calling out mysterious sounds: 'Letter A, letter A' in a sing-song voice, or 'Letter A says Ah, letter A says Ah', as the case may be. To the uninitiated I may explain that No. 1 is the beginning of spelling, and No. 2 is the beginning of word building. Hoary headed men will spend hours discussing whether 'c-a-t' or 'ker-ar-te' are the best means of conveying the knowledge of how to read cat. I must own an indifference to the point myself, and sympathise with teachers not allowed to settle it for themselves.[61]

She might express 'indifference' but the problem is that others do not. One way of understanding it is to see how closely our view of what it means to be literate relates to our view of the purpose of education and through education our beliefs about the nature of society and our place within in it. In his essay on *Modern Education and the Classics*, TS Eliot describes education as:

> A subject which cannot be discussed in a void: our questions raise other questions, social economic, financial, political. And the bearings are on more ultimate problems even than these: to know what we want in education we must know what we want in general, we must derive our theory of education from our theory of life.[62]

So Gunther Kress, for example, who has progressive views, wrote that:

> If we represent literacy, in the curriculum, as a matter of fixed, immutable rules, we encourage a different attitude to the one suggested by a representation of literacy as a set of resources shaped by society and constantly reshaped by each individual reader and writer. The former encourages an acceptance of what is; a certain attitude to authority; a limitation accepted and internalised by the individual. The latter encourages curiosity about how things have come to be as they are; a certain attitude to individual responsibility and agency; and an internalisation of the individual as active, creative and expansive.[63]

Yet in a chapter ironically subtitled 'Proper literacy' the newspaper columnist, Melanie Phillips, who is more traditional, writes, 'The revolt against the teaching of grammar becomes a part of a wider repudiation of external forms of authority'.[64] She lays the blame at the door of radical English teachers:

> English, after all is the subject at the heart of our definition of our national cultural identity. Since English teachers are the chief custodians of that identity we should not be surprised to find that revolutionaries intent on using the subject to transform society have gained a powerful foothold, attempting to redefine the very meaning of reading itself.[65]

These differences are not necessarily party political. Gove and Blunkett are on different sides of the party political fence but in the business of literacy they are as one. Brian Cox, who wrote the first national curriculum for English, described himself as a 'moderate progressive[s]'[66] despite voting Conservative for much of his adult life. For now though it would seem that synthetic phonics has won the day. Children are not only to be taught to read by this method alone but are now tested (since May 2012) at the age of six, at the end of year 1, to discover how successful they have been in acquiring phonic knowledge. This, despite the fact that there is no evidence that synthetic phonics is any better a way of teaching children to read than any other, and, according to the APPG, and many academics, might be detrimental to some. In a letter written by the United Kingdom Literacy Association in October 2011, they said that:

> "This confirms our previously expressed worry that the use of a test of only the decoding aspect of reading could actually harm standards in the longer term, with able readers mistakenly identified as needing further teaching of phonetics and being held back as a result.[67]"

So far the coalition has not responded.

Notes

1. Brighouse, T. (2011) Decline and fall: are state schools and universities on the point of collapse? Keynote lecture, Lady Margaret Hall, Oxford 16 September.
2. Ibid.
3. Cox, B. (1995) *Cox on the Battle for the English Curriculum* (p. 37). London: Hodder & Stoughton.
4. Departmental Committee of the Board of Education (1921) *The Teaching of English in England: Being the Report of the Departmental Committee Appointed by the President of the Board of Education to Inquire into the Position of English in the Educational System of England* [Newbolt Report]. (Ch. 3, para. 77: 72) London: Her Majesty's Stutionery Office (HMSO).
5. Ibid.
6. Cox, B. op. cit., p. 3.
7. Ibid., p. 38.
8. *Evening Standard* cited in All-Party Parliamentary Group for Education (2011) *Report of the Enquiry into Overcoming the Barriers to Literacy*. London: HMSO.
9. Ibid.
10. Gove, M. (2010) *Failing Schools Need New Leadership*. Availabel online at www.conservatives.com/News/Speeches/2009/10/Michael_Gove_Failing_schools_need_new_leadership.aspx (accessed 4 December 2010).
11. Blunkett, D. (1999) Commentary: moaners who are cheating your children, *Daily Mail*, 19 July.
12. Brooks, G. (1997) *Trends in Standards of Literacy in the United Kingdom 1948–1997*. Paper preserved at the British Educational Research Association Conference, University of York, 11–14 September.

13. Twist, L., Sainsbury, M., Woodthorpe, A. and Whetton, C. (2003) *Reading All Over the World: Progress in International Reading.* Literacy Study (PIRLS) National Report for England. Slough: National Foundation for Educational Research (NFER).
14. Mary Hilton (2006) Measuring standards in primary English: issues of validity and accountability with respect to PIRLS and National Curriculum test scores, *British Educational Research Journal*, 32(6): 817–37; Mary Hilton (2007) A further brief response from Mary Hilton to: 'Measuring standards in primary English: the validity of PIRLS – a response to Mary Hilton' by Chris Whetton, Liz Twist and Marian Sainsbury, *British Educational Research Journal*, 33(6): 987–90.
15. OECD (2010) *Programme for International Student Development.* Available online at www.pisa.oecd.org/document/61/0,3746,en_32252351_32235731_46567613_1_1_1_1,00.html (accessed 14 December 2010).
16. Department for Education and Skills (DfES) (2006) *Independent Review of the Teaching of Early Reading: The Final Report.* [Rose Report] London: HMSO.
17. Department for Children, Schools and Families (DCSF) (2008) *Independent Review of the Primary Curriculum: Final Report.* Available online at www.publications.education.gov.uk/eOrderingDownload/Primary_curriculum_Report.pdf (accessed 8 December 2010).
18. DfES, op. cit., p. 4.
19. Ibid., p. 4.
20. Ibid., p. 36.
21. Department for Education and Employment (DfEE) (1997) *The National Literacy Strategy.* London: HMi.
22. Watson, E. and Johnston, R. (2005) *Accelerating Reading Attainment: The effectiveness of synthetic phonics.* St. Andrews: University of St. Andrews.
23. Ellis cited in Rosen, M. (2006) Available online at www.michaelrosen.co.uk/kingstalk.html (accessed 3 December 2010).
24. Ibid.
25. Ibid.
26. National Institute of Child Health and Human Development (NIH, DHHS) (2000) *Report of the National Reading Panel: Teaching Children to Read (00-4769).* Washington, DC: US Government Printing Office.
27. All-Party Parliamentary Group for Education (2011) *Report of the Enquiry into Overcoming the Barriers to Literacy.* London: HMSO.
28. Ibid., p. 6.
29. Ibid., p. 4.
30. Ibid., p. 14.
31. Alexander, R. (2009) *Children, Their World, Their Education: Final Report and Recommendations of the Cambridge Primary Review.* London: Routledge.

32. Ibid., p. 269.
33. Alexander, R. (2006) *Education as Dialogue: Moral and Pedagogical Choices for a Runaway World.* Cambridge: Dialogos.
34. Ibid., p. 5.
35. Dewey, J. (1966) *Experience and Education* (p. 18). London: Collier Books.
36. Street, B. and Street, J. (1991) The schooling of literacy, in D. Barton and R. Ivanich (eds) *Writing in the Community*. London: Sage Publications.
37. Freire, P. and Macedo, D. (1987) *Literacy: Reading the Word and the World* (p. 41). London: Routledge.
38. Aronowitz and Giroux, cited in Ball, S.J., Kenny, A. and Gardiner, D. (1990) Literacy policy and the teaching of English, in I. Goodson and P. Medway (eds) *Bringing English to Order* (p. 61). London: Falmer.
39. Heath, S. (1983) *Ways With Words.* Cambridge: Cambridge University Press.
40. Gee, cited in Corden, R. (2000) *Literacy and Learning Through Talk* (p. 27). Maidenhead: Open University Press.
41. Hoggart, R. (1998) Critical literacy and creative reading, in B. Cox (ed.) *Literacy Is Not Enough: Essays on the Importance of Reading* (p. 60). Manchester: Manchester University Press.
42. Meek, M. (1988) *How Texts Teach What Readers Learn.* Stroud: Thimble Press; Meek, M. (1991) *On Being Literate.* London: Bodley Head.
43. Barnes, D., Britten, J. and Rosen, H. (1972) *Language, the Learner and the School.* Middlesex: Penguin Books.
44. Britton, J. (1974) *Language and Learning.* Middlesex: Penguin Books.
45. Corden, op. cit., p. 8.
46. Vygotsky, L. (1978a) *Thought and Language.* Cambridge, MA: MIT Press.
47. Bruner, J. (1985) Vygotsky: a historical and conceptual perspective, in J. Wertsch (ed.) *Culture, Communication and Cognition: Vygotskian Perspectives.* Cambridge: Cambridge University Press.
48. Dewey, J. op. cit., pp. 28–29.
49. Ibid., p. 29.
50. Barrs, M. and Cook, V. (2002) *The Reader in the Writer.* London: CLPE.
51. Office for Standards in Education (Ofsted) (2005a) *English 2000–5: A Review of the Inspection Evidence.* London: HMSO.
52. Bell, D. (03.03. 2005) A good read., in a speech to mark World Book Day.
53. Ofsted, op. cit.
54. Ofsted (2005b) *The Literacy and Numeracy Strategies and the Primary Curriculum: HMCI* (p. 16). London: HMSO.
55. Ibid., pp. 16–17.
56. Twist, L., Sainsbury, M., Woodthorpe, A. and Whetton, C. (2003) op. cit., p. 22.
57. Bullock Report (1975) cited in Ofsted (2005a) *English 2000–5. A Review of the Inspection Evidence* (p. 24). London: HMSO.

58. OECD (2002) *Reading for change: a report on the programme for international Student Assessment*, cited in Ofsted (2005a) *English 2000–5* (p. 2). London: HMI.
59. Ofsted (2004) Reading for purpose and pleasure, cited in Ofsted (2005a) *English 2000–5* (p. 23). London: HMI.
60. OECD (2010) *Programme for International Student Development*. Availabel online at www.pisa.oecd.org/document/61/0,3746,en_32252351_32235731_46567613_1_1_1_1,00.html (accessed 14 December 2010).
61. Bathurst, cited in van der Eyken, W. (1973) *Education, the Child and Society: A Documentary History 1900–1973* (p. 121). London: Penguin.
62. Elliot, cited in Tate, N. (1998) *What is Education For? The Fifth Annual Education Lecture* (pp. 3–4). London: King's College.
63. Kress, G. (1995) *Writing the Future: English and the Making of a Culture of Innovation* (p. 75). Sheffield: NATE Papers in Education.
64. Phillips, M. (1997) *All Must have Prizes* (p. 69). London: Little, Brown and Co.
65. Ibid., p. 69.
66. Cox, B. (1992) *The Great Betrayal: Memoirs of a Life in Education* (p. 112). London: Hodder & Stoughton.
67. UK Literacy Association (UKLA) (2011) Letter to Michael Gove, 21 October.

Is informal education better than formal education?

Justin Dillon

Introduction

Here is an argument that you might find plausible. The evidence suggests that the more students experience 'formal' science education at school, the more they dislike it. However, take them into an 'informal' setting such as a science centre or an outdoor environmental centre and they become enthralled and fascinated by the authentic experience. *Ergo*, if we can find out what young people like about science outside schools and then translate it into the school experience then we will make science education much more interesting.

However, there are several assumptions implicit in that argument that are not altogether supported by the evidence. The first is that there are two types of learning, formal and informal. The second is that informal learning is better than formal learning in some way. The third is that it is both possible and desirable to transfer the good aspects of informal education into the formal school system. This chapter challenges all three assumptions. An examination of what young people *do* think about science in and out of school does suggest that while there may be much to learn about why science centres and museums are popular, transposing strategies from one location to another is unlikely to succeed. It might be far more effective for schools and other science education institutions to work in partnership in a sustained cooperation.

Formal and informal what?

Since the first schools opened there have been school critics. Criticisms of schools and schooling range from ill-informed sweeping generalizations to accurate and perceptive insights. Some critics are convinced that the whole formalized process of education, whether it be in schools or, later in life, in universities or training facilities, is bordering on being a waste of time. Here, for example, is Jay Cross, a management consultant, introducing his book, *Informal Learning: Rediscovering the Natural Pathways that Inspire Innovation and Performance*:

> Workers learn more in the coffee room than in the classroom. They discover how to do their job through informal learning: talking, observing others, trial and error, and simply working with people in the know. Formal learning – classes and workshops – is the source of only 10 to 20 percent of what people learn at work. Corporations overinvest in formal training programs while neglecting natural, simpler informal processes.[1]

Cross does note that 'formal' and 'informal' learning 'both involve building new neural connections in the brain and adapting to new conditions. They are very much the same. They coexist.'[2] Cross explains the difference between the two phenomena as follows:

> Imagine a spectrum of learning. One band along the continuum is formal. It frequently takes an industrial-age approach. It's regimented. Instructions come down from above. Inspectors check on productivity. Frequently, it's a production-line approach to learning. It's useful for indoctrinating groups of people with similar needs, for example, novices in a technical environment.
>
> Another band on the continuum is informal. It's the way people have learned for eons: through observation, trial and error, listening to grandma's stories. In my view, the defining characteristic is that informal learning does not have a curriculum. Nor does it usually have grades or certification. Often it's impromptu rather than scheduled.[3]

Actually, reading Cross's thoughts it sounds as though he is talking more about education than about the mental process of learning. That is, he is talking about the context in which learning takes place rather than about what it is that's learned or how it's learned. Dichotomies such as these appeal to some business leaders and politicians. The problem, of course, is that life is much more complicated and therefore reasoning about issues has to be much more sophisticated.

The way that Cross conceptualizes formal and informal learning is rather different to the distinction made by many other people. In 1990, Jerry Wellington wrote that 'there are two areas of learning which must be considered in examining science education, the public understanding of science and the advancement of science itself. These', he added, 'may be called formal and informal learning'.[4] Wellington constructed a table showing what he described as the features of formal and informal learning in science (Table 8.1).

Wellington, who was writing specifically about the role of science centres, noted that the features 'can both conflict or help, or be mutually helpful'.[5] Nevertheless, overall the table suggests that the two types of learning are quite far apart and represent educational activities underpinned by significantly different philosophical positions. As with Cross's position, Wellington seems to be talking more about context than about process or content.

Table 8.1 Features of formal and informal learning in science

Informal learning	*Formal learning*
Voluntary	Compulsory
Haphazard, unstructured, unsequenced	Structured and sequenced
Non-assessed, non-certificated	Assessed, certificated
Open-ended	More closed
Learner-led, learner-centred	Teacher-led, teacher-centred
Outside of formal settings	Classroom- and institution-based
Unplanned	Planned
Many unintended outcomes (outcomes more difficult to measure)	Fewer unintended outcomes
Social aspect central (e.g. social interactions, between visitors)	Social aspect less central
Low 'currency'	High 'currency'
Undirected, not legislated for	Legislated and directed (controlled)

Wellington was convinced that in the 1990s, 'informal learning in science will take place in a variety of contexts and through an increasing number of media' which turned out to be the case. What he did not predict was the level of interest in the impact of learning in contexts other than schools that has developed in recent years. This change has partly come about because we live in an era of accountability in education and elsewhere. So, for example, if the UK's Association for Science and Discovery Centres wishes to make a case for government funding of their members' institutions, then they need to present evidence of impact to the Secretary of State. In this context, impact refers to gains in learning or improvements in attitudes towards science. It seems as though funding bodies see learning simply as a matter of adding new bricks to a wall rather than strengthening the mortar to make the wall stronger.

In 2002, Helen Colley, Phil Hodkinson and Janice Malcolm reviewed a number of different discourses around formal, non-formal and informal learning. After looking in detail at eight ways of conceptualizing learning in different contexts they found that there were few, if any, learning situations where either informal or formal elements were completely absent. Their conclusions, which are remarkably shrewd, have not had as much impact subsequently as one might have hoped:

> “Firstly, in many of them (but not all), informal learning is defined by what it is not – formal. Secondly, many of the lists (but not all) carry value assumptions, implicit or explicit, that one form or another is inherently superior – sometimes morally, sometimes in terms of effectiveness. Thirdly, there is an overlapping body of writing about non-formal and informal education, which cannot be easily or clearly separated off from learning. All this throws serious doubts about the possibility and advisability of seeking clear definitional distinctions between these different types of learning or education.[6]”

Colley and colleagues note that 'at the centre of these debates lie conflicting claims about the inherent superiority of one or the other.'[7] Why else, one might ask, would anyone spend time on listing the characteristics of 'formal' or 'informal' learning? It would be better if we could stop denoting the formal or informal context adjectively and simply talk about learning as taking place in specific contexts or settings, thus:

> Learning in informal settings refers to the opportunities and environments for learning that exist beyond traditional or 'formal' schooling. Such opportunities and environments include those provided by museums, galleries, science centers, zoos, botanic gardens, and wildlife parks. They may also be considered to include afterschool programs, Saturday science clubs, as well as those afforded by books, television programs, new media, and the Internet.[8]

The benefits of learning outside the classroom

Criticisms of formal schooling have at times been very harsh. Here, for example, is Frank Oppenheimer, one-time scientific director of the Manhattan Project, who was the founder and first director of the Exploratorium in San Francisco, the most well-known, if not actually the first, science centre in the world:

> . . . no-one ever flunks a museum or a television program or a library or a park, while they do flunk a course–they do 'flunk out of school'. Only schools can certify students; only certified students can progress. As a result only schools are conceived as public education. I would like to suggest that the current mechanisms for certification are not only stifling to educational progress but that they are also extraordinarily costly and wasteful. Certification is an impediment.[9]

Whatever the motivation for providing alternative venues for learning they have become part of everyday life. Science centres, museums, botanic gardens and other such institutions are increasingly seen as places that provide more than a pleasant day out. While their initial claims to be places of learning were met by resistance from some educationalists who labelled what happened in the centres as little more than 'edutainment', increasing research evidence has shown them to offer a wide range of affordances. It has become clear, though, that the learning is affected by a number of factors some of which are outlined below.

Factors associated with different contexts

The learning that takes place in out-of-school contexts can be affected by a range of factors including the novelty of the situation, the lack of a fixed curriculum and the ability to choose one's own route through an exhibition. Another factor to consider is that most visitors have chosen to engage with the learning and, in some cases, actually pay for it. This level of commitment and motivation may well impact on the degree of learning that occurs. One of the challenges facing educators in informal settings is that the time that visitors have available can be short and there is virtually no time to get to know them. Consequently, museum educators need to be adept at using specimens and objects to grab people's attention before they find out what level of knowledge or experience the visitors have about the topic. Educators in these informal contexts need a skill set quite different from that demonstrated by school teachers.[10] They need to be able to use 'particular modes of talk – re-voicing, repeating, summarizing – to guide, structure, and scaffold learner engagement'.[11] A final point to consider is that learning in out-of-school contexts often has a very social dimension. Whether it be the class visit or the family outing, the mediating impact of the other members of the group can have a huge influence on the quality of the learning that takes place. The role of the family or friends – who do know the learner well – can be critical to the learning and engagement.

Museums have come to realize that school visits can provide a direct or an indirect source of income and have developed their offer so that it meets teachers' needs that are usually curriculum-focused. Perhaps ironically, museums and outdoor centres are becoming more like schools with classrooms, laboratories, paid teachers and activities focused on curriculum topics. They provide materials to help school teachers prepare for visits and can help with follow-up activities; for example, through the provision of websites holding images selected by the students during their visits. In some cases school students are actually involved in co-curating displays and in leading public tours.[12] The boundaries between formal and informal contexts have never been more blurred.

We are entering an era when relationships between schools and museums, science centres, galleries and gardens are seen as essential rather than desirable. The trend is more established in the USA[13] than in the

UK but the gap is beginning to close. In the UK, the Teaching and Learning Research Programme (TLRP) has stated that learning in informal contexts 'such as learning out of school, should be recognised as at least as significant as formal learning and should therefore be valued and appropriately utilised in formal processes'.[14]

Learning outdoors – shifting the locus of learning

So far the focus of the chapter has been mainly on museums, science centres and similar venues. However, a good deal of education outside the classroom takes place in school grounds, in local parks and open spaces and at residential centres usually in the countryside in the UK or even overseas.

Advocates of outdoor education are sometimes guilty of over-generalising about its value. Tim Brighouse, a well-known educationalist, is quoted as saying 'One lesson outdoors is worth seven inside',[15] while Graham Smith wrote that 'the importance of fieldwork to geographers is beyond question'.[16] And the head of Eton College is of the belief that 'pupils learn more outside the classroom than they do inside'.[17] A consideration of the research evidence suggests that a more cautious view of the value of learning in the outdoors might be more accurate.

The most authoritative survey of research into learning outside the classroom was carried out by Rickinson et al. in 2004. The authors concluded that:

> “Substantial evidence exists to indicate that fieldwork, properly conceived, adequately planned, well taught and effectively followed up, offers learners opportunities to develop their knowledge and skills in ways that add value to their everyday experiences in the classroom.[18]”

More recently, the national schools' inspectorate, the Office for Standards in Education (Ofsted), commented that 'When planned and implemented well, learning outside the classroom contributed significantly to raising standards and improving pupils' personal, social and emotional development'.[19] While Ofsted's report was not based on a thorough research study, it nevertheless confirms a growing view that some schools are failing to appreciate what the outdoors offers students.

The Rickinson et al. review identified four areas of impact on students that have been the focus of significant research: cognitive, affective; social/inter-personal; and physical behavioural. Those categorizations, however, reflected the literature reviewed that generally had a narrow approach more in keeping with research into learning in schools. A more recent study found that the value in England of learning in natural environments included enhanced educational attainment, attitudes to other children, awareness of environment and natural science skills, behavioural outcomes and social cohesion, health benefits, school staff morale and a more attractive school (aesthetically and to prospective parents).[20]

Some caveats

While it is true that substantial evidence exists of the potential benefits of fieldwork, it is not true that these benefits apply equally to all students in all settings. Two issues, in particular, are worth discussing; the value of novel settings and students' attitudes towards the outdoors.

While it might be thought that the more novel an experience, the more educative and experience it might provide, some evidence suggests otherwise. Australian researchers who studied high school science students during visits to a marine theme park noted that 'teachers need to ensure that students are not distracted by the novelty of the location'.[21] Too much novelty can be a bad thing though there is, as in many things, a balance to be maintained between novelty and preparedness. Ellis, on the basis of positive feedback from students nine months after a field trip to Norway, argued that less preparation than might normally take place could lead to more authentic responses to landscape from students.[22] It would be difficult, though, to imagine that many teachers would feel comfortable reducing the amount of preparation that they gave students.

Although many young people love the outdoors and messing about in streams and ponds, some do not. While many books aimed at children of primary school age focus on the outdoors as being exciting, books for older students are just as likely to show the outdoors as a place of danger so it is no wonder that some children harbour a fear of the countryside. In the USA, Bora Simmons interviewed children from Chicago focusing on their attitudes towards going outside. The children identified a range of natural hazards and expressed concerns about threats posed by strangers as well as indicating that they felt more physically comfortable indoors.[23] In studies by other researchers, children expressed fears about getting lost or about being harmed by snakes or poisonous plants.[24] These fears and phobias can have a negative impact on children's learning in the outdoor classroom. Children with a high 'disgust sensitivity' prefer to take part in activities that do not involve handling organic matter and they would rather work in sites with clear water, no algae and easy access rather than wading into muddy streams.[25]

Why don't more teachers make use of the outside classroom?

There has been concern for some time that children's access to nature is on the decline. The issue is more complex than that statement suggests as research has found that not only are children losing their connection with the natural environment but also that it is children in urban environments who are particularly disadvantaged.[26] Another disturbing statistic is that only 10 per cent of children play in the natural environment compared to 40 per cent of adults who played in natural environments when they were young.[27]

The conventional wisdom is that schools do not take their students on so many visits to the natural environment for three reasons: cost, health and safety concerns and lack of adequate supply cover. While these reasons may be true for some schools the arguments do not stand up to much scrutiny. How is it that some schools do take their students on visits and others do not? A deeper set of issues might explain the variation.

Looking first at the issue of cost, in 2005 the House of Commons Education and Skills Committee investigated education outside the classroom. In their report, they were dismissive: 'we do not believe that cost alone is responsible for the decline of education outside the classroom, or that simply throwing money at the problem would provide a solution'. By way of explanation, they added:

> This conclusion is supported by evidence from the DfES London Challenge programme. As part of this initiative, the Field Studies Council offered full funding to schools to support an off-site educational visit. One third of schools did not take up this offer despite it being effectively free of charge. It seems therefore that an increase in funding alone would not be enough to persuade schools to change their behaviour . . .[28]

In terms of the risks of taking students on visits, the Committee was equally dismissive:

> Many of the organisations and individuals who submitted evidence to our inquiry cited the fear of accidents and the possibility of litigation as one of the main reasons for the apparent decline in school trips. It is the view of this Committee that this fear is entirely out of proportion to the real risks.[29]

The risks have been exaggerated for many years. They are linked to 'a prevailing social trend, not only towards making things safer, but also towards seeking compensation for acts or omissions that result in personal injury'.[30]

The real barriers

Another set of barriers must exist to explain the differences between individual teachers and schools. Studies of teachers' responses to curriculum change and professional development suggest that a number of factors impact on teachers' pedagogical choices; that is, how and what they decide to teach. These factors are as follows:

- teachers' view of the nature of their subject;
- teachers' views of the role of education;
- teachers' views of effective pedagogy;
- teachers' self-efficacy;

- teachers' working practices (planning, teaching and evaluation);
- teachers' and "school leaders' commitment" to school-community links;
- the relationship between schools and providers.[31]

Any attempt to encourage teachers to use the outdoors might benefit from taking these factors into account. Professional development that treats teachers as individuals working in unique contexts may be the answer. This is the approach taken by the Natural Connections Demonstration Project that was due to commence in autumn 2012.

Conclusion: towards synergy rather than competition

The false dichotomy of formal and informal learning emerged at a time when it was realized that museums and science centres offered great potential not just for enthusing people about science but facilitating science learning. It has taken some time for advocates of learning outside the classroom to realize that partnerships between schools and other institutions might offer a better way forward than competition. Museums, science centres, botanic gardens and other outdoor classroom institutions have produced pre- and post-visit resources to provide an experience that brings together what they can offer and what schools can offer. There is still a long way to go but examples of good practice continue to emerge. What is required now is funding to strengthen and expand existing partnerships, develop new links and research what the advantages of these partnerships are to learners, teachers and the schools and institutions themselves. At its heart, this is an issue of equitable access to the range of learning experience that collaboration can provide.

Notes

1. Cross, J. (2007) *Informal Learning: Extending the Impact of Enterprise Ideas and Information*. Available online at www.adobe.com/resources/elearning/pdfs/informal_learning.pdf.
2. Cross (op. cit.).
3. Cross (op. cit.).

4. Wellington, J. (1990) Formal and informal learning in science: the role of interactive science centres, *Physics Education*, 25(5): 247–52: p. 247.
5. Wellington (op. cit.).
6. Colley, H., Hodkinson, P. and Malcolm, J. (2002) *Non-formal Learning: Mapping the Conceptual Terrain. A Consultation Report*. Leeds: University of Leeds.
7. Colley et al. (op. cit.).
8. King, H. and Dillon, J. (2012) Learning in informal settings, in N. Seel (ed.) *Encyclopedia of the Sciences of Learning* (Part 12, 1905–1908, p. 1905). New York: Springer.
9. Oppenheimer, F. (1975) The Exploratorium and other ways of teaching physics, *Physics Today*, 28(9): 9–13: 11.
10. Tran, L. and King, H. (2007) The professionalization of museum educators: the case in science museums, *Museum Management and Curatorship*, 22(2): 129–47.
11. King, H. and Dillon, J. (op. cit.), p. 1906.
12. See, for example, www.wallacecollection.org/education/specialprojects.
13. Bevan, B. with Dillon, J., Hein, G.E., Macdonald, M., Michalchik, V., Miller, D., Root, D., Rudder, L., Xanthoudaki, M. and Yoon, S. (2010) *Making Science Matter: Collaborations Between Informal Science Education Organizations and Schools. A CAISE Inquiry Group Report*. Washington, DC: Center for Advancement of Informal Science Education (CAISE).
14. Cambridge Primary Review (2008) *Learning and Teaching in Primary Schools: Insights from TLRP*. Available online at www.tlrp.org/themes/documents/PRresearchsurvey.pdf, p. 18.
15. Tim Brighouse, quoted in May, S., Richardson, P. and Banks, V. (1993) *Fieldwork in Action: Planning Fieldwork* (p. 2). Sheffield: Geographical Society.
16. Smith, G. (1999) Changing fieldwork objectives and constraints in secondary schools in England, *International Research in Geographical and Environmental Education*, 8(2): 181–89: 181.
17. Tony Little, quoted in Eyres, H. (2008) Bold Etonians, *Financial Times*, 23 May, p. 1.
18. Rickinson, M., Dillon, J., Teamey, K., Morris, M., Choi, M. Y., Sanders, D. and Benefield, P. (2004) *A Review of Research on Outdoor Learning*. Preston Montford: Field Studies Council.
19. Office for Standards in Education (Ofsted) (2008) *Learning Outside the Classroom. How Far Should You Go?* London: Ofsted.
20. eftec (2011) Assessing the benefits of learning outside the classroom in natural environments. Final Report for King's College London.
21. Burnett, J., Lucas, K.B. and Dooley, J.H. (1996) Small group behaviour in a novel field environment: senior science students visit a marine theme park, *Australian Science Teachers' Journal*, 42(4): 59–64: 63.

22. Ellis, B. (1993) Introducing humanistic geography through fieldwork, *Journal of Geography in Higher Education*, 17(2): 131–39.
23. Simmons, D.A. (1994) A comparison of urban children's and adults' preferences and comfort levels for natural areas, *International Journal of Environmental Education and Information*, 13(4): 399–413; Simmons, D.A. (1994) Urban children's preferences for nature: lessons for environmental education, *Children's Environments*, 11(3): 194–203.
24. Wals, A.E.J. (1994) Nobody planted it, it just grew! Young adolescents' perceptions and experiences of nature in the context of urban environmental education, *Children's Environments*, 11(3): 177–93; Bixler, R.D., Carlisle, C.L., Hammitt, W.E. and Floyd, M.F. (1994) Observed fears and discomforts among urban students on field trips to wildland areas, *Journal of Environmental Education*, 26(1): 24–33.
25. Bixler, R.D. and Floyd, M.F. (1999) Hands on or hands off? Disgust sensitivity and preference for environmental education activities, *Journal of Environmental Education*, 30(3): 4–11.
26. Thomas, G. and Thompson, G. (2004) *A Child's Place: Why Environment Matters to Children*. London: Green Alliance/DEMOS.
27. England Marketing (2009) *Report to Natural England on Childhood and Nature: A Survey on Changing Relationships with Nature across Generations*. Warboys: England Marketing.
28. House of Commons Education and Skills Committee (2005) *Education Outside the Classroom*. Available online at www.publications.parliament.uk/pa/cm200405/cmselect/cmeduski/120/12002.htm, p. 21.
29. House of Commons Education and Skills Committee (op. cit.), p. 29.
30. Harris, I. (1999) Outdoor education in secondary schools: what future? *Horizons*, 4: 5–8.
31. Dillon, J. (2010) *Beyond barriers to learning outside the classroom in natural environments*. Available online at www.theoutdoorsnation.files.wordpress.com/2010/11/lotc-barriers-analysis-final.pdf.

The social and emotional aspects of learning (SEAL) programme

Neil Humphrey

Introduction

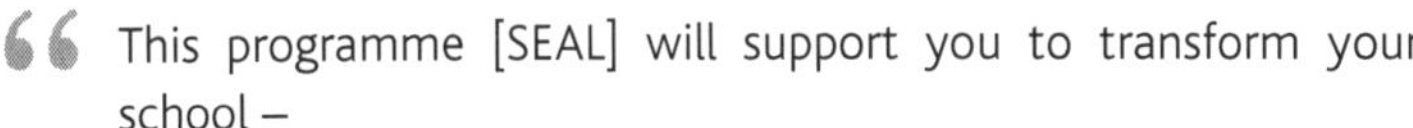

> This programme [SEAL] will support you to transform your school –
>
> *(National Strategies Website, 2010)*

Following its launch as part of the Behaviour and Attendance Pilot in 2003, the social and emotional aspects of learning (SEAL) programme swept through the English education system. By 2010 it was estimated that SEAL was being implemented in 90 per cent of primary schools and 70 per cent of secondary schools.[1] SEAL was a flagship New Labour initiative that was promoted as a panacea for schools. It was claimed that SEAL would improve academic results, behaviour, attendance, and a variety of other important outcomes, and was funded to the tune of at least £30 million.[2] However, far from being a universal remedy, close inspection of the various independent evaluations of SEAL suggest that it has failed to achieve the majority of its intended outcomes. This chapter explores the reasons behind this failure, considering such issues as the intellectual and academic basis for SEAL, the role of independent evaluation in the development and refinement of educational policy, and the broader evidence base for approaches to social and emotional learning (SEL). It concludes by using Stich's[3] four-factor model for the promotion of unfounded ideas as a lens through which to consider how SEAL rose to such prominence in the English education system.

What is SEAL?

SEAL is described as, 'a comprehensive approach to promoting the social and emotional skills that underpin effective learning, positive behaviour, regular attendance, staff effectiveness and the emotional health and wellbeing of all who learn and work in schools'.[4] It is based upon the framework of emotional intelligence (EI) popularized by Goleman.[5] SEAL's constituent components are: (a) the use of a whole-school approach to create a positive school climate and ethos; (b) direct teaching of social and emotional skills in whole-class contexts; (c) the use of teaching and learning approaches that support the learning of such skills; and (d) continuing professional development for school staff.[4] Implementation of SEAL follows the 'waves of intervention' model promoted by the National Strategies, outlined in Figure 9.1.

SEAL implementation in schools was supported by a number of guidance documents and materials pertaining to its different components (e.g. 'family SEAL', 'SEAL small groupwork') and versions (e.g. 'primary SEAL', 'secondary SEAL'), and training offered in local authorities (LAs)

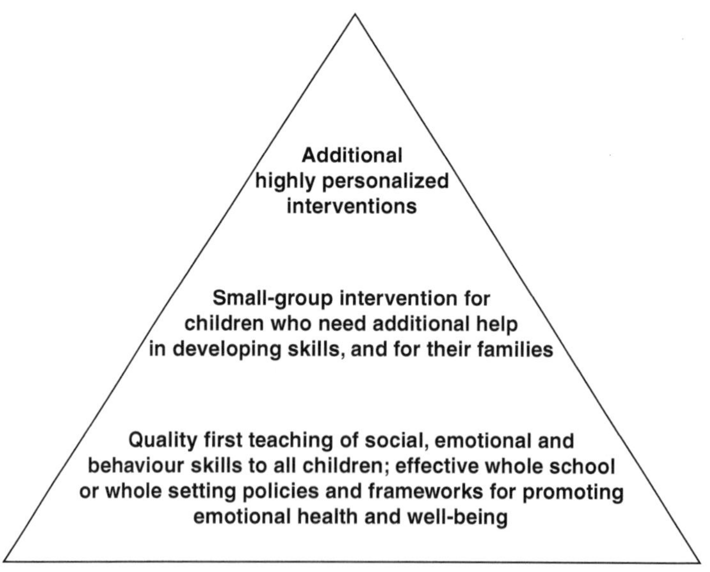

Figure 9.1 National Strategies' 'waves of intervention' model applied to SEAL[6].

by behaviour and attendance consultants and other professionals working in children's services. As a programme, it is somewhat unusual in relation to the broader literature on approaches to SEL in that it is envisaged as a loose enabling framework for school improvement[7] rather than a structured 'package' to be applied in schools. Schools – particularly in secondary SEAL – were actively encouraged to explore different approaches to implementation that supported identified school improvement priorities rather than following a single model. This philosophy was reflected in the absence of materials for some components (e.g. in the primary SEAL small groupwork guidance, materials were only available for four of the seven themed interventions, with school staff encouraged to develop their own),[8] and the inclusion of a variety of contrasting implementation case studies in the guidance produced for schools.[4] In some cases, this led to an 'anything goes' model with, for example, some children being taught that their bodies had seven 'energy centres', each with a different colour, as part of the SEAL programme.[2]

The emergence of SEAL – a brief overview of the New Labour policy context

SEAL emerged from the confluence of a number of related influences and factors. At the policy level, New Labour were under pressure to redress the technicism in the English education system embodied by the 'standards agenda' (e.g. narrowly focused league tables, targets and inspection regimes).[9] In the early part of the decade, they began to develop more holistic policy directives with a focus on promoting well-being (e.g. *Every Child Matters*).[10] Around the same time, Weare and Gray published an influential review, funded by the Department for Education and Skills (DfES), entitled *What Works in Promoting Children's Emotional and Social Competence and Wellbeing*?.[11] One of the key recommendations of their report was the prioritization, development and implementation of a national, school-based programme to promote social and emotional skills in pupils and staff. Finally, Daniel Goleman's bestseller had brought the concept of EI (and its claimed importance in education, the workplace and life in general) into the public consciousness. These factors ultimately led to the DfES commissioning a new National Strategy as part of the Behaviour and Attendance Pilot, and SEAL was born to a great fanfare with the claims made that the programme could produce:

> “better academic results for all pupils and schools; more effective learning . . . higher motivation; better behaviour; higher school attendance; more responsible pupils, who are better citizens and more able to contribute to society; lower levels of stress and anxiety; higher morale, performance and retention of staff; [and] a more positive school ethos.”

It was ostensibly designed around the key principles of ‘what works’ from many years of research conducted in the field of SEL in the USA and elsewhere, and as such was adopted unquestioningly by LAs and schools across England.

The emperor has no clothes – a critical analysis of SEAL

As a central component of the policy drive around childhood well-being[12] and with the apparent backing of the SEL evidence base, the SEAL programme enjoyed a honeymoon period in which critics were few and far between – indeed, aside from this chapter, to date only Craig,[8] Ecclestone and Hayes,[13, 14] and Humphrey[15] have ever published critiques of the programme. Those who raised objections to the SEAL orthodoxy had their concerns dismissed as being, ‘based on ideology and anecdote rather than any robust data.’ However, as this section of the chapter shows, the problems with the SEAL programme are in fact brought to light by close scrutiny of the evidence.

The evidence base for SEAL

‘The temptation to form premature theories upon insufficient data is the bane of our profession’ (Sherlock Holmes in *The Valley of Fear*, Arthur Conan Doyle, 1915).

Currently, seven studies have been conducted that have evaluated at least one component of SEAL in some way. These are listed in Table 9.1.

Table 9.1 Published evaluations of the SEAL programme

SEAL component	*Original study*	*Related publications*
Primary – curriculum	16	17
Secondary – pilot	18, 19	
Primary – small groupwork	20	21, 22, 23, 24, 25
Secondary – whole school	1	26
Primary – family	27	
Primary/secondary – whole school	19	

Inspection of these studies and their associated publications reveals several key themes. The first of these is the *lack of methodological rigour*. Of the five studies that purported to assess the impact of SEAL (the two studies of the secondary pilot being primarily concerned with assessment of process), three lacked a control/comparison group,[16] and one also lacked a longitudinal element. However, this did not prevent the greatly *overstated impact* of the SEAL programme. Take, for example, the conclusion drawn by Hallam et al.,[16] that the primary SEAL programme, 'had a major impact on children's wellbeing, confidence, social and communication skills, relationships, including bullying, playtime behaviour, pro-social behaviour and attitudes towards schools'. The analyses presented in the report simply do not support such a statement, with statistically significant changes only in certain variables, and marginal effect sizes across the board.[13]

Another important theme is the *null results* reported in several studies. Humphrey, Lendrum and Wigelsworth, Downey and Williams,[17] and Humphrey et al. (in relation to parental ratings and maximal measures of social and emotional competence)[28] each failed to find a measurable impact of SEAL. Perhaps more worryingly, one study found potentially *negative findings* with academic performance declining (for children in Key Stage 1) and attitudes to school (for children in Key Stage 2) worsening during the course of SEAL implementation in Hallam et al.'s evaluation of primary SEAL.[16] Although one study – Humphrey et al.'s evaluation of the primary small groupwork element[20] – did report a measurable impact of SEAL in some domains using a methodologically defensible design, this was the exception to the rule.

The role of research in policy development – use and abuse

The SEAL programme provides an exemplar of the strange role commissioned research often plays in educational policy development. Used properly, independent research can help to refine policy as part of the process of improving the education system. However, under New Labour, this research was often little more than window dressing; if a given evaluation was perceived as supporting the policy directive in question, it was celebrated. If the study findings were seen as undermining policy, there were attempts to manipulate evidence[19] or the academics leading the research were vilified.[29,30] In the case of SEAL, the DfEs were so keen to capitalize on the EI zeitgeist that they did not bother to wait for the results of pilot evaluations before launching the programme nationally. Hence, the primary SEAL guidance for schools was published in May 2005,[31] a full 10 months before the pilot evaluation findings were reported in February 2006. Similarly, the secondary SEAL guidance for schools was published in April 2007,[4] three months before the two pilot evaluations reported their findings. The immediate and obvious problem this created was that there was no opportunity to learn from the pilot evaluation findings. As a result, key issues raised in pilot data – such as variability in implementation, workload challenges, attitudes and understanding, and slowing down of activity during the course of implementation in the case of secondary SEAL[18,32] – subsequently emerged during the national rollout.[1]

The academic and intellectual basis for SEAL

As noted earlier, Daniel Goleman's book on EI was a key influence in the development of SEAL, and this is evidenced clearly in the guidance provided for schools. The framework of social and emotional skills promoted through SEAL (empathy, self-awareness, self-regulation, motivation and social skills) is identical to Goleman's typology of EI, and indeed his work is cited throughout the various documents pertaining to the different components of the programme. However, Goleman's work has been heavily criticized by a variety of influential academics in the field of EI (e.g. Mayer, Salovey, Sternberg, Zeidner, Roberts and

Matthews). Craig's[13] critique of SEAL summarizes the main problems well, including the rather vague definition of EI, a shaky evidence base, overstated claims of the importance of EI, and its promotion as a panacea for social problems.

Given these issues, why was the populist notion of EI espoused by Goleman so influential? It may come down to two factors. First, Goleman's definition of EI is extremely wide-ranging and protean. In addition to the aspects of emotional ability extrapolated in the more respectable models of EI,[33] Goleman infuses characteristics such as warmth, persistence and optimism.[5] The sheer breadth of the character facets covered immediately increases the intuitive appeal of this framework – there is something for everyone. Perhaps more importantly though, Goleman's EI model may have been used as the lynchpin for SEAL purely because it was so popular, and could therefore be used as a 'hook' to entice educators. Few teachers in English schools would have heard of Salovey and Mayer, but many more would be familiar with Goleman. As Sternberg[34] states, Goleman's work 'stirred the imaginations of many people'.

The design of SEAL and evidence of 'what works' in the field of SEL

Implicit throughout the SEAL guidance is the idea that the design of the SEAL programme reflects the evidence of best and most effective practice in SEL.[15] However, there are in fact a number of fundamental differences in the *nature* of the SEAL and the SEL interventions for which there is a strongest evidence base. First, as previously mentioned, SEAL was designed as a 'loose enabling framework'.[17] This 'bottom-up' approach was taken because, 'too much top-down prescription and emphasis on programme fidelity can lead to a lack of ownership, disempowerment of those involved, and, ultimately, a lack of sustainability'.[7]

The approach described above contrasts sharply with that taken in the USA, where the emphasis has been on prescribed programmes, and where research has shown that programme fidelity – that is, the extent to which an intervention is delivered as intended, judged as the amount of deviation from a core model – is crucial in determining the success and impact of interventions. For example, Durlak and DuPre's seminal review concluded that 'higher levels of fidelity are significantly related to programme outcomes'.[35] Similarly, other reviews[36,37] have demonstrated that, 'the fidelity with which an intervention is implemented affects how well it succeeds'.[36] Programmes that have a strong evidence base in the SEL literature also provide structure and consistency in delivery.[38] SEAL – both as conceived and as subsequently delivered in schools – lacks these features, with no central model of implementation, and indeed, school actively encouraged to 'take from it what they wish'[7].

The divergence of the SEAL model from the SEL evidence base does not stop at the top-down versus bottom-up approach to implementation. The overall conceptualization of SEAL is as a 'whole-school' approach; that is, a universal, multi-component (e.g. curriculum, environment/ethos, parents/community) intervention that involves, 'thinking holistically, looking at the whole context including organization, structures, procedures and ethos, not just at individual pupils or at one part of the picture only'.[4] The secondary SEAL guidance makes the claim that whole-school approaches have been shown conclusively to be more effective than single component interventions in improving outcomes for children. This is based upon the proposition that the broader focus of multi-component programmes that extend beyond the classroom should better support the development of new skills.[39] However, as before, if we examine the research base thoroughly, we see that the evidence simply does not stack up.

High-quality studies of whole-school, multi-component SEL interventions are thin on the ground. For example, two recent systematic reviews conducted on behalf of the National Institute for Health and Clinical Excellence could not find evidence for *any* programmes that contained elements involving the curriculum, environment/ethos *and* parents/community.[40,41] Furthermore, where evidence has been available, analysis in which effect sizes associated with different types of programmes were systematically compared found no advantage for multi-component programmes over those that made use of a single component.[39,42] Given this, one might question why a whole-school, multi-component model for SEAL was so heavily promoted? As with the bottom-up versus top-down schism, it may simply reflect the fact that whole-school approaches were *de rigeur* in educational policy development when SEAL was being created. The reason this is an important issue is that – aside from misrepresenting the evidence base – those determined to further the cause for whole-school approaches may actually be putting schools in a position where most are unlikely to succeed. We know, for example, that complex interventions requiring action at multiple levels and the commitment of multiple participants take longer to implement successfully,[35] are more likely to be discontinued,[43] and typically become greatly diluted due to their broader scope.[42] These issues, combined with the additional efforts required and lack of clear guidance associated with a bottom-up model, mean that the risk of implementation failure is greatly increased for programmes like SEAL.[44]

Broader issues in the field of social and emotional learning

The broader field of SEL is also not without its inherent problems. The discourse in this area makes reference to 'social and emotional learning' or 'SEL' as though it is a single, consistently definable and agreed upon entity that is understood in the same way by all who use the term. The reality is very different. SEL – like Goleman's definition of EI – is a protean and often intangible term that is used to describe a myriad of processes and programmes, many of which bear little or no relation to one another, and sometimes contain little in the way of social and/or emotional content. Durlak et al.[39] provide a reasonably tight definition, describing SEL as the process of 'acquiring core competencies to recognise and manage emotions, set and achieve personal goals, appreciate the perspectives of others, establish and maintain positive relationships, make responsible decisions, and handle interpersonal situations constructively'. However, to be considered a SEL programme a given intervention only has to emphasize the development of *one* or more of these competences, meaning that any number of approaches that differ wildly in their nature, content, audience, settings and expected outcomes can be classified within the framework.[1] Hoffman[45] rightly suggests that this causes ambiguity and conceptual confusion, as programmes drawing from public and mental health, conflict resolution, moral and character education and juvenile justice perspectives are all subsumed under the same banner. Such definitions enable the gradual incorporation of increasingly diverse sources of evidence about programmes that bear less and less resemblance to any fundamental concept of social and/or emotional competence, at least as it is articulated and understood by developmental psychologists.[46]

The SEAL guidance states that the evidence base for SEL interventions, upon which the programme is ostensibly based, is overwhelming.[4] As with other such claims examined in this chapter, interrogation of the literature paints a different picture. Setting aside the issue of conceptual incoherence inherent in the SEL field (see above), the lack of methodological rigour and questionable interpretations in many studies published make it difficult to draw any firm conclusions. Notable problems include a lack of control/comparison groups, lack of longitudinal assessment, and failure to control for school effects.[1] A recent meta-analysis by Durlak et al.[39] highlights even more methodological shortcomings. This article represents the most up-to-date and comprehensive analysis of the evidence base for SEL, with 207 studies included, representing outcomes for nearly a quarter of a million children and young people. The authors reported a high level of variability in the quality of studies, with 53 per cent relying solely on child self-report (raising issues of reliability), 42 per cent not monitoring implementation in any way (meaning that fidelity to treatment models had to be assumed, limiting the attribution of any successful outcomes), 20 per cent being unpublished reports (and therefore not subjected to academic scrutiny), 25 per cent using measures with no reported reliability (meaning that they may not tap consistent responses over time), and 50 per cent using measures with no reported validity (meaning that they may not measure what they purport to measure). On the basis of this, the authors (ibid.) concluded, 'current findings are not definitive'.

Two further problems present critical issues in the translation of the SEL evidence base into English educational policy and practice. First, the vast majority of the evidence base stems from the USA, with only a smattering of studies from the UK context (e.g. in Blank and Guillaime's[41] review, only 3 of 40 studies were conducted in the UK). The issue of transferability of findings needs to be approached with caution. The education system in the USA differs from the UK in key areas such as size and growth rate of school-age population, funding and expenditure, curriculum structure and pedagogical approaches.[47] Thus, we cannot assume that what has worked in one country will also work in another, and there is a clear need to develop the evidence base in the UK.

Finally, we have the problem of 'efficacy' versus 'effectiveness' in the SEL literature. Most studies report efficacy trials; that is, programmes delivered under well-controlled circumstances with high levels of resources to promote implementation and monitor fidelity. This is very different to judging the effectiveness of an intervention when it is taken 'to scale'; that is, a more pragmatic evaluation of practice delivered in real-life settings. The potential dangers of such disparity were highlighted by Shucksmith et al. :[48]

> “studies . . . have seen the investment of massive sums of money in large multi-component longitudinal trials. The results that emerge from these are very useful and are showing the way towards the design of more effective interventions, yet there must be serious doubts as to the availability of such resources within normal education budgets.”

These concerns are echoed by other authors such as Greenberg et al. The bottom line is that the age-old trade-off between internal validity and external validity has meant that many trials of SEL interventions actually tell us much less than we think about whether they will be effective in the complex, messy world of educational practice.

Concluding thoughts: SEAL and the promotion of unfounded ideas

The chapter has sought to challenge the orthodoxy of SEAL in the English education system, and in doing so highlight a range of critical issues relating to the programme itself and the broader field of SEL from which it emerged. To the extent to which these aims have been achieved, a logical next question is, *'How?'*. That is, how did SEAL manage to rise to such prominence given everything that has been outlined above?

In attempting to answer this question, I borrow from Waterhouse's[49] critique of emotional intelligence by proposing Stich's[3] four-factor model of the promotion of unfounded ideas. The first factor, *fraud*, is typically applied to describe the act of deliberately misleading people in service of a particular goal. While this is highly unlikely to have happened in relation to the development of SEAL, the notion of *self-fraud* is perhaps pertinent. Thus, those involved in lobbying so strongly build a well-intentioned but ultimately misconceived model of the potential of a national, school-based programme to promote social and emotional skills to effect widespread change across the entire education system. Such ideas, Waterhouse explains, can take hold for three reasons – credo consolans (an unproven idea provides comfort if it predicts a good outcome), immediate gratification (the idea offers instant solutions for difficult problems) and easy explanations (the idea is accepted if it offers a simple story for something complex or difficult to understand).

Stich's second factor, *anxiety*, can be seen throughout the literature in this area. If SEAL and programmes like it are the *solution*, there needs to be a *problem*. In service of this, a 'moral panic' of sorts is generated in which a rationalist education system and society more generally are dramatically painted as sources of emotional distress, and children and young people are cast as unwitting and disempowered victims (what Ecclestone and Hayes[14] refer to as the 'diminished' view of the human subject). As a case in point, consider that at the most recent annual secondary SEAL conference, a keynote speaker drew upon an account of a Holocaust survivor, which beseeched future educators to avoid producing '*learned monsters, skilled psychopaths,* [and] *educated Eichmanns*' as part of her thesis about the importance of SEAL.[50] Thus, those seeking to promote the benefits of SEAL become the equivalent of 'moral entrepeneurs'[51] in this analogy.

Stich's third factor, *absent evidence*, is reflected in the lack of evidence to support two central strata of the SEAL model – the 'bottom-up' philosophy and the accompanying whole-school, multi-component approach to implementation. In neither case is there anything approaching the 'overwhelming' evidence that is claimed in the programme guidance. The final factor in the model, *ignoring evidence*, completes our understanding of the rapid expansion of SEAL. As outlined earlier, evaluations that have directly assessed the impact of SEAL have produced mixed, null and/or negative findings, but have been selectively reported (or even completely ignored) by policy-makers and SEAL proponents – see, for example, Tew).[52] Alongside this, studies that illuminated issues around implementation, particularly in relation to the pilot versions of SEAL, were not properly utilized in refining later iterations of the initiative as the rush to bring the programme to scale took hold. Ultimately, SEAL can be seen as an exemplar of the type of approach that Topping, Holmes and Bremner[53] cautioned against over a decade ago:

> “Policy and practice in education have often been shaped by 'what feels right' to teachers, by contagious fashions that sweep in and then leave without trace, and by the short-term expedients of politicians who feel the need to be seen to be doing something in order to secure votes.”

Notes

1. Humphrey, N., Lendrum, A. and Wigelsworth, M. (2010) *Social and Emotional Aspects of Learning (SEAL) Programme in Secondary Schools: National Evaluation*. Nottingham: Department for Education.
2. BBC (2011) *Analysis – Testing the Emotions*. Available online at www.bbc.co.uk/programmes/b00z5bqd.
3. Stich, S. (1993) *The Fragmentation of Reason: Preface to a Pragmatic Theory of Cognitive Evaluation*. Boston, MA: MIT Press.
4. Department for Children Schools and Families (DCSF). (2007) *Social and Emotional Aspects of Learning (SEAL) Programme: Guidance for Secondary Schools*. Nottingham: DCSF Publications.
5. Goleman D. (1996) *Emotional Intelligence: Why It Can Matter more than IQ*. New York: Bloomsbury Publishing PLC.
6. DCSF (2017), see note 4.
7. TeachFind (2011) *The Waves of Intervention Model*. Available online at www.teachfind.com/national-strategies/waves-intervention-model; Weare K. (2010) Mental health and social and emotional learning: evidence, principles, tensions, balances, *Advances in School Mental Health Promotion*, 3: 5–17.
8. Department for Education and Skills (DfES) (2006) *Excellence and Enjoyment: Social and Emotional Aspects of Learning (Key Stage 2 Small Group Activities)*. Nottingham: DfES Publications.
9. Ainscow, M., Booth, T. and Dyson, A. (2006) Inclusion and the standards agenda: negotiating policy pressures in England, *International Journal of Inclusive Education*, 10: 295–308.
10. Department for Education and Skills (DfES) (2003) *Every Child Matters*. Nottingham: DfES Publications.

11. Weare, K. and Gray, G. (2003) *What Works in Promoting Children's Emotional and Social Competence and Wellbeing?* Nottingham: DfES Publications.
12. Ecclestone, K. and Hayes, D. (2009) Changing the subject: the educational implications of developing emotional well-being, *Oxford Review of Education*, 35: 371–89.
13. Craig, C. (2007) *The Potential Dangers of a Systematic, Explicit Approach to Teaching Social and Emotional Skills (SEAL)*. Glasgow: Centre for Confidence and Well-Being.
14. Ecclestone, K. and Hayes, D. (2008) *The Dangerous Rise of Therapeutic Education*. London: Routledge.
15. Humphrey, N. (2009) SEAL: insufficient evidence? *School Leadership Today*, 1.
16. Hallam, S., Rhamie, J. and Shaw, J. (2006) *Evaluation of the Primary Behaviour and Attendance Pilot*. Nottingham: DfES Publications.
17. Hallam, S. (2009) An evaluation of the social and emotional aspects of learning (SEAL) programme: promoting positive behaviour, effective learning and well-being in primary school children, *Oxford Review of Education*, 35: 313–30.
18. Office for Standards in Education (Ofsted) (2007) *Developing Social, Emotional and Behavioural Skills in Secondary Schools*. London: Ofsted.
19. Banerjee, R. (2010) *Social and Emotional Aspects of Learning in Schools: Contributions to Improving Attainment, Behaviour and Attendance*. Sussex: University of Sussex.
20. Humphrey, N., Kalambouka, A., Bolton, J., Lendrum, A., Wigelsworth, M., Lennie, C. et al. (2008) *Primary Social and Emotional Aspects of Learning: Evaluation of Small Group Work*. Nottingham: DCSF Publications.
21. Humphrey, N., Lendrum, A., Wigelsworth, M. and Kalambouka, A. (2009) Primary SEAL group interventions: a qualitative study of factors affecting implementation and the role of local authority support, *International Journal of Emotional Education*, 1: 34–54.
22. Humphrey, N., Kalambouka, A., Wigelsworth, M. and Lendrum, A. (2010) Going for goals: an evaluation of a short, social-emotional intervention for primary school children, *School Psychology International*, 31: 250–70.
23. Humphrey, N., Kalambouka, A., Wigelsworth, M., Lendrum, A., Lennie, C. and Farrell, P. (2010) New Beginnings: evaluation of a short social-emotional intervention for primary-aged children, *Educational Psychology*, 30: 513–32.
24. Lendrum, A., Humphrey, N., Kalambouka, A. and Wigelsworth, M. (2009) Implementing primary social and emotional aspects of learning (SEAL) small group interventions: recommendations for practitioners, *Emotional and Behavioural Difficulties*, 14: 229–38.

25. Humphrey, N., Lendrum, A., Wigelsworth, M. and Kalambouka, A. (2009) Implementation of primary social and emotional aspects of learning (SEAL) small group work: a qualitative study, *Pastoral Care in Education*, 27: 219–39.
26. Wigelsworth, M., Humphrey, N. and Lendrum, A. (2011) A national evaluation of the impact of the secondary social and emotional aspects of learning (SEAL) programme, *Educational Psychology*, iFirst: 1–26.
27. Downey, C. and Williams, C. (2010) Family SEAL – a home-school collaborative programme focusing on the development of children's social and emotional skills, *Advances in School Mental Health Promotion*, 3: 30–41.
28. Humphrey, N., Kalambouka, A., Bolton, J., Lendrum, A., Wigelsworth, M., Lennie, C. et al. (2008) *Primary Social and Emotional Aspects of Learning (SEAL): Evaluation of Small Group Work*. Nottingham: DCSF Publications.
29. Thomson, P. and Gunter, H. (2006) Stories from commissioned research. In: *Proceedings from the British Educational Research Association Conference*. Warwick: 2006.
30. Baty, P. and Shepherd, J. (2006) Ministers vilify researchers, *Times Higher Education Supplement*. Available online at www.timehighereducation.co.uk.
31. Department for Education and Skills (DfES) (2005) *Excellence and Enjoyment: Social and Emotional Aspects of Learning*. Nottingham: DfES Publications.
32. Smith, P., O'Donnell, L., Easton, C. and Rudd, P. (2007) *Secondary Social, Emotional and Behavioural Skills Pilot Evaluation*. Nottingham: DCSF Publications.
33. Salovey, P. and Mayer, J. (2008) Emotional intelligence, *Imagination, Cognition and Personality*, 9: 185–211.
34. Sternberg, R. (2002) Foreword, in G. Matthews and M. Zeidner (eds) *Emotional Intelligence: Science and Myth*, pp. xi-xv. Boston, MA: MIT Press.
35. Durlak, J.A. and DuPre, E.P. (2008) Implementation matters: a review of research on the influence of implementation on program outcomes and the factors affecting implementation, *American Journal of Community Psychology*, 41: 327–50.
36. Carroll, C., Patterson, M., Wood, S., Booth, A., Rick, J. and Balain, S. (2007) A conceptual framework for implementation fidelity, *Implementation Science*, 2: 40–49.
37. Greenberg, M., Domitrovich, C., Graczyk, P. and Zins, J. (2005) *The Study of Implementation in School-based Preventive Interventions: Theory, Research, and Practice*. Washington, DC: US Department of Health and Human Services.

38. Catalano, R.F., Berglund, M.L., Ryan, J.A.M., Lonczak, H.S. and Hawkins, J.D. (2004) Positive youth development in the United States: research findings on evaluations of positive youth development programs, *The Annals of the American Academy of Political and Social Science*, 591: 98–124.
39. Durlak, J.A., Weissberg, R.P., Dymnicki, A.B., Taylor, R.D. and Schellinger, K.B. (2011) The impact of enhancing students' social and emotional learning: a meta-analysis of school-based universal interventions, *Child Development*, 82: 405–32.
40. Adi, Y., Kiloran, A., Janmohamed, K. and Stewart-Brown, S. (2007) *Systematic Review of the Effectiveness of Interventions to Promote Mental Wellbeing in Children in Primary Education*. Warwick: University of Warwick.
41. Blank, L., Baxter, S., Goyder, L., Guillaume, L. and Wilkinson, A.S.H. et al. (2010) Promoting wellbeing by changing behaviour: a systematic review and narrative synthesis of the effectiveness of whole secondary school behavioural interventions, *Mental Health Review Journal*, 15: 43–53.
42. Wilson, S.J. and Lipsey, M.W. (2007) School-based interventions for aggressive and disruptive behavior: update of a meta-analysis, *American Journal of Preventive Medicine*, 33: S130–43.
43. Yeaton, W.H. and Sechrest, L. (1981) Critical dimensions in the choice and maintenance of successful treatments: strength, integrity, and effectiveness, *Journal of Consulting and Clinical Psychology*, 49: 156–67.
44. Lendrum, A. Implementing social and emotional aspects of learning (SEAL) in secondary schools in England: issues and implications. Unpublished PhD thesis: University of Manchester.
45. Hoffman, D.M. (2009) Reflecting on social emotional learning: a critical perspective on trends in the United States, *Review of Educational Research*, 79: 533–56.
46. Saarni, C. (1999) *The Development of Emotional Competence*. New York: Guilford Press.
47. US Department of Education (USDE) (2005) *Comparitive Indicators of Education in the United States and Other G8 countries*. Washington, DC: USDE.
48. Shucksmith, J. (2007) Mental wellbeing of children in primary education (targeted/indicated activities). Teeside: University of Teeside.
49. Waterhouse, L. (2006) Multiple intelligences, the Mozart effect, and emotional intelligence: a critical review, *Educational Psychologist*, 41: 207–25.
50. Gross, J. (2010) *SEAL and the changing national education agenda*. In: 4th Annual Secondary SEAL Conference. London: Optimus Education.
51. Becker, H. (1963) *Outsiders: Studies in the Sociology of Deviance*. New York: The Free Press.

52. Tew, M. (2011) Ignore the Nay-sayers: Commitment to Enhancing Relationships will Lead to Improved Behaviour and Learning. Available online at www.antidote.org.uk.
53. Topping, K., Holmes, E.A. and Bremner, W. (2000) The effectiveness of school-based programs for the promotion of social competence, in R. Bar-On, and J. Parker (eds) *The Handbook of Emotional Intelligence: Theory, Development, Assessment, and Application at Home, School, and in the Workplace* (pp. 411–32). San Francisco, CA: Jossey-Bass.

Computers good, calculators bad?

Jeremy Hodgen

Introduction

As the Coalition Government in the UK embarks on another reform of the national curriculum, ministers are keen to review the use of technology, calculators and computers in schools. Calculators, we are told, are bad. Nick Gibb, the current Minister for Schools, for example, is concerned that young children's arithmetic may be suffering because they are too reliant on calculators:

> Children can become too dependent on calculators if they use them at too young an age. They shouldn't be reaching for a gadget every time they need to do a simple sum. They need to master addition, subtraction, times tables and division, using quick, reliable written methods. This rigour provides the ground-work for the more difficult maths they will come across later in their education.[1]

This view echoes a previous (Labour) Secretary of State for Education, David Blunkett, who, in 1997, called for a ban on calculators:

> Mental arithmetic is a key skill which children must learn. They must also understand the basis on which the calculations are being made. Calculators should not be introduced until later in primary schools than is often the case at present. So that once

> the foundations of mental arithmetic are already in place, they can master how to use them more effectively. Numerate pupils must know how to use calculators sensibly and must be able to make a decision about when to use a calculator. We must ensure that no child is totally reliant on a calculator.[2]

These views reflect a widespread belief among politicians and others that calculators hinder the learning of mathematics, particularly in primary schools. Computers, on the other hand, are often believed to be good for learning. Michael Gove, the Secretary of State for Education, while bemoaning the current ICT[3] curriculum, argues that technology is bringing about a 'profound change in education' and that the 'traditional' model of a teacher 'may well be extinct in ten years':

> Imagine the dramatic change which could be possible in just a few years, once we remove the roadblock of the existing ICT curriculum. Instead of children bored out of their minds being taught how to use Word and Excel by bored teachers, we could have 11 year-olds able to write simple 2D computer animations using an MIT tool called Scratch. By 16, they could have an understanding of formal logic previously covered only in University courses and be writing their own Apps for smartphones.[4]

Again, this positive view of computers and technology is shared by previous Labour politicians. In 1999, Tony Blair, for example, declared education and technology to be 'the best economic policy we have'[5] and, as a result, made substantial investments to increase access to technology in both primary and secondary schools. One effect of this investment is that almost all classrooms in England are fitted with an Interactive White Board, a technology that might be more amenable to the traditional role of the teacher that Michael Gove suggests is outdated.

In this chapter, I examine the evidence on the effects of calculators and computers on learning. Given my focus on calculators and the government's particular interest in arithmetic and numeracy, my focus is largely on mathematics education.

Calculators and attainment: the international evidence

It is often claimed that the use of calculators is banned in countries with high mathematical attainment and that this is one of the factors in the success of these systems. So, for example, responding to a parliamentary question on calculators, Nick Gibb said:

> The international evidence is also clear. High-performing jurisdictions around the world ... limit the use of calculators in the primary mathematics classroom. Guiding principles for the Massachusetts, Singapore and Hong Kong curricula state that calculators should not be used as a replacement for basic understanding and skills. ... Elementary students learn how to perform basic arithmetical operations without using a calculator. Evidence from the most successful educational systems around the world suggests that calculators should be introduced only once pupils have a thorough grounding in number facts or number bonds, including knowing their multiplication tables by heart, and that calculators should be used only to support the teaching of mathematics where the aim is to focus on solving a problem rather than on the process of calculation.[6]

This statement is somewhat misleading about both England's performance in mathematics and the availability of calculators in English primary schools. In fact, at primary school level, England is one of the highest performing systems in the most recent Trends in International Mathematics and Science Study (TIMSS) mathematics survey.[7] As a result of the introduction of the National Numeracy Strategy in 1999, the use of calculators is restricted in England. Calculators are only introduced to most children in Year 5 in upper primary school at around age 9.[8] This was the case for the year group surveyed in TIMSS, hence it is hardly surprising that calculator use is extremely high. Of the three systems highlighted by Gibb, only Singapore institutes a ban on calculator use at primary, while in Massachusetts, only 8 per cent of Grade 4[9] students are in classrooms in which calculator use is not permitted. Evidence suggests that mathematical attainment in England is more problematic at secondary school than at primary school. Attainment at TIMSS for

Year 9 students is slightly above average (and is below what might be expected given students' performance at primary), while performance of 15-year-olds in the Organization for Economic Co-operation and Development's (OECD's) Programme for International Student Assessment (PISA) survey is not better than average.[10] Again, in secondary mathematics the policies of systems with the highest mathematical attainment are different. While calculator use is not permitted in a significant minority of classrooms in Taiwan, South Korea and Japan, in Singapore and Hong Kong almost all students, like those in England, have access to calculators.[11]

The TIMSS survey provides evidence on calculator use across a variety of systems, both high and low performing. The proportion of students in classrooms where calculator use is not permitted varies widely across these systems. While many of the systems provide curricular guidance on the use of calculators, the decision as to whether to permit calculators is largely taken at a local level, by teachers, schools and education districts, rather than nationally.[12]

In Figure 10.1, the percentage of Grade 4[13] students in classrooms where calculators are not allowed is plotted against average TIMSS score for each system. There is a slight negative effect overall. In other words,

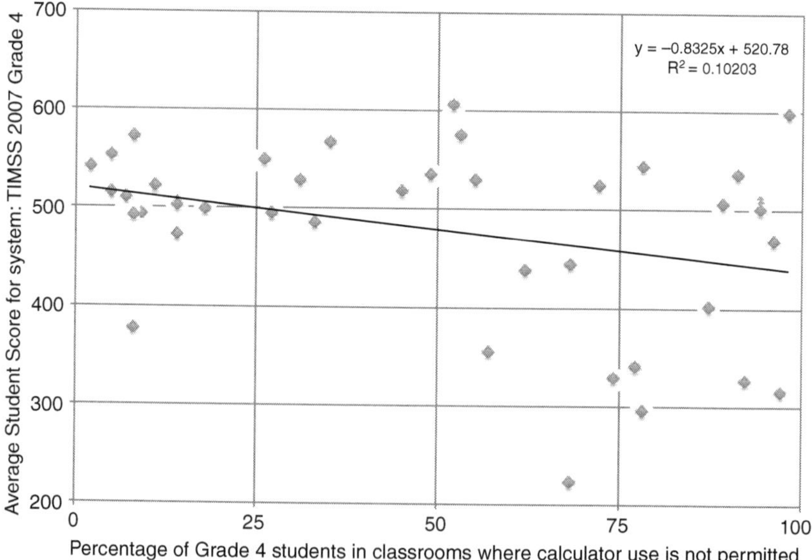

Figure 10.1 Attainment and a ban on calculator use at Grade 4 in TIMSS 2007

there is a slight tendency for attainment in mathematics at Grade 4 to be lower the more calculator use is discouraged. In many primary classrooms, however, the use of calculators is 'restricted' rather than banned. In other words, teachers allow children to use calculators at particular times and for particular tasks, and, at other times, focus on other approaches to calculation. Again, in the 2007 TIMSS survey, the attainment of students in classrooms where calculator use was unrestricted was significantly lower than those where calculator use was either restricted or banned. Although attainment for restricted use of calculators was slightly higher, there was no statistically significant difference between this and a ban.[14] These data would suggest that for upper primary classrooms, while there is an advantage to controlling the use of calculators in primary classrooms, there is no gain in attainment associated with an outright ban.

The negative effect of a calculator ban is more pronounced for the secondary students (see Figure 10.2). Indeed, in contrast to the findings at primary, there is no statistical difference between students in classrooms with restricted and unrestricted use of calculators, but the attainment of students in classrooms where calculators are banned is lower.[15] The evidence would suggest that, in lower secondary classrooms, access to calculators is beneficial, while a ban is not.

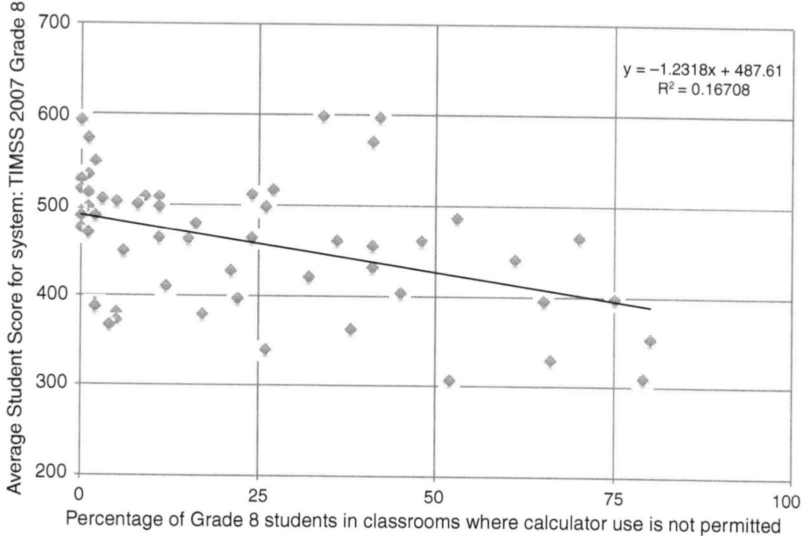

Figure 10.2 Attainment and a ban on calculator use at Grade 8 in TIMSS 2007

International survey evidence needs to be interpreted with caution and the biggest factor in success in these surveys is the extent to which a system's curriculum matches the curriculum that is tested.[16] I note that relationships highlighted above indicate associations not causations between calculator use and attainment. There is a great danger of cherry-picking policies from successful systems out of context.[17] Nevertheless, the TIMSS results provide little support for a ban on the use of calculators at any level of schooling.

Can calculator use improve learning?

International surveys such as TIMSS simply provide evidence of calculator use in general, but provide limited detailed evidence about the effects. Since calculators began to become widely available in the 1970s, there have been a number of intervention studies that have examined the use and effects of calculators in depth.

The Calculator Aware Number (CAN) project led by Hilary Shuard at Cambridge set out to develop a mathematics curriculum designed around calculator use in primary schools in England. Between 1986 and 1989, the project worked with a number of schools and teachers. A follow-up study conducted in 1995/6 examined the effects of this curriculum on children who had begun school in 1989 and had thus experienced a 'calculator aware' curriculum throughout their primary schooling.[18] These students' attainment was compared to a control group of similar schools with a more traditional curriculum. The calculator aware students' understanding and fluency were better but in addition, and somewhat counter-intuitively, they used calculators less than the control group. These students used mental methods more often and more effectively and tended to use calculators only when appropriate. Mental methods *are* faster than calculators for some calculations (e.g. multiplications involving numbers to one significant figure). The intervention students knew this because they had been taught when, and *when not*, to use calculators.

A meta-analysis[19] of 54 studies found that calculator use did not hinder attainment in mathematics in general and there were no statistically discernible differences between different grades (elementary compared to middle or senior grades).[20] However, when assessment involved the use of calculators, students taught with calculators outperformed those who had not been taught with calculators. This is a powerful argument for using calculators since a central aim of mathematics education is to teach students to be mathematically literate in a world in which they are expected to use calculators.

A perhaps more surprising finding is the effect on students' attitudes to mathematics. Students taught with calculators had more positive attitudes towards mathematics.[21] Evidence suggests that students do not study mathematics because they perceive it to be dull and boring. If using calculators can counter this perception, then this is a further reason for using calculators in teaching.

The Leverhulme Numeracy Research Programme conducted by Professor Margaret Brown and others at King's College London tracked more than 2,000 children in two cohorts across primary schooling in England between 1997 and 2002.[22] The study identified different effects for different uses of calculators in primary classrooms. Allowing students access to calculators most days had a negative association with attainment (effect size: −0.31).[23] However, if calculators were only used *rarely* to develop familiarity with number operations, this negative effect was even greater (effect size: −0.41). Allowing primary children either too much or too little access to calculators is likely to reduce attainment, whereas using calculators proactively to teach children about number is likely to raise attainment.

Hence, how calculators are used matters and this observation is particularly true at primary. The evidence suggests that where calculators are used to develop children's understanding of, and fluency with, number, the effects are likely to be beneficial. For primary, the evidence suggests that it is important to regulate, but not ban, the use of calculators.

I now turn to examine the evidence on the use of computers.

Computers and attainment: the international evidence

TIMSS does suggest that systems that allow greater access to computers tend to be higher attaining. In Figure 10.3, the percentage of primary (Grade 4) teachers reporting that computers are available is plotted

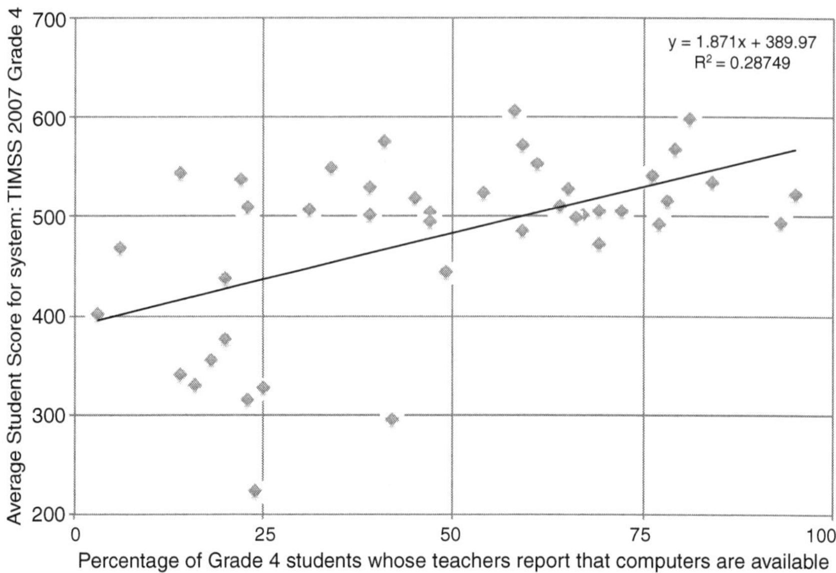

Figure 10.3 Attainment and computer availability at Grade 4 in TIMSS 2007

against the average score for each system. There is a positive effect for availability. The relationship at secondary (Grade 8) is similar. I note that the analysis in Figure 10.3 is relatively simplistic and other analyses are more equivocal. One study, for example, found that increased use of technology was associated with increased attainment in Brazil, but not in Norway, while in Japan it was associated with lower attainment.[24] Similarly, an analysis of the US National Assessment of Educational Progress (NAEP) survey from 1996 suggests that high levels of computer use are not associated with increased attainment for either Grade 4 or Grade 8 students.[25] In the UK, the ImpaCT2 study found that, although attainment was higher for primary and secondary students in classrooms where (ICT) use was high, this difference was not significant.[26]

However, it is important to note here that availability does not necessarily translate into increased use. Indeed, another international survey, the Second Information Technology in Education Study (SITES), conducted in 2006,[27] found that, since 1998, although most systems had increased investment in technology and access to computers had greatly improved, the use of technology and computers was low. Moreover,

SITES found no correlation between access to computers and teachers using technology in their teaching. Computer use varied across subjects, with mathematics teachers using ICT less frequently than science teachers, for example. This finding might suggest that the finding from the TIMSS data about the availability of computers and attainment might partially be explained with the wealth and gross domestic product (GDP) of the system. Certainly, there is little international evidence to support the claim that computers are likely to completely transform education in the near future.

Can computer use improve learning?

Many studies indicate that interventions involving technology can improve learning in and understanding of mathematics. A meta-analysis of 46 studies indicates a positive effect in general, although the effect was greater for primary students than for secondary.[28] The effect was also smaller in more traditional classrooms. Significant claims are made for graphing and dynamic geometry software and these claims are very persuasive for knowledgeable users.[29] Spreadsheets, condemned as 'boring' in Gove's British Educational Training and Technology (BETT) speech,[30] have been shown to increase children's understanding of mathematics.[31]

It is difficult, however, to disaggregate the effects of technology from improvements in pedagogy. Indeed, there is a strong argument that gains in attainment are achieved where technology use is the focus for changes in pedagogy.[32] In other words, technology *can* make a difference, but it is how teachers use it that is crucial. Professor Ken Ruthven of Cambridge University, for example, argues that teachers' use of technology tends to align with and strengthen teachers' existing pedagogical practices.[33] This conservative tendency is supported by Nicola Bretscher's survey of 89 mathematics teachers' technology use.[34] She found that teachers made frequent use of graphing software themselves, but allowed students to use the same software rarely. In contrast, the technology that students used most frequently was MyMaths.co.uk, primarily a revision website. Of course, revision is beneficial and there is evidence that this type of computer use can be beneficial.[35] However, this type of use is hardly a radical departure from existing practice.

Bretscher's survey also documents a very significant use of Interactive White Boards (IWBs). The increased use of IWBs, as I noted above, is a direct result of the Labour Government's investment in technology. Several studies have examined the effect of IWBs on learning in mathematics and in general, although none has investigated the effect on attainment. One study found that IWBs encouraged a more interactive approach to teaching together with increased pace. Compared to lessons without IWBs, students answered questions more frequently, but these responses were shorter and did not impact on the proportion of teacher talk.[36] Another found that interactivity often involved simply 'getting kids up to the board', particularly for lower-attaining classes and this slowed the pace of the lesson.[37] Another study compared the use of IWBs to other technologies and found that lessons with IWBs resulted in poorer quality questioning and more teacher talk.[38] These findings echo Ruthven's argument that, in the absence of support to do otherwise, technology use tends towards the conservative.

So, computers *can* improve learning, but these improvements are far from guaranteed and are dependent on changes to pedagogy. Like any pedagogical reform, access and availability is not sufficient for change to take place and teachers need the support and professional development opportunities.[39]

Conclusion

Calculators are often held to blame for poor numeracy skills, while it is asserted that computers will transform education. The evidence suggests these views are wrong. Calculator use can improve children's arithmetic and internationally there is no evidence to support a national ban on the use of calculators in primary education. Similarly, computers can improve children's learning, although experience and evidence to date suggests that such improvements are likely to be incremental rather than transformative.

Simply focusing on the effects of technology on mathematical attainment misses the point. Studies of adult numeracy show that adults rarely use the pencil and paper methods traditionally taught in schools.[40] Adults rely instead on calculators, spreadsheets and mental methods. To ignore or delay the introduction of technology such as calculators is tantamount to burying our heads in the sand. Education needs to prepare children for the world they will live and work in. This 'real world' is a technological world – one in which people rely on calculators, computers and mental arithmetic for the calculations that they do. A curriculum for such a world needs to embrace technology. It is shocking that, in 2008, the Office for Standards in Education (Ofsted) found that computer use had *reduced* over the previous seven years.[41]

As Stuart Plunkett argued almost 40 years ago in his seminal paper, 'Decomposition and all that rot':

> The advent of calculators has provided us with a great opportunity. We are freed from the necessity to provide every citizen with methods for dealing with calculations of indefinite complexity. So we can abandon the standard written algorithms, of general applicability and limited intelligibility, in favour of methods more suited to the minds and purposes of the users . . . Children should be helped to acquire sensible methods for calculating, and for the majority of calculations met in everyday use these will be mental methods . . . More importantly children will acquire a better understanding of number from using their own mental algorithms than from the repeated application of standard algorithms they do not comprehend. With mental methods occupying their proper place as the principal means for doing simple calculations, the position of calculators is clear. They are the sensible tool for difficult calculations, the ideal complement to mental arithmetic.[42]

Research over the past 40 years shows that achieving Plunkett's vision is far from straightforward. This experience also suggests that overstating the power of computers to transform education and viewing calculators as a hindrance to arithmetic are unlikely to support the development of such a curriculum. A more effective strategy would be to promote a mathematics curriculum in which technology is integral to arithmetic. Ruthven presents a powerful argument for such a curriculum.[43] We may have to wait until the majority of our politicians themselves rely more on calculators and mental methods until such a curriculum can be a political reality.

Notes

1. Subtracting calculators adds to children's maths abilities, *The Guardian*, 1 December 2012.
2. Tables turn on children's calculator culture, *The Independent*, 1 April 1997.
3. Information and communication technology (ICT) is a term used to cover a broad range of technologies including computers and calculators as well as digital technologies.
4. Goves' speech to BETT Show, 11 January 2012.
5. Cited in Kritt, D.W. and Winegar, L.T. (eds) (2007) *Education and Technology: Critical Perspectives, Possible Futures*. Plymouth: Lexington Books.
6. Hansard, 30 November 2012.
7. Mullis, I.V.S., Martin, M.O., Foy, P., Olson, J.F., Preuschoff, C., Erberber, E. and Galia, J. (2008) *TIMSS 2007 International Mathematics Report*. Chestnut Hill, MA: TIMSS and PIRLS International Study Center, Boston College. TIMSS surveys students at Grade 4 and Grade 8. These are equivalent to Year 5 (age 9–10) and Year 9 (age 13–14) in England.
8. Department for Education and Employment (DfEE) (1999) *The National Numeracy Strategy: Framework for Teaching Mathematics from Reception to Year 6*. London: DfEE.
9. In fact, the policy in Singapore has recently changed to encourage some use of calculators in upper primary.
10. Bradshaw, J., Ager, R., Burge, B. and Wheater, R. (2010) *PISA 2009: Achievement of 15-Year-Olds in England*. Slough: NFER. See also Hodgen, J., Brown, M., Küchemann, D. and Coe, R. (2011) Why have educational standards changed so little over time: The case of school mathematics in England. Paper presented at the British Educational Research Association (BERA) Annual Conference, Institute of Education, University of London.
11. Mullis et al. (op. cit.).
12. Eurydice (2011) *Mathematics Education in Europe: Common Challenges and National Policies*. Brussels: Education, Audiovisual and Culture Executive Agency (EACEA P9 Eurydice); Mullis, I.V.S., Martin, M.O., Olson, J.F., Berger, D.R., Milne, D. and Stanco, G.M. (Eds) (2008) *Timss 2007 Encyclopedia: A Guide to Mathematics and Science Education Around the World* (Vol. 1). Chestnut Hill, MA: TIMSS and PIRLS International Study Center, Lynch School of Education, Boston College.
13. Mullis et al. (op. cit.).
14. Average scale score for Grade 4 students in classrooms with unrestricted use of calculators (450), restricted use (476) and in which calculators were not permitted (472). Significance tests generated using the TIMSS International Data Explorer. Available online at www.nces.ed.gov/timss/idetimss/ (accessed 16 Mach 2012).

15. Average scale score for Grade 8 students in classrooms with unrestricted use of calculators (447), restricted use (450) and in which calculators were not permitted (438). Significance tests generated using the TIMSS International Data Explorer (op. cit.).
16. Burstein, L. (ed.) (1992) *The IEA Study of Mathematics III: Student Growth and Classroom Processes.* Oxford: Pergamon Press.
17. Askew, M., Hodgen, J., Hossain, S. and Bretscher, N. (2010) *Values and Variables: A Review of Mathematics Education in High-performing Countries.* London: Nuffield Foundation.
18. Ruthven, K. (1998) The use of mental, written and calculator strategies of numerical computation by upper primary pupils within a 'calculator-aware' number curriculum, *British Educational Research Journal,* 24(1): 21–42.
19. Meta-analysis is a statistical technique for aggregating the effects of a number of related studies.
20. Ellington, A.J. (2003) A meta-analysis of the effects of calculators on students' achievement and attitude levels in precollege mathematics classes, *Journal for Research in Mathematics Education,* 34(5): 433–63.
21. Ellington (ibid.).
22. Brown, M., Askew, M., Hodgen, J., Rhodes, V., Millett, A., Denvir, H. and Wiliam, D. (2008) Individual and cohort progression in learning numeracy ages 5–11: results from the Leverhulme 5-year longitudinal study, in A. Dowker (ed.) *Children's Mathematical Difficulties: Psychology, Neuroscience and Education* (pp. 85–108). Oxford: Elsevier.
23. Effect size is the difference between group means, divided by the standard deviation, resulting in a measure of effect in standard deviations. Effect sizes are commonly used to evaluate the impact of educational initiatives and interventions. Effect sizes of less than 0.2 are generally regarded as small or negligible.
24. Guzel, C.I. and Berberoglu, G. (2005) An analysis of the programme for international student assessment 2000 (PISA 2000) mathematical literacy data for Brazilian, Japanese and Norwegian students, *Studies in Educational Evaluation,* 31(4): 283–314. doi: 10.1016/j.stueduc.2005.11.006.
25. Wenglinsky, H. (1998) *Does it Compute? The Relationship Between Educational Technology and Student Achievement in Mathematics.* Princeton: Policy Information Service.
26. Harrison, C., Comber, C., Fisher, T., Haw, K., Lewin, C., Lunzer, E. and Watling, R. (2003) *ImpaCT2: The Impact of Information and Communication Technologies on Pupil Learning and Attainment.* Coventry: BECTA.
27. Law, N., Pelgrum, W.J. and Plomp, T. (2008) *Pedagogy and ICT Use in Schools Around the World: Findings from the IEA SITES 2006 Study.* Hong Kong: CERC-Springer. Note that England did not take part in the SITES survey.

28. Li, Q. and Ma, X. (2010) A meta-analysis of the effects of computer technology on school students' mathematics learning, *Educational Psychology Review*, 22(3): 215–43.
29. See, for example, Jones, K. (2000) Providing a foundation for deductive reasoning: students' interpretations when using dynamic geometry software and their evolving mathematical explanations, *Educational Studies in Mathematics*, 44(1): 55–85.
30. Gove (op. cit.).
31. Ainley, J., Bills, L. and Wilson, K. (2005) Designing spreadsheet-based tasks for purposeful algebra. *International Journal of Computers for Mathematical Learning*, 10(3): 191–215.
32. Higgins, S. (2003) *Does ICT Improve Learning and Teaching in Schools? A Professional User Review of UK Research Undertaken for the British Educational Research Association*. Nottingham: BERA.
33. Ruthven, K. (2009) Towards a naturalistic conceptualisation of technology integration in classroom practice: the example of school mathematics, *Education & Didactique*, 3(1): 131–52.
34. Bretscher, N. (2011) *A survey of technology use: the rise of interactive whiteboards and the MyMaths website*. Paper presented at the CERME 7 Seventh Congress of the European Society for Research in Mathematics Education, Rzezsow, Poland 12 January.
35. Higgins (op. cit.).
36. Smith, F., Hardman, F. and Higgins, S. (2006) The impact of interactive whiteboards on teacher–pupil interaction in the National Literacy and Numeracy Strategies, *British Educational Research Journal*, 32(3): 443–57.
37. Moss, G., Jewitt, C., Levacic, R., Armstrong, V., Cardini, A. and Castle, F. (2007) *The Interactive Whiteboards, Pedagogy and Pupil Performance Evaluation: An Evaluation of the Schools Whiteboard Expansion Project – the London Challenge*. London: Institute of Education.
38. Zevenbergen, R. and Lerman, S. (2008) Learning environments using interactive whiteboards: new learning spaces or reproduction of old technologies? *Mathematics Education Research Journal*, 20(1): 108–26.
39. Spillane, J.P. (1999) External reform initiatives and teachers' efforts to reconstruct their practice: the mediating role of teachers' zones of enactment, *Journal of Curriculum Studies*, 31(2): 143–75.
40. See, for example, Cockcroft, W.H. (1982) The mathematical needs of adult life, in W.H. Cockcroft (ed.) *Mathematics Counts* (pp. 5–11). London: Her Majesty's Stationery Offie (HMSO), Hoyles, C., Noss, R. and Pozzi, S. (2001) Proportional reasoning in nursing practice, *Journal for Research in Mathematics Education*, 32(1): 4–27.
41. Office for Standards in Education (2008) *Mathematics: Understanding the Score*. London: Ofsted.

42. Plunkett, S. (1979) Decomposition and all that rot, *Mathematics in School*, 8(3): 2–5.
43. Ruthven, K. (2001) Towards a new numeracy: the English experience of a 'calculator-aware' number curriculum, in J. Anghileri (ed.) *Principles and Practice in Arithmetic Teaching* (pp. 165–88). Maidenhead: Open University Press.

PART 3

Learners

CHAPTER

Left-brain, right-brain, brain games and beanbags: neuromyths in education

Corinne Reid and Mike Anderson

And men ought to know that from nothing else but thence come joys, delights, laughter and sports, and sorrows, griefs, despondency, and lamentations. And by this, in an especial manner, we acquire wisdom and knowledge, and see and hear, and know what are foul and what are fair, what are bad and what are good, what are sweet, and what unsavory... And by the same organ we become mad and delirious, and fears and terrors assail us... All these things we endure from the brain...

(Hippocrates, 460–370 BC)

Introduction

In this chapter we explore a number of neuromyths that have contributed to bad education. These myths range from the idea that we only use 10 per cent of our brain, that some of us are left-brain thinkers while others are right-brained and that some simple exercises (like playing video games or throwing beanbags) can change children's brains in ways that aid their ability to learn in school. However, we also explore a more general myth; namely, that the science of learning should ultimately be the science of the brain. In so doing we tackle the question of why modern neuroscience is so alluring for educators and discuss some of the dangers of taking a too brain-centric view of education.

The co-evolution of neuroscience, neuropraxis and neuromyths

For centuries, philosophers, scientists, physicians, psychologists and educators have been seduced by the possibility of understanding the mysteries of human nature and intellect by unlocking the enigma that is the brain. Along the way we have made incredible leaps in our knowledge of what the brain does and how it relates to who we are and how we live our lives. We have made marked improvements in understanding how we process our world through sensory channels enabling innovative technology such as bionic ears and synthetic vision for the blind. We have, at the same time, been beguiled by a range of 'neuromyths' that, with the passage of time, seem, literally, unbelievable, yet which have left a significant footprint on our professional and social communities. Some myths have turned out to be essentially harmless. Philosopher, scientist and physician Qusta ibn Luqa (864–923), for example, wrote a treatise which argued that:

> “people who want to remember look upwards because this raises the worm-like particle [of the pineal gland in the brain], opens the passage, and enables the retrieval of memories from the posterior ventricle. People who want to think, on the other hand, look down because this lowers the particle, closes the passage, and protects the spirit in the middle ventricle from being disturbed by memories stored in the posterior ventricle.
> *(Constantinus Africanus 1536, p. 310, reported in Lokhorst, 2011).*[1] ”

Other neuromyths have had far more serious consequences for individual patients and for us as a society. In the 1700s, Franz Gall, a German physician and father of phrenology, proposed that moral and intellectual faculties were located in specific areas of the brain and further that these correspond to scalp topography.[2] So committed was he to this idea that he proposed both medical and moral treatment for adolescents who had the 'bumps' associated with having criminal or aggressive tendencies. Notably, he argued for the gentle treatment of criminals and the mentally ill on the basis that their behaviour was of somatic origin and to some degree beyond their responsibility.

Sakas and colleagues report on the evolution of psychosurgery as a method to redress a range of extreme behavioural, emotional and intellectual symptoms throughout the ages.[3] Stone Age man carefully drilled holes in skulls to release harmful spirits residing in the brain. Almost 30 000 frontal lobotomies were performed in the UK and the USA by early 1950s, again, with palliative or curative intent to destroy areas of the brain thought to be malfunctioning in patients committed to asylums and hospitals. Even Rosemary Kennedy, who was born into the American political dynasty, was given a frontal lobotomy to treat intellectual and behavioural problems.[4] So well established and highly valued was this practice that half of the Nobel Prize for Physiology or Medicine of 1949 was awarded to Antonio Egas Moniz for the 'discovery of the therapeutic value of leucotomy in certain psychoses'. Lobotomy was superseded by ECT or shock therapy in which electrical current is used to stimulate brain circuitry and so the story goes on. The moral of the story is that in all ages there have been advocates of these techniques that now may seem ridiculous if not barbaric. Even given this history, the tangibility of the brain and the seemingly hard quality of anatomic and neuroscientific evidence continues to prove seductive for scientists, educators, therapists and many other health professionals – perhaps never more so for educators. Google Books *n*-gram viewer chart in Figure 11.1 illustrates how the publication of material at the intersect of neuroscience and education has grown rapidly since the mid-1990s. And, while neuroscience and education have not had quite such a dramatic history together as psychiatry and neuroscience, the partnership

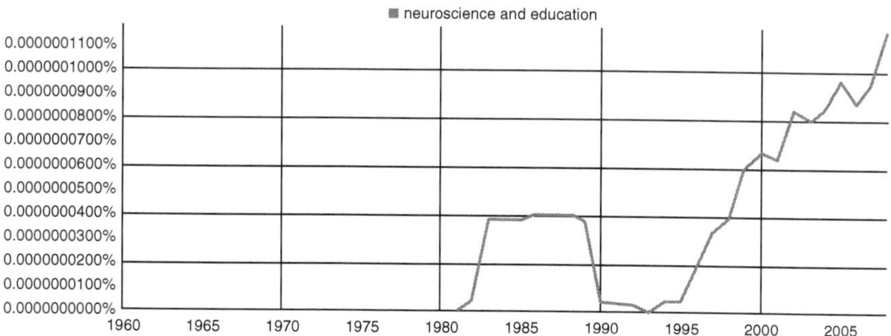

Figure 11.1 Growth of publication of material in neuroscience and education

has the potential to be equally as influential on the lives of children in our care, for good and ill.

Neuromyths in education

Along with the great interest in emerging links between neuroscience and education come concerns from both fields about the robustness of the available evidence.[5] Two factors have been identified as contributing to this concern: (1) the known challenges of bringing together two disciplines that have a different language, different approaches to knowledge development and to research design; and (2) examples of misapplication of neuroscientific findings to educational practice creating a range of stubborn neuromyths.[6] As we have seen in the historical examples given at the beginning of this chapter, such myths can manifest or evolve into exceedingly harmful policies and practices.

Neuromyth 1: We use only 10 per cent of our brain

While no one is quite sure of the provenance of this myth, it has resulted in a large and burgeoning market in brain training programs to 'unlock the potential of your brain'. This is in spite of considerable evidence contrary to the claim and no evidence to support it. Beyerstein (1999) summarizes some of the key arguments[7] and evidence, noting that:

1. Our brain is organised into functional areas that are activated during different kinds of tasks or activities. Years of brain mapping would suggest that no functionless areas exist in normal brains.
2. A long history of studies of brain damage highlight the depth and breadth of deficits that occur following even minor assault to one region of the brain or another. Indeed, the evidence would suggest that there is no region of the brain that can be damaged without loss of abilities.
3. Various forms of brain mapping technology (EEG, PET, fMRI) consistently show activity occurring across all areas of the brain. Only in cases of severe brain pathology or brain injury might there be areas where there is no activity. Even when we are asleep, functional

magnetic resonance imaging shows that there is activity occurring in our brain.

4. Autopsy of healthy brains does not reveal the degree of differential degeneration that would be expected if significant parts of the brain were not utilised. Our body typically works on a use or lose it principle and so we should see diminishment in much of the brain structure if only 10% were being used.
5. Evolution would dictate the selective reproduction of smaller brain and head size if there was redundancy in its function. The risk of larger human head circumference for childbirth would ensure that this was the case. We have retained our large brains because we need them for our survival.

This is a myth that demonstrates how an idea can take hold in the complete absence of evidence or even of a conceptual base!

Neuromyth 2: Some people are left-brain thinkers while others are right-brain thinkers and each needs a different form of learning instruction

This popular myth posits that some people are left-brain or logical thinkers and others are predominantly right-brain or intuitive thinkers who learn better through non-verbal or spatial means. Left-brain thinkers have been said to be good at analytical tasks and language-based thinking while right-brain thinkers are said to be stronger at spatial tasks, art and mathematics.[14] Related to this myth is the idea that people have dominant sensory learning preferences or different types of intelligences and that students consequently have preferences for particular modes of information presentation.[8] The VARK system for example, proposes four major sensory modes of learning: visual, aural, reading/writing and kinaesthetic. Each of these sensory preferences is said to contribute to differences in learning styles, supposedly reflecting the neural system with which a learner prefers to receive information. Current examples of this belief system guiding educational practice include curriculum development in single sex schools guided by a belief that boys and girls learn differently;[9] and the development of more tailored e-learning environments to accommodate 'brain differences' in learning style.[10]

However, the evidence for brain lateralization is based not on research into normal brain functioning but on historical research with patients who had their corpus callosum severed through accident or surgery. For these patients, as for current patients with brain injury, lateralization was a symptom of this severe pathology rather than the brain's preferred and optimal mode of functioning. In normal brains, while there is some degree of localization of function, there is overwhelming evidence of multisensory input and integration of functions drawing on both sides of the brain for almost every daily task.[11] Language and spatial information can even be processed differently, but simultaneously, by the two hemispheres. So intervention that targets one hemisphere over another is difficult if not impossible to achieve, but even if it were possible, by doing so we may prevent learning of all-important ability to integrate hemispheric processing. Moreover, there is no brain-based evidence that interventions targeting these styles are successful in enhancing learning.[12]

Neuromyth 3: There are critical periods in brain development during which enhanced learning can take place

It is undoubtedly a truism to say that the brain changes and develops with age. There is even neuroscientific evidence that supports the existence of critical periods for experience-expectant brain plasticity related to sensory-motor issues such as the development of 3D vision. However, there is no evidence that this is generally true for experience-dependent areas of brain plasticity such as those involved in the many aspects of learning addressed at school.[13] While it is true, for example, that there is an unparalleled period of very rapid synaptic growth and increased neural density from birth to the age of 3[14] this does not, contrary to popular belief, provide evidence to support the explosion of international policy developments in formalizing, even making compulsory, early childhood education. It is a conceptual and evidentiary leap to assume that such synaptic growth represents a unique openness to learning and a further leap still that such openness will optimally respond to formal education in a school setting.[15] Current evidence would suggest that changes in brain structure and function are likely to parallel openness to different kinds of learning at different developmental stages rather than different rates of learning. There is no evidence that the number of synapses relates to better learning. Further, while there is growing evidence to suggest that children from disadvantaged backgrounds benefit significantly from quality centre-based care and education in early childhood[16] and even that home-based support may be less beneficial for these groups of children,[17] there is no evidence that non-disadvantaged groups of children will experience enhanced learning under these circumstances. Indeed, there is even some evidence that children from middle-class backgrounds show less progress in a full-time early learning context than at home. In a study of 14 000 kindergarteners in the USA, white middle-class children in daycare showed delays in their social development compared to children kept at home.[18] While these delays disappeared by Grade 3 it does question the veracity of interpretation of the evidence base guiding these major international trends in policy-making and social intervention.

Neuromyth 4: Physical activities that involve cross-lateralization and coordination can enhance brain development and learning

A number of brain-based,[19] brain-compatible,[20] brain-friendly,[21] or brain-targeted[22] instructional approaches have been developed over the past decade. Most systems are based around a suite of core principles highlighting the importance of individualized instruction, challenging opportunities to expand our learning and the importance of the mind/brain/body connection in providing integration of all learning systems.[23] These same principles have led to a range of teaching techniques that have a strong common-sense appeal, such as introducing movement in the classroom, encouraging self-regulation, scaffolding for transfer of information into long-term memory and using mnemonic devices. However, often these methods defy a connection with the neuroscientific evidence base broadly invoked to support them.[24] There are some wild claims that are largely dismissed by educators, such as Tate's (2004; see note 19) claim that her brain compatible instruction can 'grow dendrites'.[25] However, others provide a seemingly respectable rationale and point to a range of evidence. An example is the claim that voluntary gross motor activities activate cross-lateralization of the brain, increasing language reception and acquisition, and in turn supporting reading.[26] Despite evidence to the contrary, games such as throwing beanbags and balance exercises have been proffered as ways of improving cross-lateral integration for the purpose of improving reading and learning. These claims require significant inferential leaps between evidentiary pillars, to support an activity that could be justified on the basis of enjoyment or physical health. When paired with a neurodevelopmental claim, they acquire an ethical responsibility to be evidence-based.

One controversial program based on a suite of physical activities to address a range of learning disabilities is the ddat (dyslexia dyspraxia attention treatment) or Dore programme. The rationale provided by the programme is that:

> “The cerebellum is key to the learning process, making skills become automatic through practice. But if the cerebellum is not working efficiently then it is very likely you will struggle with one or more of the following – poor reading and writing, concentration, co-ordination or social skills. Dore's drug-free programme consists of daily physical exercises that aim to improve balance, co-ordination, concentration and social skills.
> *(www.dore.co.uk/learningdifficulties/, accessed 28 January 2012).*”

While there is no evidence that the cerebellum can be effectively developed through such physical activities, the program gained considerable media attention and international currency among parents. Five editors of a scientific journal resigned over the publication of what they considered to be a flawed study on the treatment that suggested that the treatment was effective. A number of prominent academics spoke out against the program and its evidence base. Yet it was in commercial operation in a number of countries for a number of years.

Another difficulty in evaluating many brain-based learning approaches is that they develop into an omnibus suite of techniques and interventions despite a quite specific theoretical origin, which then becomes exceedingly difficult to test. Neurolinguistic programming (NLP) is arguably one of these instances. Tosey and Mathison suggest that

'NLP' reflects the principle that a person is a whole mind–body system,[27] with consistent, patterned connections between neurological processes ('neuro'), language ('linguistic') and learned behavioural strategies ('programming').[28] Carey and colleagues reviewed the literature on NLP and identified more than 77 basic NLP techniques.[29] While they could report some evidence of the effectiveness of programs that identified themselves as NLP, in about 30 per cent of the 110 studies they reviewed, there was no way to discern what elements of the program contributed to their success. Further, as with all other evaluations of brain-based learning programs, there was no attempt to use targeted brain-based outcome measures.

Neuromyth 5: Brain training can enhance learning

Despite the many commercially available brain training computer games and activities making claims about their ability to enhance your learning and make you more intelligent, the jury is still out on whether this is possible. As schools and parents continue to outlay significant sums of money in the hopes of changing a child's learning trajectory, a long history of programs have not borne the close scrutiny of scientific evaluation.[30] However, there have been more positive recent attempts at scientific and ethical accountability. Training in executive functioning appears to have the best current theoretical support from neuroscience and potentially the greatest impact in practice. When conceptualizing working memory as part of executive functioning, one carefully performed study (albeit with adults) claims a dose-related impact of a computer-based working memory training task.[31] Increasing general intelligence is the Holy Grail of most neuro-educational interventions, not least because effects will not be limited to arcane activities in the classroom but will have wide-ranging effects across the lifespan. Moreover, of all interventions designed to improve intelligence, the training of executive functions has the most developed scientific rationale through the established associations between the executive ability to maintain task goals, the operation of the frontal lobes of the brain and performance on measures of fluid intelligence. Klingberg and colleagues also reported preliminary success in training working memory in children with attention deficit hyperactivity disorder (ADHD) with broader impacts on complex reasoning skills and parent-rated symptoms of ADHD.[32] Thorell and colleagues noted the importance of early intervention efforts for children with executive functioning challenges and attempted training of preschoolers on working memory and inhibition computer tasks.[33] Each of these studies are preliminary. Two involve children but neither incorporated comprehensive profiling of participants that would allow careful investigation of outcomes measures nor a theoretical framework through which to interpret findings and investigate the critical mechanisms of change.

Why does it matter in the classroom?

Perhaps it is relevant to ask at this point why it matters if neuromyths are promulgated in the education system. Does it matter that kids are spending time throwing beanbags to one another or playing computer games? At one level these activities seem harmless enough. Yet the waste of precious educational dollars on interventions for which we have no evidence for their effectiveness is surely something we should avoid (for a classic example see McIntosh and Ritchie for a story of how educational authorities spent considerable sums on providing coloured lenses for reading difficulties).[34] Moreover, in the examples discussed in this chapter we have seen how important social and economic decisions about classroom philosophy can be influenced by seemingly harmless myths; for example, the age at which to start compulsory education and whether boys and girls should be segregated at school. In our clinics we also see children who have had secondary failure experiences at school as a result of a classroom philosophy underpinned by a belief that all children have the same potential if we can just 'find the key' to unlock their 'learning style' or 'intelligences'. These misinterpretations of neuroscientific research can leave us with praxis driven by inaccurate expectations about childrens' abilities. This can place children with learning challenges even further at risk in the school system and distract us from pursuing evidence-based solutions to guide everyday teaching practice. It is pause for thought that in 2010, Howard-Jones surveyed 158 graduate teachers to discover that 82 per cent considered teaching children in their preferred learning style could improve learning outcomes; 65 per cent considered that coordination exercises could improve integration of left–right hemispheric function; and 20 per cent thought their brain would shrink if they drank less than six to eight glasses of water a day.

What is the solution?

Challenging individual neuromyths is one way to provide a counterbalance to their proliferation and impact in the classroom. However, looking at general errors of thinking or practice underlying these myths may provide a firmer footing on which to move forward in forging productive links between the disciplines and indeed to answer the question of whether the science of learning should be the science of the brain.

Common methodological and professional challenges underlying educational neuromyths

Building bridges between disciplines

To further answer the question of whether education should be brain-based, greater contact is required between the disciplines of education, neuroscience and psychology. There are those who argue strongly for a reductionist position in which all behavioural phenomenon can be explained by the brain, while others question why we privilege brain-based explanations at all over psychological or behavioural explanations.[35] While there are many philosophical arguments to be had, ultimately it will be interdisciplinary relationship-building between practitioners and researchers that will afford the opportunity to evaluate whether relevant questions, methods of investigation and interpretive frameworks can be agreed upon.

Building bridges between different levels of explanation

Most neuromyths result from making inferential leaps between different levels of explanation. Education typically operates at the behavioural level, while neuroscience operates at the biological level. We have found in our own research with primary school-aged children that behavioural and biological measures of learning and error processing can give different outcomes, and suggest different explanations for how a child is best able to learn from errors.[36] We have been able to differentiate and evaluate these hypotheses by reference to a cognitive theory that draws together and makes sense of biological and behavioural observations. Understanding the difference and means of making contact between the behavioural, cognitive and biological levels is an important intermediary step in interpreting brain data in an educational context.[37] Cognitive theories of the relationship between cognitive functioning, brain development and learning behaviour or achievement provide a critical pathway on which we can move between the levels.[38]

Building bridges between laboratory-based and school-based research

All neuroscientifically based educational interventions should have some basis in standard laboratory-based scientific research. But a successful experiment or fruitful theoretical construct does not necessarily translate to making a difference in schools. Increasingly we are adopting methodological approaches that span standard laboratory-based research and settings where real children conduct the real business of learning. In our own research we have prioritized the development of a research model that can address each of these concerns in an integrated and comprehensive way. We have called this model Project KIDS. This model takes seriously the need for prioritizing contextually valid, longitudinal research opportunities. Our multidisciplinary team has involved psychologists, teachers, neuroscientists and paediatricians. Together, we have designed a neurocognitive profiling program that is embedded within a 'play day' framework. Up to 24 children attend our specially designed child-research facility that includes playgrounds and craft areas; event-related potential's (ERP) designed as astronaut training; psychometric assessment of abilities designed as space games; and information processing tasks designed as computer games. School-based achievement tasks are also completed as games as are measures of social and emotional development. All tasks are administered in a standardized way by a highly trained paediatric assessment team but are at the same time presented as games that earn tokens to be exchanged for craft materials for use in a team activity involving all children and staff. And so, over two consecutive days, we collect biological, cognitive and behavioural measures of a range of abilities and skills. We draw the data together through the lens of a well-defined theory of cognitive development, Anderson's Minimal Cognitive Architecture, which is our connecting bridge between the three levels of explanation captured by our data.[39]

Caution in interpretation and inferential use of brain data

There is currently a tendency to over interpret brain scan data. Alferink and colleagues report the case of brain scans that appeared in Newsweek comparing PET scans of 'normal' and 'neglected' children. Apparent differences in these scans were interpreted by child advocacy groups as having significant social policy implications. However, these scans were withheld from publication in a peer-reviewed journal because they were not statistically different, even though it was 'obvious' to the uncritical reader that they were.[40] Further, if a section of the brain lights up in a scanner it is assumed to be in a causal way associated with the event occurring. Not only may it not be causal, it may not be a primary feature of the behaviour, nor even a primary marker, and most certainly not a unique and solitary marker. At best we can confidently say that is likely to be a necessary but not sufficient marker of the function, ability or behaviour that we are exploring. Activation may also not always be a sign of positive activity – if we scanned a child while they were being caned, we would in all likelihood see localized activity that we could interpret as 'learning' but this probably would not lead us to promote caning.

Our tendency to overinterpret brain data is also ably illustrated by a study by Weisberg and colleagues in which data was shown to adults either with or without spurious brain-related imagery and information.[41] Brain imagery increased the reported confidence in the veracity of the data. Diener also questions whether we fully understand what brain imaging is telling us and what it cannot tell us, foreshadowing the possibility that it may in time come to be seen as the new phrenology.[42] Notably, there is very little educational research that includes brain-based measures of change to evaluate the effectiveness of different learning options.

Caution in interpretation of non-human research

Much of neuroscientific research is conducted on monkeys, cats and mice. This includes the synaptogenesis research that is so widely drawn upon – it was conducted largely on rhesus monkeys. Similarly, research on critical periods in development is based on research such as cats having their eyes sewn shut to see how it will affect their later ability to see. Not only is such research targeting severe deprivation rather than normal development, we also have many examples of where the brain structure, function and development in animals is markedly and critically different than in humans. Not to mention the research that knocks out target genes in mice thought to be at risk of dyslexia!

Caution in making inferences from research based on pathology to practice in a classroom with typically developing children

Much of the research in neurosciences is conducted with clinical samples in which there is some kind of brain pathology. This is particularly true for research with children as we typically only receive ethical permission to perform brain scans on children who have a clinical need for the procedure. As we have seen from the lateralization research, what is true for people with brain injury or illness is often not true for a non-clinical population. This is a particularly important issue in education. In times past when psychiatry misapplied research evidence in practice, it was with a small minority of the population, containing the horrific impact to a few. In education, policies built on misinterpretation of neuroscientific evidence affect all children. The example of the age of beginning education demonstrates how the pre-emptive leaping between evidentiary pillars has the potential to affect millions of children around the world.

Caution in making inferences from laboratory-based research

Neuroscientific research and brain scanning is almost entirely conducted in the laboratory, almost none in the classroom. This is a significant obstacle in bringing neuroscience to educational policy and practice. How a child's brain reacts to a very isolated event in a carefully designed experimental task, under controlled conditions, is unlikely to be how it reacts in a real-world setting where there are multiple competing inputs and many distractions. Contextual validity is a critical factor to consider for the future.

Conclusion

As teachers and psychologists we have, more than any other professions, the privilege and the responsibility of supporting each of our students to realize their full potential. In future it is likely that neuroscience will have an even greater presence in our classrooms. In addition to helping us understand the learning needs of our children, it is being called upon to explain their social challenges and behaviours such as bullying, violence and the emotional challenges of mental illness.[43] The decade of the brain is rapidly morphing into the century of the brain and as new technology develops, it offers us the same potentials as it has offered medicine to explore mechanisms of illness and disease through the use of empirical tests. Indeed, while our discussion of neuromyths should invoke caution, it should be noted that many of the psychosurgical, phrenological and electroconvulsive techniques of the past are forerunners to what we currently consider to be the best neurosurgical practice. Neuromyths often hold a grain of truth. But if we are to continue the dance with neuroscience then we need to be firmer in our demand for contextualized, theory-driven evidence gathering, to develop ontologies that describe the structure of mental process so that it is possible to evaluate their responsiveness to real-life learning contexts.[44] We need to be clearer and more collegial in thinking about how best to gather the data and we need to be both cautious and rigorous in critically evaluating the robustness of the links between our brain-based data and school-based learning behaviour. Neuromyths are sometimes inevitable consequences of a discipline unfolding. The limits of our knowledge define points of vulnerability. However, neuromyths also arise out of carelessness and a lack of appreciation of the potential cost of overeagerness in application. Rosemary Kennedy is a good reminder.

Notes

1. Lokhorst (2011) Constantinus Africanns, 1536, De animoe et spiritus discrimine liber, in: Constantini Africanni Opera, pp:308–17, Basel. (In Latin) referenced by Lukhorst, Gert-jan, 'Descartes and the Pineal Gland'. The stanford Encyclopedia of Philosophy (Summer 2011 Edition), Edward N. Zalta (ed.), http://photo.stanford.edu/archives/sum2011/entries/pinealslaul/. Accessed 28 May 2012.
2. Gall, F.J., letter to Retzer, 1798. Translated in D.G. Goyder (1857), *My Battle for Life: The Autobiography of a Phrenologist* (pp. 143–52). Oxford: Bodleian Library. Available online at www.historyofphrenology.org.uk/stexts/retzer.htm.
3. Sakas, Damianos, E., Panourias, L.G., Singounas, E. and Simpson, B.A. (2007) Neurosurgery for psychiatric disorders: from the excision of brain tissue to the chronic electrical stimulation of neural networks, in Damianos E. Sakas and B.A. Simpson (eds) *Operative Neuromodulation. Functional Neuroprosthetic Surgery: An Introduction* (pp. 365–74). New York: Springer.
4. Shorter, E. (2000) *The Kennedy Family and the Story of Mental Retardation*. Philadelphia, PA: Temple University Press.
5. Ansari, D. (2011) Culture and education: new frontiers in brain plasticity, *Trends in Cognitive Sciences*, 16(2): 93–95; Christodoulou, J.A. and Gaab, N. (2009) Using and misusing neuroscience in education-related research, *Cortex*, 45(4): 555–57; Della Sala, S. (1999) *Mind Myths: Exploring Popular Assumptions About the Mind and Brain*. Chichester: John Wiley & Sons Ltd; Della Sala, S. and Anderson, M. (2012) Neuroscience in education: an (opinionated) introduction, in S. Della Sala and M. Anderson (eds) *Neuroscience in Education: The Good the Bad and the Ugly*. Oxford: Oxford University Press; Goswami, U. (2006) Neuroscience and education: from research to practice? *Nature Review of Neuroscience*, 7(5): 406–11; Howard-Jones, P. (2010) *Introducing Neuroeducational Research: Neuroscience, Education and the Brain from Contexts to Practice*. New York: Routledge; Purdy, N. (2008) Neuroscience and education: how best to filter out the neurononsense from our classrooms? *Irish Educational Studies*, 27(3): 197–208; Willingham, D. (2009) Three problems in the marriage of neuroscience and education, *Cortex*, 45: 544–45.
6. Beauchamp, M.H. and Beauchamp, C. (2012) Understanding the neuroscience and education connection: themes emerging from a review of the literature, in S. Della Sala and M. Anderson (eds) *Neuroscience in Education: The Good the Bad and the Ugly*. Oxford: Oxford University Press.
7. Beyerstein, B. (1999) Whence cometh the myth that we only use 10% of our brains? In S. Della Sala (ed.) *Mind Myths: Exploring Popular Assumptions About the Mind and Brain*. Chichester: John Wiley & Sons Ltd.

8. Fleming, N.D. (1995) I'm different; not dumb: modes of presentation (VARK) in the tertiary classroom, in A. Zelmer (ed.) Research and development in higher education, Proceedings of the 1995 Annual Conference of the Higher Education and Research Development Society of Australasia (HERDSA), *HERDSA*, 18: 308–13; Gardner, H. (1993) *Multiple Intelligences: The Theory and Practice*. New York: Harper Collins.
9. Keller, S. (2011) Teaching methods at single sex high schools: an analysis of the implementation of biological differences and learning styles. Senior Theses, Trinity College, Hartford, CT; Trinity College Digital Repository. Available online at www.digitalrepository.trincoll.edu/theses/48.
10. Wolf, C. (2007) Construction of an adaptive e-learning environment to address learning styles and an investigation of the effect of media choice, Ph.D. thesis, School of Education, RMIT University.
11. Goswami (2012) Principles of learning, implications for teaching? Cognitive neuroscience and the classroom, in S. Della Sala and M. Anderson (eds) *Neuroscience in Education: The Good the Bad and the Ugly*. Oxford: Oxford University Press.
12. Dembo, M.H. and Howard, K. (2007) Advice about the use of learning styles: a major myth in education, *Journal of College Reading and Learning*, 37(2): 101–09; Kratzig, G.P. and Arbuthnott, K.D. (2006) Perceptual learning style and learning proficiency: a test of the hypothesis, *Journal of Educational Psychology*, 98: 238–46.
13. Bruer, J.T. (1997) Education and the brain: a bridge too far, *Educational Research*, 26(8): 1–13; Anderson and Della Sala (2012), see note 4.
14. Davis, A. (2011) (ed.) *Handbook of Pediatric Neuropsychology*. New York: Springer Press.
15. Alferink, L.A. and Farmer-Dougan, V. (2010) Brain-(not) based education: dangers of misunderstanding and misapplication of neuroscience research and brain based education, *Exceptionality*, 18(1): 42–52.
16. Schweinhart, L.J., Barnes, H. and Weikart, D. (1993) *Significant Benefits: The High/Scope Perry Preschool Study Through Age 27*. Ypsilanti, MI: High-Scope Educational Research Foundation, Monograph #10; Loeb, S., Bridges, M., Bassok, D., Fuller, B. and Rumberger, R. (2005) How much is too much? The influence of preschool centers on children's social and cognitive development. NBER Working Paper No. 11812, December, JEL No. I2, I3.
17. Miller, S., Maguire, L.K., Macdonald, G. (2011) Home-based child development interventions for preschool children from socially disadvantaged families, *Cochrane Database of Systematic Reviews*, 12, Art. No. CD008131. DOI:10.1002/14651858.CD008131.pub2.
18. Loeb, S., Bridges, M., Bassok, D., Fuller, B. and Rumberger, R. (2005) How Much is Too Much? The Influence of Preschool Centers on Children's

Social and Cognitive Development. National Bureau of Economic Research Working Paper No. 11812, http://www.nber.org/papers/w11812.

19. Jensen, E. (2008) A fresh look at brain-based education, *Phi Delta Kappa*, 89(6): 408–17; Laster, M.T. (2007) *Brain-Based Teaching for All Subjects: Patterns to Promote Learning*. Lanham, MD: Rowman & Littlefield Education (ISBN: 978-1578867226); Dennison, P. (2006). *Brain Gym and Me: Reclaiming the Pleasure of Learning*. Ventura, CA: The Educational Kinesiology Foundation; Caine, G. and Caine R.N. (2010) Overview of the systems principles of natural learning [PDF document]. Retrieved from Caine Learning Online Web Site: http://www.cainelearning.com/files/Summary.pdf; Kiedinger, M. (2011) Brain-based Learning and its Effects on Reading Outcome In Elementary Aged Students. Masters Thesis. University of Wisconsin-Stout.
20. Ronis, D. (2007) *Brain Compatible Assessments*. 2nd edition. Los Angeles, CA: Corwin Press; Tate, M. (2004) *Sit and get won't grow dendrites*. Los Angeles, CA: Corwin Press.
21. Perez, K. (2008) *More Than 100 Brain-friendly Tools and Strategies for Literacy Instruction*. Los Angeles, CA: Corwin Press.
22. Hardiman, M. (2003) *Connecting brain research with effective teaching: the Brain-targeted Teaching Model*. Lanham, MD: Scarecrow Press.
23. Caine, G. and Caine, R.N. (2010) *Overview of the Systems Principles of Natural Learning* [PDF document]. Available online at www.cainelearning.com/files/Summary.pdf.
24. Coltheart, C. and McArthur, G. (2012) Neuroscience, education and educational efficacy research, in S. Della Sala and M. Anderson (eds) *Neuroscience in Education: The Good the Bad and the Ugly*. Oxford: Oxford University Press.
25. Alferink & Farmer-Dougan, (2010); see note 15.
26. Lyons, C.A. (2003) *Teaching Struggling Readers: How to Use Brain-based Research to Maximize Learning*. Portsmouth, NH: Heinemann; Shaywitz, S.E. (2003) *Overcoming Dyslexia*. New York: Random House Inc.; Wolfe, P. (2009) *Building the Reading Brain: PK-3* (2nd edn). Thousand Oaks, CA: Corwin.
27. Tosey, P. and Mathison, J. (2010) Neuro-linguistic programming as an innovation in education and teaching, *Innovations in Education and Teaching International*, 47(3): 317–26.
28. Dilts, R., Grinder, J., Bandler, R. and DeLozier, J. (1980) *Neuro-linguistic Programming*, Volume 1: *The Study of the Structure of Subjective Experience*. Capitola, CA: Meta Publications.
29. Carey, J., Churches, R., Hutchinson, G., Jones, J. and Tosey, P. (2010) *Neurolinguistic Programming and Learning: Teacher Case Studies on the Impact of NLP in Education*. Reading: CfBT Education Trust.

30. Howard-Jones, P. (2010) *Introducing Neuroeducational Research: Neuroscience, Education and the Brain from Contexts to Practice*. New York: Routledge.
31. Jaeggi, S.M., Buschkuehl, M., Jonides, J. and Perrig, W.J. (2008) Improving fluid intelligence with training on working memory, *Proceedings of the National Academy of Sciences of the United States of America*, 105(19): 6829–33.
32. Klingberg, T., Fernell, E., Olesen, P., Johnson, M., Gustafsson, P., Dahlström, K., Gillberg, C.G., Forssberg, H. and Westerberg, H. (2005) Computerized training of working memory in children with ADHD – a randomized, controlled trial, *Journal of the American Academy of Child and Adolescent Psychiatry*, 44(2): 177–86.
33. Thorell, L.B., Lindqvist, S., Bergman, S., Bohlin, G. and Klingberg, T. (2009) Training and transfer effects of executive functions in preschool children, *Developmental Science*, 12(1): 106–13.
34. McIntosh & Ritchie, (2012) Rose tinted? The use of coloured filters to treat reading difficulties, in Della Sala & Anderson (eds) *Neuroscience in Education: The Good the Bad and the Ugly*. Oxford: Oxford University Press.
35. Miller, G. (2010) Mistreating psychology in the decades of the brain. *Perspectives on Psychological Science*, November 5: 716–43, doi:10.1177/1745691610388774.
36. Anderson, M. and Reid, C. (2009) Don't forget about levels of explanation, *Cortex*, 45: 560–61.
37. Cragg, L., Fox, A., Nation, K., Reid, C., and Anderson, M., (2009) Neural correlates of successful and partial inhibition in children: An ERP study. *Developmental Psychobiology*, 51: 533–43; Richardson, C., Anderson, M., Reid, C. and Fox, A.(2011) Neural indicators of error processing and intraindividual variability in reaction time in 7 and 9 year-olds. *Developmental Psychobiology*, 53: 256–65,. doi:10.1002/dev.20518.
38. Coltheart and McArthur (2012), see note 23.
39. Anderson, M. (1992) *Intelligence and Development: A Cognitive Theory*. Oxford: Blackwell.
40. Bruer, J.T. (1999) *The Myth of the First Three Years: A New Understanding of Early Brain Development and Lifelong Learning*. New York: Free Press.
41. Weisberg, D.S., Keil, F., Goodstein, J., Rawson, E. and Gray, J.R. (2008) The seductive allure of neuroscience explanations, *Journal of Cognitive Neuroscience*, 20: 470–77.
42. Diener, E. (2010) Neuroimaging: voodoo, new phrenology, or scientific breakthrough? Introduction to special section on fMRI, *Perspectives on Psychological Science*, 5(6): 714–15.

43. Viding, E., McCrory, E.J., Blakemore, S-J. and Frederickson, N. (2011) Behavioural problems and bullying at school: can cognitive neuroscience shed light on an old problem? *Trends in Cognitive Neuroscience*, 15(7): 289–334.
44. Poldrack, R. (2010) Mapping mental function to brain structure: how can cognitive neuroimaging succeed? *Perspectives on Psychological Science*, 5(6): 753–61.

From fixed IQ to multiple intelligences

Philip Adey

Introduction

One can see where Howard Gardner got the motivation to develop his theory of multiple intelligences. In 1994, two other Harvard professors, Richard Herrnstein and Charles Murray, published a book called *The Bell Curve*[1] which soon became notorious in educational circles. Named after the Gaussian curve of normal distribution familiar to anyone in the social sciences, *The Bell Curve* promoted an extreme hereditist view of intelligence in which a person's life chances were determined more by his or her genetic make-up at conception than by anything else. This view was, not surprisingly, an anathema to most educators. If our students' abilities are fixed before they even come into our classrooms, what are we supposed to do about it? Gardner's multiple intelligence theory arose in reaction to Herrnstein and Murray's fixed intelligence position and as such is laudable, but opposition to a false theory alone is insufficient reason to be able to support multiple intelligence. Unfortunately many of multiple intelligence's proponents working in schools have used the theory uncritically to promote some curriculum nonsenses.

In this chapter, I try to steer a narrow course between the Scylla of fixed, highly hereditable intelligence and the Charybdis of Multiple Intelligences. Once those dangers are avoided, we will see a clear sea beyond, with a bright, overarching aim for the whole educational system.

Let us start with the fixed intelligence idea.

Intelligence is largely inherited

> 'She is really very able'
> 'His ability is quite limited'
> '. . . the top ability set'

These expressions are commonplace in schools and generally go unchallenged as the meaning seems quite clear to most teachers. However, I would like to question the meaning of 'ability' as commonly used in schools, to unpack some of the implications of its use and to offer an alternative vision of the whole purpose of education.

For many years I have been asking teachers what they understand by the term 'intelligence' or 'general ability'. What sort of behaviours does a child show that demonstrate intelligence? The answers are surprisingly consistent across different subjects and in many countries. These are some of the things which teachers recognize as intelligent behaviour:

- making connections between different ideas;
- seeing patterns in data;
- applying a principle being learned today to a different context;
- asking probing questions;
- going beyond the given;
- thinking 'outside the box'.

These are all to do with making connections between different concepts, and seeing the relationships between different areas of knowledge. As such this characterization by professionals of the nature of general ability is quite consistent with psychologists' traditional definitions of intelligence as the ability to extract relationships from data and to make predictions based on patterns of data. It is what intelligence tests attempt to measure and express as an 'intelligence quotient' (IQ). Neither teachers nor psychologists have a problem with an idea of general ability that is largely context-free; that is, which is really *general* in that it can be applied to learning mathematics, French, or history – and some would say to plumbing, football and dance also. So far, so good. But what is also implied in the common conception of ability is that it is somehow an inborn characteristic of an individual. Whereas we are content to believe that, with a bit of effort, almost all children can learn some basic information such as dates, tables and spellings, we attribute the ability to comprehend abstractions and use higher-level critical thinking only to a minority. But where do we think these differences come from? Are they determined by the genes, inbuilt into the micro-physiology of the individual and immune to change by education? The casual use of the word ability, as in the quotes above, often carries an implication that there is not much that a school or teachers can do about such a fundamental property of the individual, but that it must be taken as a given to be worked with.

The weakness of this position becomes clear if you take it to its limit: If general ability is really immune to influence, what are we doing in education? The role of the education system would be reduced to some Brave New World nightmare of pigeon-holing children into schools and classes according to their 'ability' and devising a multi-level curriculum so that each sub-sub-set of children was taught what was seen as material appropriate to their level, with no opportunity for individuals to move from one level to another. This, indeed, is the principle underlying selection at 11+ years to allocate children to different types of schools, a practice thankfully abandoned in most parts of the UK in the 1960s (but still stubbornly persisting in some local authorities). It is also the principle underlying the practice of streaming or setting, dealt with in Chapter 3. And it is fundamentally misguided.

Time was, not that long ago, when the 'nature-nurture' debate ran hot (are we a product of our genes or our environment?) but a contemporary understanding of genetics has largely taken the wind out of the sails of the argument. Genes themselves determine very little directly. They act as templates for building proteins but the actual proteins that are built, how they are deployed, and their effect on lifestyle are absolutely not predetermined. It is relatively meaningless to talk in absolute terms, as was common up to 10 years ago, of fixed 'proportions' of IQ or that is determined by genes and environment respectively. We are a product of gene-environment interaction and that interaction is enormously complex and cannot be simplistically broken down into components.

Robert Plomin and his co-workers in the Institute of Psychiatry at King's College London have been studying twins for years, comparing IQ scores of monozygotic and dizygotic pairs as they grow up in various environments. The monozygotic (identical) twins, of course, have identical genetic make-up while the dizygotic (fraternal) twins share no more genes than other siblings (on average, 50 per cent). By comparing traits of these two types of twins, Plomin is able to explore the interaction of genes and environment in spite of the fact that the two potential sources of variation are hopelessly confounded (parents provide both genes and environment). Plomin proposes that 'about 20% of variance (in IQ) is accounted for by the genes at birth, but this rises to 60% by the age of 14'.[2] The suggestion is that from soon after conception any latent potential in the genetic make-up is amplified by a parental environment that is itself influenced by genes so that after some years it appears that the genes have a far larger effect than can fully be attributed to them. In effect, gene-environment interaction precludes the sort of simplistic analysis that was attempted by Cyril Burt in the 1930s – even before he started inventing data to boost his hypotheses.[3] Matt Ridley's *Nature via Nurture*[4] offers a readable account of the issue and Malcolm Gladwell's *Outliers* makes a strong case for the impact of the social and cultural environment on genius. Even Mozart, even Bill Gates, needed 10 000 hours of practice to become the geniuses that they were.[5]

One of the dangers of holding, even subconsciously, the belief that there is not much we can do about a child's fundamental ability is that it becomes self-fulfilling. If we assume that the bottom set can not cope with difficult ideas, and keep everything simple for them to manage with little effort, we are robbing them of the opportunity to grow intellectually. Of course tasks must be tailored, taking account of current capabilities, but that does not mean spoon-feeding; it means setting challenges which, with some help, are attainable. I return to this issue of cognitive stimulation towards the end of the chapter.

Moreover, if both the teacher and the child believe that intelligence is more or less fixed, then fixed it will be. Carol Dweck has shown how children develop ideas of intelligence quite early in their school careers.[6] Broadly speaking, some develop what is essentially a fixed view of their own ability, believing, for example, that there is not much they can do to become smarter, that there is little point in working harder or making any effort to improve their thinking abilities, or believing that their success is due to innate ability and that they need make little effort. And yet other children take a completely different view of their own abilities. They believe that by making an effort and meeting challenges head-on they can improve their general ability to solve problems or that however successful they are currently, extra effort will bring even greater achievement. It is not difficult to imagine the types of intellectual environment that fosters each of these self-views of intelligence. Here are two scenarios, both of which I have witnessed at first hand:

Scenario 12.1

A Year 7 science class. The teacher has explained, not very clearly, what he wants the class to do. He asks 'Now does everyone understand that?'

Pupil (hesitantly) 'No, sir, I didn't quite understand . . .'
T: (crossly) 'What's the matter with you? Weren't you listening at all? Was I talking Martian or something?'

Scenario 12.2

A Year 7 science class. They have finished an activity about control of variables and the teacher has summed up what they have discovered. 'Now does everyone understand that?'

Pupil (hesitantly) 'No sir, we (indicating his partner) don't really get it'
T: 'Oh thank you for telling me. Why don't you talk with (indicates two other pupils), see if they can explain it to you better than I did. Come back to me if you're still stuck.'

Now, in which of those two classrooms are the students more likely to develop a sense that with a bit of effort and help from their friends they can improve, not only their knowledge, but their ability to understand things? Which classroom promotes a fixed, and which a flexible view of the nature of intelligence?

Before we leave the idea of fixed intelligence, it should be made clear that I am not proposing total flexibility of intellectual growth. If I have overstated the case for the plasticity of intelligence, it is by way of countering the prevailing tendency to underestimate the extent to which general intelligence can be modified. In reality, there do remain limits to how much we can raise a child's general intelligence – but I believe it is better to underestimate those limits than to use them as a prop to justify lazy teaching.

Reaction to the idea of one fixed intelligence: multiple intelligences?

'It is necessary to advance a hypothesis, or theory, and then to test it. Only as the theory's strengths – and limitations – become known will the plausibility of the original postulation become evident'. So writes Howard Gardner in his book proposing the theory of multiple intelligences, *Frames of Mind* (1993: 59). Amen to that.

From the last section we can conclude that the notion of a largely fixed general intelligence is untenable. So how should we react against it? One reaction that has taken on a life of its own in many schools is Gardner's idea that intelligence is not one, but many. His theory of multiple intelligences, which argues against the premise of *The Bell Curve* on the grounds that there is no such thing as general intelligence (since Spearman's time, often referred to as *g*), but that intelligence is multifaceted. Originally in *Frames of Mind* Gardner identified seven 'intelligences' each of which was characterized by reference to one or more genius exponents of that intelligence.[7] The seven intelligences and some representatives were:

Logical-mathematical	Albert Einstein, John von Neumann
Verbal	T.S. Elliot, William Shakespeare
Spatial	Pablo Picasso, Francis Crick and James Watson
Musical	Wolfgang Amadeus Mozart, Yehudi Menhuin
Kinaesthetic	Isadora Duncan, Marcel Marceau
Interpersonal	Mahatma Gandhi, Lyndon Johnson
Intrapersonal	Sigmund Freud, Marcel Proust

More recently there have been suggestions that emotional intelligence, environmental intelligence and spiritual intelligence might be added to the list. Gardner never claimed that the original list was exhaustive but he did offer criteria for what might properly count as an 'intelligence', which include:

- association with a particular brain locality;
- existence of prodigies in that field;
- distinct operations, developmental history and evolution;
- psychometric independence.

John White has made a comprehensive philosophical critique[8] of these criteria but here I will focus more on the psychology. Brain localization, and the existence of *idiot savants* play a particularly important part in justifying the theory and each will be considered in turn.

Brain localization

It is the case that different parts of the brain are implicated in different functions. Even before the advent of brain scanning, it was known that damage to certain parts of the brain through stroke or injury would lead reliably to impairment of certain functions. Thus, the left temporal and frontal regions are associated particularly with language, the occipital lobe with vision, and so on. The development of scanning methods such as functional magnetic resonance imaging (fMRI) have broadly confirmed the functions of these areas but it has also provided a great deal of detail and allowed us to see that any one function such as language, vision, spatial awareness and so on are served by many areas of the brain. For example, while the left temporal area is associated with language, there are many other areas also implicated in language comprehension, analysis, synthesis and production. It turns out that the idea that different parts of the brain are uniquely responsible for particular functions (associated with the seven or nine intelligences) is, at best, an oversimplification.

But even if the picture was simple – one brain locality for one function – does this preclude the existence of an overarching general controller, or conductor, of all the localities responsible for particular functions? In fact it has been shown[9] that if subjects are given problems with either a largely spatial demand, or a verbal demand, the corresponding areas of the brain do show increased activity. But in both cases, the same area of the prefrontal cortex also showed increased activity, as if this was managing at a higher level the particulars of either verbal or spatial processing. The power and efficiency of this general manager would correspond to a general intelligence, and the development of the general processor with maturation and stimulation would account for the process of general cognitive development. The prefrontal cortex seems to be the seat of this 'executive function', which fulfils the general function of planning and selecting and orchestrating the brain's functions in all cognitive areas. The facts that this part of the brain is relatively much bigger in humans than any other primates, and that the final phases of wiring in the prefrontal cortex is the last stage of brain development, occurring around 13–15 years of age in humans, reinforce the notion that this could be the, or at least an important, seat of general intelligence.

But the idea that brain localization implies multiple intelligences runs into another problem. If one part of the brain is damaged, with corresponding impairment of its associated functioning, very often other parts of the brain develop capability in the missing function. Stroke victims do not generally experience repair to the parts of their brains that have been damaged, and yet they often recover speech and mobility to a remarkable degree as other parts of the brain take over the functions of the damaged area. This again implies an orchestrating principle, something that detects impairment in a vital function and directs an alternative route by which that function may be executed – at least to some degree. We have to conclude that brain localization itself falls far short of providing evidence for independent multiple intelligences.

Savantism

The existence of a small number of individuals who have a truly remarkable ability in one area while remaining seriously deficient in general mental functioning is a source of wonder and great interest. These are individuals who may have remarkable powers, for example, in arithmetical calculation, memory, music or drawing but who in other respects have serious learning and social deficits. Often, but not always, they are autistic.

Well-known examples include Derek Paravicini (1979–), a musical genius who has absolute pitch and can play a piece of music perfectly after hearing it once. He started playing the piano at the age of two but in other respects has severe learning difficulties. He is blind and autistic. Stephen Wiltshire has extraordinary drawing abilities, being able accurately to reproduce a detailed city scene after viewing it once. He is autistic and has no other notable abilities. Kim Peek (1951–2009) who was the inspiration for the film *Rain Man* (although Peek was not autistic) in spite of serious brain damage had a phenomenal memory. He could read a book in an hour and memorize it completely, recalling it in detail years later but he could not function normally in the world, being unable even to dress himself. Other savant individuals are calendrical calculators; they can tell you the day of the week immediately from a historical date (e.g. 'May 9th 1765?' – 'Tuesday').

The existence of such individuals is cited as evidence that one of the multiple intelligences may become developed to genius level while leaving other intelligences far behind, and thus the intelligences are independent of one another. The difficulty here is that a model of multiple intelligences supposedly applicable to the whole population is being constructed on the basis of a tiny number of extremely unusual individuals. It is estimated that no more than about 100 individuals with savant capacities have *ever* been reliably reported, and that not more than 50 such individuals are alive today. Indeed their abilities are quite extraordinary, and there has, as yet, been no satisfactory explanation for the savant phenomenon. But just because we cannot yet provide a plausible explanation, that does not mean that we have to accept *any* explanation. To invest belief and curriculum resources in the theory of multiple intelligences, as many schools have done, is to use a miniscule minority of very special people to determine the educational pathway to be followed by the general population. It makes no sense.

Correlation between intelligences

It is not difficult to understand why teachers and others took to the theory of multiple intelligences with such enthusiasm. It seemed to deal a body blow to the idea of a single, fixed intelligence which, for good reason, is objectionable to most educators. What is more, it allowed teachers, who on the whole are kind liberal-minded people, to believe that everyone could be good at something. OK, so Fred isn't too hot at reading and writing but his interpersonal skills are brilliant, he's going to grow up to be another Richard Branson. Everyone's a winner. Unfortunately, an argument against an unpalatable viewpoint, however much we want to cheer it on, is not necessarily valid. Laudable though objection is to the idea of a fixed inherited intelligence, the validity of multiple intelligences as an alternative is not supported by the evidence.

The theory of multiple intelligences is predicated on the idea that the seven, or nine, intelligences are independent of one another, that each develops along its own pathway unconstrained by the others or by a general intelligence. But, in fact, there is always correlation between different abilities; that is, there is a tendency for an individual who is strong in one area to be strong in all areas, what is known as a 'positive manifold'. Taken over the population as a whole, the positive correlation among different specialized abilities argues strongly for the existence of an underlying general intelligence. It has been argued that the emergence of 'g' from measures of particular abilities is just a statistical artefact, and that alternative mathematical modelling would yield a solution with multiple independent intelligences, but more sophisticated analysis (known as path analysis or structural equation modelling) makes it clear that by far the most plausible explanation for the correlation is the existence of a real general intellectual factor underlying all special abilities, represented in Figure 12.1. A student's performance on any particular task will depend on both special abilities and general ability, the proportions of each varying from task to task. Such hierarchical models of intelligence, consisting of a general factor plus a number of special factors, have been around for nearly a century and have appeared in various guises.

One of the most elaborate of these models was produced by John Carroll (Harvard again) following a massive reanalysis of thousands of test results collected from the 1930s to the 1970s. John Carroll rather gently chides[10] Gardner's model of multiple intelligences for omitting the general factor.

In rare cases, an individual may develop a special ability to a remarkable degree, eclipsing the others and apparently drowning out the general factor. Thus, a child who shows an early talent for music may be

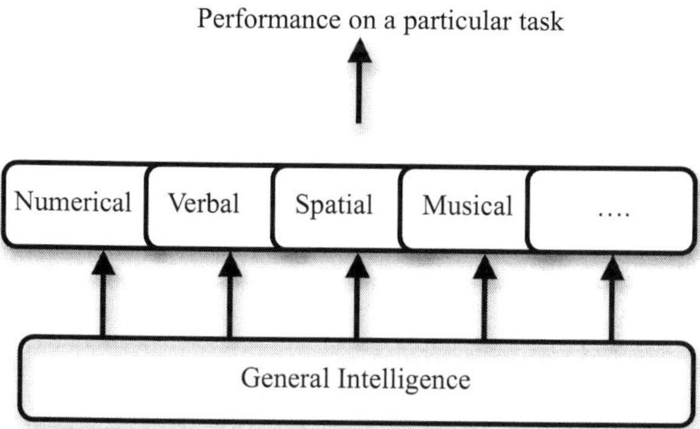

Figure 12.1 A general intellectual factor underlying special abilities

encouraged to put in phenomenal hours of practice (and indeed enjoy it) so that she grows into a musical prodigy, neglecting literature, the arts and other special abilities. The young footballer, likewise, may devote himself so totally to developing ball skills that schoolwork is neglected and he ends up being labelled a 'dumb footballer', not for any lack of general intelligence, but because the single-minded pursuit of excellence in one area precludes developing potential across a wider front. But over the population as a whole, abilities in different areas are correlated, and the feeling one may have of being, say, 'good at writing but useless at maths' may be attributed to the self-fulfilling prophesy of expectations of students and teachers.

To summarize this section, there is no doubt that we can distinguish operationally and logically different sorts of abilities – numerical, linguistic, spatial, kinaesthetic, and so on. The problem arises from claims that these special abilities are entirely independent of one another. All psychological measurement and common experience shows that underlying a person's special abilities is one common general intelligence factor.

Plasticity of intelligence

So if we cannot unseat intelligence from its general throne, what valid objection can we make to the fixed general intelligence idea? Multiple intelligence has led us astray by attacking the wrong bit of 'general, fixed' intelligence; it has targeted the general bit, which actually has some plausibility, and ignored the fixed bit, which is far more vulnerable. Once we realize that intelligence, even general intelligence, can change significantly under the influence of the environment (upbringing, teaching, nutrition, and so on), it loses its sting. Instead of being a deterministic brake on what our students can achieve, it offers us a great opportunity to raise achievement across the board with quite limited, but well-targeted intervention.

What evidence can be offered that intelligence is, indeed, modifiable?

The Flynn effect

Data from IQ tests administered over many years shows that the average IQ of the population is rising steadily, at the rate of abut 3 points every 10 years,[11] although some evidence suggests that in Scandinavian countries mean IQ scores have reached a peak and are no longer rising. The reasons why population IQ should rise is a matter for speculation: more children going to school and staying longer? More general stimulation from computer games and so on? Better nutrition? All these hypotheses and many more can be generated but experimental, or even epidemiological, evidence to support one over another is very difficult to come by. Whatever the cause, the fact that population intelligence is rising over the years shows that intelligence is not fixed, but is amenable to change.

The anti-Flynn effect

Notwithstanding the general trend noted above, recent measurements by Michael Shayer indicate that the general reasoning power of the school population in England has actually decreased significantly over the past 20 years.[12] In the 1970s Shayer and his team conducted a survey of the levels of cognitive development of 9-16-year-olds in England and Wales, sampling 14 000 students and carefully ensuring that the sample was representative of the population as a whole. The two striking outcomes of this survey were (1) that the range of measured cognitive abilities at any age were far wider than had previously been believed and (2) that not more than 30 per cent of students at the school leaving age of 16 demonstrated the use of abstract thinking. (Oh and one might add a third surprising outcome – that this massive and important survey caused so little stir among educators, journalists or politicians. Heads remained firmly in the sand, but that is another story.) Then, in 2008-09, Shayer was able to obtain results on the same tests he had used in the 1970s with a new representative sample. Boys had dropped an average of 1.4 standard deviations (sd) and girls had dropped 0.55 sd.

Once again, we can speculate about the reasons for this decline (National curriculum? Teaching to the test? Computer games?) but the evidence of the decline itself again shows intelligence is not a fixed quantity in the population.

Teaching thinking

Perhaps the most convincing evidence of the plasticity of intelligence is provided by programmes which have successfully demonstrated that better thinking can be positively affected by appropriate teaching strategies. Many curriculum programmes and pedagogies have been devised with the aim of directly teaching children to think better; that is, to be more intelligent. Unfortunately, many of these programmes have failed to show any convincing evidence of an effect and have tended to bring the 'teaching thinking' game into disrepute. But there are some notable exceptions: A recent evaluation of the *Philosophy for Children*[13] programme in one local authority's primary schools showed an effect size on cognitive abilities of 0.48 after a year and a half intervention of one hour per week. More importantly, the gains made by the experimental group over the controls was maintained for at least two years after the intervention, after the pupils had transferred to secondary schools. And the *cognitive acceleration* (CA) approach has been demonstrating big effects for years. To mention just two from the many reports[14] of the effects of CA:

1. In the original experiment, reported in 1991, students who used CA in science during their Years 7 and 8, when followed up for three further years, scored about 1 grade higher in their GCSE science, mathematics and English compared with matched controls. Effect sizes varied from 0.35 to 1.1.

2. Pupils who used Year 1 and 2 CA activities in mathematics showed gains in Key Stage 1 levels with an effect size of 0.51. When followed up for a further four years they showed significantly greater gains in Key Stage 2 national test levels in English than parallel classes that had not experienced CA (effect size 0.36).

The important point is that gains were obtained in subject areas far removed from that in which the thinking lessons were set. If the different types of thinking were truly distinct, one would not get this crossover. Transfer provides evidence for the underlying general intelligence. The mechanism is that the intervention, working through, say, science stimulates the students' general intelligence and that this, in turn, benefits learning in all areas including, say, English.

Conclusion

In this chapter I have argued, uncontroversially, that the nineteenth and early twentieth century idea that intelligence is more or less fixed by the lottery of heredity is quite untenable. But I have also argued that the idea of multiple intelligences, proposed as an antidote to hereditary general intelligence, is equally flawed as a model of human abilities. 'Evidence' from brain localization and *idiot savants* do not justify the proposition that a number of independent intelligences exist, and the persistent correlation between tests of different types of ability shows that a hierarchical model consisting of special abilities underpinned by a general intellectual processor offers by far the most plausible structure of human intelligence. School curriculum designs based on the theory of multiple intelligences are misguided.

Finally, I showed that there is substantial reason to believe that students' general intelligence can be enhanced by appropriate curriculum intervention. Far from general intelligence being a millstone around educators' necks, once one accepts that it is modifiable it becomes the great educational opportunity. Information can always be obtained from books and the web, but how to process that information, including critically evaluating it, making connections between different concepts and relating it to a particular issue at hand, that depends on intelligence. The main function of the education process from nursery school – maybe as far as first degree level – should be to develop students' general intelligence.

Notes

1. Herrnstein, R. and Murray, C. (1994) *The Bell Curve: Intelligence and Class Structure in American life*. New York: Free Press.
2. Plomin, R. (2001) Genetics and behaviour, *The Psychologist*, 14(3): 134–39.
3. See www.indiana.edu/~intell/burtaffair.shtml.
4. Ridley, M. (2003) *Nature via Nurture*. London: Harper Perennial.
5. Gladwell, M. (2011) *Outliers; The Story of Success*. New York: Back Bay Books.
6. Dweck, C.S. and Bempechat, J. (1983) Children's theories of intelligence: consequences for learning, in S.G. Paris, G.M. Olson and H.W. Stevenson (eds) *Learning and Motivation in the Classroom* (pp. 239–56). Hillsdale, NJ: Lawrence Erlbaum.
7. Gardner, H. (1993) *Frames of Mind* (2nd edn.). New York: Basic Books.
8. White, J. (2008) Illusory intelligences? *Journal of Philosophy of Education*, 42(3–4): 611–30.
9. Duncan, J., Seitz, R.J., Kolodny, J., Bor, D., Herzog, H. and Ahmed, A. (2000) A neural basis for general intelligence, *Science*, 289: 457–59.
10. Carroll, J.B. (1993) *Human Cognitive Abilities*. (p. 641). Cambridge: Cambridge University Press.
11. Flynn, J.R. (1994) IQ gains over time, in R.J. Sternberg (ed.) *Encyclopedia of Human Intelligence* (pp. 617–23). New York: Macmillan.
12. Shayer, M., Coe, R. and Ginsburg, D. (2007) 30 years on – a large anti-'Flynn effect'? The Piagetian test *Volume & Heaviness* norms 1975–2003. *British Journal of Educational Psychology*, 77(1): 25–41; Shayer, M. and Ginsburg, D. (2009) Thirty years on – a large anti-Flynn effect? (II): 13- and 14-year olds. Piagetian tests of formal operations norms 1976–2006/7, *British Journal of Educational Psychology*, 79(3): 409–18.
13. Topping, K.J. and Trickey, S. (2007a) Collaborative philosophical enquiry for school children: cognitive effects at 10–12 years, *British Journal of Educational Psychology*, 77(2): 271–78; Topping, K.J. and Trickey, S. (2007b) Collaborative philosophical enquiry for school children: cognitive gains at 2-year follow-up, *British Journal of Educational Psychology*, 77(4): 787–96.
14. Summarized in Adey, P. and Shayer, M. (2011) *The effects of cognitive acceleration*. Paper presented at the The Socialization of Intelligence. Available online at www.kcl.ac.uk/sspp/departments/education/research/crestem/CogAcc/Cognaccel.aspx

For a more comprehensive approach to the idea of intelligence in education, see:

Adey, P., Csapo, B., Demteriou, A., Hautamäki, J. and Shayer, M. (2007) Can we be intelligent about intelligence? Why education needs the concept of plastic general ability, *The Educational Research Review*, 2(2): 75–97.

Shayer, M. (2008) Intelligence for education: As *described* by Piaget and *measured* by psychometrics, *British Journal of Educational Psychology*, 78(1): 1–29.

Learning styles: unreliable, invalid and impractical and yet still widely used

Frank Coffield

Introduction

In 1580 in his Essays, Michel de Montaigne wrote: 'We are, I know not how, double within ourselves.' He went on to describe himself by juxtaposing nine sets of diametrically opposite adjectives, all of which he felt applied to himself: 'bashful, insolent; chaste, lascivious; talkative, taciturn; tough, delicate; clever, stupid; surly, affable; lying, truthful; learned, ignorant; liberal, miserly'.[1] Let us now move forward almost 300 years to 1862 when the Russian novelist Dostoevsky visited Charles Dickens in London. Years later Dostoevsky wrote an account of their meeting in which he reported that Dickens felt that 'There were two people in me . . . one who feels as he ought to feel and one who feels the opposite. From the one who feels the opposite I make my evil characters, from the one who feels as a man ought to feel I try to live my life. Only two people I asked?'.[2]

Let us now suppose in an admittedly outrageous flight of fancy that Michel de Montaigne and Charles Dickens are invited to complete Kolb's *Learning Style Inventory*, where they would have to choose for each of 12 items one of four words to describe their learning style. If they completed the task, and it is a very big 'if', because they are most likely to have recoiled in amazement at the naiveté and simplicity of the thinking behind it, they would have been assigned to an active *or* a reflective, an abstract *or* a concrete learning style – after, I repeat, circling no more than 12 adjectives.

Honey and Mumford's Learning Style Questionnaire certainly probes further with its 80 items, but the process and the outcome are the same. Those who put a tick or a cross against items such as 'I'm always interested to find out what people think' are then told they are 'activists' as opposed to 'reflectors', or 'theorists' as opposed to 'pragmatists'. As Rose argued: 'These oppositions are textbook-neat, but . . . are narrow and misleading'.[3] Stan Ivie reminds us that John Dewey rejected 'either-or' thinking because it creates false dichotomies which 'trick us into believing that sharp distinctions exist where in reality there is merely a continuum of experience'.[4]

At least Kolb and Honey and Mumford based their approaches on an explicit theory, which is more than can be said for many of the learning style inventories still being used in schools, colleges and universities, which have been devised by tutors themselves without any consideration of the validity or reliability of their instrument. So, for example, students are invited to choose whether they would prefer to learn how to cook by *either* 'looking at instruction cards' *or* 'listening to someone else telling about what to do' *or* 'getting stuck in and having a go'. Only one choice is allowed and so the person who sensibly uses all three methods of learning to cook is forced into an artificial and false selection. In this way, students are quickly 'shoe-horned' into being either a 'visual', 'auditory' or 'kinaesthetic' learner. In these ways, some psychologists are failing to recognize the complexity and contrariness of human nature that was so obvious to Montaigne and Dickens; and they are also ignoring the obvious point that the context often powerfully shapes how we behave. In the course of any one day we will be required to be 'activists', 'reflectors', 'theorists' *and* 'pragmatists' as we respond to the various challenges and opportunities that life presents us with.

The research

This chapter is based on research carried out by David Moseley, Elaine Hall, Kathryn Ecclestone and myself over a period of 18 months. We conducted a systematic and critical review of learning styles and their implications for methods of teaching. The research was commissioned by the Learning and Skills Development Agency and two complementary reports were produced in 2004. The first, called *Should we be Using*

Learning Styles? What Research has to Say to Practice[5] is aimed at students, teachers, school managers and inspectors. The second, more detailed, report entitled *Learning Styles and Pedagogy in Post-16 Learning: A Systematic and Critical Review*[6] is intended for researchers, academics and anyone with a deep interest in the topic. Both reports can be downloaded free of charge from www.LRSC.ac.uk.

This chapter describes the four key questions we set out to answer, the methods we used to conduct the review, and how each model of learning styles was analysed; I then discuss what I call 'the dark side' of learning styles, describe some of their most glaring deficiencies and end with some positive recommendations.

Four key questions

We set out to answer the following questions:

- What are the leading models of learning styles and what are potentially the most influential?
- What empirical evidence is there to support the claims made for these models?
- What are their implications for teaching methods?
- What empirical evidence is there that these models of learning styles have an impact on students' learning?

We wanted to get behind the claims made by the developers of learning style instruments to the evidence found by independent researchers.

Methods

The first surprise, which was not wholly welcome, was the huge size of the literatures involved. For example, David Kolb's wife, Alice, drew up a bibliography of all the research studies into his experiential learning theory and his Learning Style Inventory: it runs to 1,004 items up to January 2000.

From this vast literature we selected 13 of the most influential (or potentially influential) models of learning styles from the 70 we came across (see Figure 13.1). The fact that there are in existence as many

- Allinson and Hayes' Cognitive Style Index
- Apter's Motivational Style Profile
- Dunn and Dunn's Learning Style Questionnaire
- Entwistle's Approaches and Study Skills Inventory for Students
- Gregorc's Style Delineator
- Herrmann's Brain Dominance Instrument
- Honey and Mumford's Learning Styles Questionnaire
- Jackson's Learning Styles Profiler
- Kolb's Learning Styles Inventory
- Myers–Briggs Type Indicator
- Riding's Cognitive Styles Analysis
- Sternberg's Thinking Styles
- Vermunt's Inventory of Learning Styles

Figure 13.1 The 13 (out of 70) models studied

as 70 learning style instruments speaks volumes about the uncontrolled proliferation of learning style instruments within this disorganized field of study.

We needed some criteria for evaluating the huge collection of books and articles we quickly began to amass. The criteria we decided upon are as follows:

- The approach was widely quoted and regarded as central to the field as a whole.
- The model was based on an explicit theory.
- The model was representative of the literature and of the total range of models available.
- The theory has proved to be productive; that is, leading to further research by others.
- The learning style questionnaire has been widely used by teachers and managers.

The work of other contenders was rejected by applying these criteria:

- The approach was derivative and added little that was new.
- The focus of the research was on teaching styles or creativity rather than on learning styles.

- The publication was a review of the literature rather than the description of a new model.
- The study was a standard application of an instrument to a small sample of students and added nothing to either theory or practice.
- The methodology of the study was flawed.

Once we began evaluating the publications chosen for study, we were faced with a serious dilemma. The topic of learning styles is now of considerable practical importance to teachers and yet many of the debates, for example, about which type of factor analysis to use in the analysis of the data are highly technical and abstruse. The solution to our dilemma was to produce two reports; one for practitioners and a second for specialists in the field. The first aims to make our methods, findings and recommendations accessible to a broad audience; the second examines each of the 13 models in considerable detail.[7] We also sent the penultimate version of our review to the authors of the 13 models selected. Only one did not reply, while the others corrected minor errors, provided us with copies of forthcoming articles and repaired omissions in our coverage of their work, all of which helped to strengthen our conclusions.

Analysis of each model

To ensure comparability in our treatment of the 13 models, we used the same framework to evaluate each one. We described briefly the design of each model, after making some general introductory remarks about the definitions used by the authors and the scope of their instrument. We then provided details of its reliability and validity as given by the originators and compared these with the findings of independent researchers. Finally, we examined the evidence of pedagogical impact and provided an overall assessment of the model in question and a key reference. A summary also set out the strengths and weaknesses of the 13 models.

Main findings

Research into learning styles can, in the main, be characterized as small-scale, non-cumulative, uncritical and inward-looking. The literature has so far failed to provide either a common conceptual framework or a common language for the use of teachers or researchers. Our two reports provide detailed evidence of a proliferation of concepts, instruments and teaching strategies, together with a barrage of contradictory claims. In short, the research field of learning styles is theoretically incoherent and conceptually confused. That may sound like a harsh judgement, but in its defence, we listed the sheer number of dichotomies in the literature and Figure 13.2 presents all 29 of them. There is a considerable overlap among

- convergers v. divergers
- verbalizers v. imagers
- holists v. serialists
- deep and surface learning
- activists v. reflectors
- pragmatists v. theorists
- adaptors v. innovators
- assimilators v. explorers
- field-dependent v. field-independent
- globalists v. analysts
- assimilators v. accommodators
- imaginative v. analytic learners
- theorists v. humanitarians
- organizers v. innovators
- meaning-directed v. undirected
- activists v. theorists
- pragmatists v. reflectors
- non-committers v. plungers
- common sense v. dynamic learners
- concrete v. abstract learners
- random v. sequential learners
- initiators v. reasoners
- intuitionists v. analysts
- extraverts v. introverts
- sensing v. intuition
- thinking v. feeling
- judging v. perceiving
- left-brainers v. right-brainers
- lefts/analytics/inductive/successive processors v. rights/globals/deductive/simultaneous processors

Figure 13.2 Dichotomies

all these concepts, but no clarity about similarities and differences; no agreed, technical vocabulary; and no agreed theory to underpin them. The constant generation of new approaches, each with its own language, only adds muddle and clutter to existing confusion.

We also decided to match the 13 learning style models against the four minimal standards for a psychological test:

- Internal consistency; that is, do the items in the test measure the same thing?
- Test–retest reliability; that is, how similar are the scores when the same group is retested?
- Construct validity; that is, do the scores measure what they are intended to measure?
- Predictive validity; that is, do the test scores predict an expected outcome?

Figure 13.3 shows that only three of the 13 models – those of Allinson and Hayes, Apter, and Vermunt – could be said to come close to meeting these criteria. A further three – those of Entwistle, Herrman and

		Internal consistency	*Test–retest reliability*	*Construct validity*	*Predictive validity*
1	Jackson	–	–	–	–
2	Riding	x	x	x	x
3	Sternberg	x	x	x	x
4	Dunn and Dunn	x	x	x	√
5	Gregorc	x	x	x	√
6	Honey and Mumford	x	√	x	x
7	Kolb	–	√	x	x
8	Entwistle	√	–	√	x
9	Hermann	–	√	√	–
10	Myers–Briggs	√	√	–	–
11	Apter	√	√	–	√
12	Vermunt	√	√	√	x
13	Allinson and Hayes	√	√	√	√

Figure 13.3 Learning styles matched against minimal criteria

Myers–Briggs met only two of the four criteria. The Jackson model is in a different category, being relatively new and at the time we produced our two main reports no independent evaluations had been carried out.[8] The remaining six models, despite in some cases having been revised and refined over 30 years, failed to meet the criteria and so, in our opinion, should not be used in schools.

Allinson and Hayes' Cognitive Style Index – the CSI – emerged as the most robust model. We found that it had the best evidence for reliability and validity, although the pedagogical implications of the model have not been fully explored yet. The CSI was designed for use in adult organizations (e.g. businesses, small firms) and as a research tool. It is well regarded as a means of asking pertinent questions about how adults think, behave and learn in the world of work, but, unfortunately, it is not suitable for use with students in education.

The dark side of learning styles

Since our two reports were published in the summer of 2004, we have received a steady stream of emails from teachers, complaining that inspectors and senior managers continue to recommend (i.e. insist) that they 'differentiate' classes by means of learning styles. As knowledge about learning styles spreads within the teaching profession, I hope that inspectors and managers who continue to insist on their use will be asked: what particular questionnaire are you recommending and what are its scores for reliability and validity? One teacher educator wrote to say that, when visiting a local school, pupils had labels on their desks indicating their learning styles as in '*I'm a kinaesthetic learner*', '*I'm an active experimenter*' and so on. As John White, Emeritus Professor of Philosophy of Education at the Institute of Education, wrote in relating to what he described as 'the myth' of Howard Gardner's multiple intelligences:

> Putting children into boxes that have not been proved to exist may end up restricting the education they receive, leading teachers to overly rigid views of individual pupils' potentialities, and what is worse, a new type of stereotyping.[9]

Other opponents object to the commercialization of some of the leading tests, whose authors, when refuting criticism, are protecting more than their academic reputations. Rita Dunn, for example, insists that it is easy to implement her 22-element model, but that it is also necessary to be trained at considerable expense by her and her husband in a New York hotel. The basic cost in 2009 was $1,225 per trainee, excluding meals and accommodation; being trained to use their learning style instruments in research costs a further $1,000.[10]

Claims made for some of the models are clearly excessive. For example, the Dunn and Dunn model has all the appearance and arrogance of a total belief system. According to its proponents:

- It is successful with all age groups from children in kindergarten to professional adults.
- It leads to statistically significant higher scores in academic attainment, attitudes to learning and behaviour.
- It works with all types of subject areas from those taught in school to those taught in higher education.

If that was not enough, Dunn and Dunn claim that their tests 'summarize the environmental, emotional, sociological, physiological and global/analytic processing preferences that a student has for learning'.[11] All this from an instrument with only 104 items. Such overblown claims only serve to give the field of learning styles a bad name. They also make the point that it matters fundamentally which learning style inventory is chosen and how it is used: they are not all alike. It is also hard to take seriously a learning style inventory such as the one produced by Dunn, Dunn and Price that contains among its 104 statements the following: 'I think best when I feel cool'. Does this refer to temperature or with-it-ness? But worse is to come: 'I like to do things with adults' and 'It's easy for me to remember what I learn when I feel it inside me'. It is beyond parody.

Too simple, decontextualized and depoliticized

Too much is being expected of relatively simple, self-report tests. The difficulties with this type of test are well known: individuals may not be able to categorize their own behaviour accurately or objectively, they may never have reflected on how they learn or study, they may give socially desirable responses, and they may feel highly constrained by the predetermined format. We therefore advise against any teaching intervention based solely on any of the learning style instruments.

Moreover, Learning Style Questionnaires present decontextualized and depoliticized views of learning and learners. An example will best illustrate this point. One of the items from the Sternberg–Wagner Self-assessment Inventory on the Conservative Style reads as follows: '*When faced with a problem, I like to solve it in a traditional way*'.[12] Without a detailed description of the kind of problem the psychologist has in mind, the respondent is left to supply a context of his or her choosing, because methods of solving a problem depend critically on the character of that problem. The crisis in the Eurozone, gender inequality in pay and wages, conflict among colleagues and global warming are all problems, some of which may be solved in a traditional way, some of which may need new types of solution, while others still may not be amenable to solution at all. Crucially, some problems can only be resolved collectively. Nothing is added to the sum of human knowledge by individual respondents rating themselves on a 7-point scale on how well the decontextualized statement: '*When faced with a problem, I like to solve it in a traditional way*' describes them. This is spurious and useless precision.

The research tradition into learning styles has also been criticized for its depoliticized treatment of the differences between learners that stem from social class, race and gender. There is a worrying lack of research in the UK into learning styles and social class, or learning styles and ethnicity, although more of the latter has been carried out in the USA. The main charge here is that the socio-economic and the cultural context of students' lives and of the institutions where they learn is omitted from most of the learning styles literature, which tends to concentrate on factors within the individual student.

Positive recommendations

Some valuable features did emerge from our close reading of the literature and so we wish to offer some positive suggestions.

Instead of being assigned to a particular learning style, it would be more beneficial for students to appreciate the relative advantages and weaknesses of a range of different styles. The aim for teachers would be not only to study how students learn but also to show them how to enhance their learning by developing a flexible repertoire of approaches to learning rather than settling for just one. But self-knowledge is not an end in itself: students need to be shown how to use that knowledge to tackle problems they encounter when struggling to learn mathematics or history.

What kind of outcome do we as educators want from introducing students to the notion that there is a variety of ways in which to learn? The ideal result was described to me by a teacher at a conference in London. When asked by an inspector, '*What kind of learner are you?*', an 11-year-old girl replied: '*I'm all types rolled into one. And I use different styles, depending on what I'm doing and how I'm doing it.*' The nightmare reply to such a question would be: '*I'm a kinaesthetic learner and I expect the whole curriculum to be presented to me kinaesthetically. So there's no point in talking to me – I'm not an auditory learner. And there's no point in showing me diagrams, pictures or films – I'm not visual either.*'

Discussing learning with students can also provide them with a much needed 'lexicon of learning' – a language with which to discuss their own learning preferences and those of others, how people learn or fail to learn, why they try to learn, how different people conceive of learning in different ways, how they plan and monitor it, and how teachers can facilitate or hinder these processes.

There is, however, not one agreed language of learning styles, but a variety of competing vocabularies. We would recommend the language used by Entwistle[13] because he talks about deep (e.g. reading for understanding), surface (e.g. memorizing to get by), and strategic (e.g. being organized in order to achieve) approaches to learning rather than deep, surface and strategic learners. Entwistle and Peterson discuss the type of teaching activities needed to encourage a deep approach to learning; for example, keeping the broad aims, teaching methods and assessment procedures in constructive alignment with each other and 'promoting students' awareness of their own cognitive processes and approaches to studying, as well as their ability to control their motives, feelings and effort'.[14]

But a language that consists solely of three adjectives – deep, surface and strategic – will not generate much conversation. So teachers need to read other theories, such as the rich framework developed by Vermunt,[15] which discusses meaning-directed, application-directed, reproduction-directed and undirected approaches to learning. The critical shift to discussing learning will lead sooner or later to talk about the relationship with teachers and this moves the discussion away from a concentration on individuals, which learning styles tend to promote. Similarly, it is preferable to criticize the crime of *theft* than to tie the label of *thief* round the neck of a pupil. So instead of talking about different types of learner we recommend discussing different approaches to learning (e.g. building an overview, looking for concrete examples or memorizing the main points); different orientations to learning (e.g. self-improvement, vocational interest or to prove competence); different models of learning (e.g. dialogue with experts, to apply knowledge or to pass exams); and different emotions associated with learning (e.g. intrinsic pleasure, practical interest or fear of failure).

Using learning styles as a means of starting a dialogue about learning between students and teachers presupposes that those teachers are knowledgeable, not only about the serious variation in the quality of learning style instruments, but also about learning itself. If they are not, we suggest that teachers read as an introduction to the topic the brief pamphlet edited by David Hargreaves for the independent think-tank, DEMOS, entitled *About Learning*.[16] Our own two reports[17] will provide more substantial treatments of the issue as well as comprehensive bibliographies.

One of the most popular recommendations is that the learning styles of students should be linked to the teaching style of their teacher, the so-called 'matching hypothesis'. Unfortunately, the evidence from empirical studies of matching is equivocal at best and deeply contradictory at worst. Our review failed to find substantial, uncontested and hard empirical evidence that matching the styles of students and teachers improves the attainment of the students significantly. In 2009 Harold Pashler and his colleagues produced not another review of learning styles but a thorough examination of this hypothesis; namely, that students' learning is enhanced by teaching that is tailored to their learning style. Their conclusions are worth quoting in full:

> “. . . there is no adequate evidence base to justify incorporating learning styles assessments into general educational practice. Thus limited education resources would better be devoted to adopting other educational practices that have a strong evidence base, of which there are an increasing number.[18]”

Some researchers even suggest that a policy of deliberate *mismatching* should be adopted to prevent students becoming bored by having the whole curriculum presented in their preferred learning style. For instance, Vermunt[19] favours what he terms '*constructive friction*', where the teacher pushes students to take more responsibility for the content, process and outcomes of their learning.

Before deciding to introduce learning styles into their practice, teachers are also duty-bound to consider whether some other intervention may be more beneficial. In other words, the case for learning styles has to compete with arguments in favour of, say, thinking skills or peer tutoring or formative assessment. Our own view, which is explained in detail in both our reports, is that teachers would be well advised to concentrate on formative assessment rather than on learning styles because the evidence shows that it can '*produce significant, and often substantial, learning gains*'.[20] In other words, providing rich dollops of feedback to students has been shown to have much greater impact than labelling them 'left-brainers' or 'right-brainers', terms for which there is no biological justification.

Conclusion

The study of learning styles has led me to conclude that all of us need a strong dose of healthy scepticism to help us lose our reverence for some of the material that is presented to us on staff development days. In our research learning style instruments have been shown to be unreliable, invalid and of negligible impact on practice. How then are we to explain the apparently irresistible rise of learning styles? First, the notion that we all have an individual learning style appears to be highly attractive to both students and teachers. But what is happening is that, with the help of some rather simple questionnaires, too many teachers are labelling students in the belief that they have a fixed learning style that cannot be changed. Rigorous, empirical research has shown that this intuitive appeal and this belief are both dangerous and mistaken. Interestingly, this appeal to intuition is lost on the German-speaking world which has set its face against learning styles because their strong pedagogical tradition has constantly objected to the notion of styles of teaching and learning which are generalized and divorced from content, subject matter and context.

Second, learning styles continue to be popular because some instruments are freely available and easy to administer; and psychological tests have been popularized in magazines, 'help-yourself' manuals and in psychological texts written for the general reader. As Pashler et al. argue 'the idea of finding out "what kind of person one is" has some eternal and deep appeal'; and students can now attribute their lack of success to teaching that does not take account of their learning style rather than to their own lack of motivation or commitment.[21]

Third, attaching learning styles to individuals can be seen as part of the urge to understand and control the world by classifying people, but the quality of the classification system then becomes crucial and the danger of placing pupils into fixed categories becomes all the more real. What we need to avoid is 'the implication that the characteristic is "built in" to the individual (or a group) in a stable manner that extends across time and situations'.[22]

Fourth, learning style instruments offer teachers a simple solution to the complex problems of teaching and learning. Instead of always hankering after simplicity, perhaps the time has come for us all to celebrate, enjoy and study the inherent complexities of teaching and learning, which are best seen as the two sides of the same coin.

Since we published our reports in 2004, I have spoken at over 20 conferences on the subject.[23] In discussion groups I have learned that many teachers routinely administer a learning style questionnaire to all their new students at the beginning of term, analyse the responses, store the results electronically, file the forms in a drawer and then forget all about them. So they raise the expectations of students that all subsequent teaching will match their preferred learning styles, but then they dash these expectations just as quickly. I suspect that when teachers are faced with the task of dividing each of their classes into four groups depending on their learning styles and teaching the whole curriculum to them accordingly, the magnitude, not to say the impossibility, of the task is made manifest. How does one teach AS level German, or A2 level mathematics or BTEC Business Studies kinaesthetically?

Finally, I wish to take my stand with Richard Sennett who argued in a discussion of human abilities that 'inflating small differences in degree into large differences in kind legitimates the system of privilege'.[24] Individual differences in ability are not, he contends, the most important fact about human beings. Far more important is the belief that everyone possesses the ability to do good work:

> We share in common and in roughly equal measure the raw abilities that allow us to become good craftsmen: it is the motivation and aspiration for quality that takes people along different paths in their lives. Social conditions shape these motivations.

Notes

1. Quoted by Sarah Bakewell (2011) *How To Live: A Life of Montaigne in One Question and Twenty Attempts at an Answer* (p. 278). London: Vintage.
2. Quoted by Claire Tomalin (2011) *Charles Dickens: A Life* (p. 322). London: Viking.
3. Quoted by Gutierrez, K.D. and Rogoff, B. (2003) Cultural ways of learning: individual traits or repertoires of practice, *Educational Researcher*, 32(5): 19–25.
4. Ivie, S. (2009) Learning styles: Humpty Dumpty revisited, *McGill Journal of Education*, 44(2): 177–92.
5. Coffield, F., Moseley, D., Hall, E. and Ecclestone, K. (2004a) *Should we be Using Learning Styles? What Research has to Say to Practice*. London: Learning and Skills Research Centre, LSDA.
6. Coffield, F., Moseley, D., Hall, E. and Ecclestone, K. (2004b) *Learning Styles and Pedagogy in Post-16 Learning: A Systematic and Critical Review*, London: Learning and Skills Research Centre, LSDA.
7. I have also written a much shorter, eight-page summary of our research: Coffield (2005) Learning styles: help or hindrance? *Research Matters*, 26, Autumn, Institute of education: National Schools Improvement Network. Available online at www.nsin.org.

8. Jackson, C.J., Hobman, E.V., Jimmieson, N.L. and Martin, R. (2009) Comparing different approach and avoidance models of learning and personality in the prediction of work, university and leadership outcomes, *British Journal of Psychology*, 100(2): 283–312.
9. White, J. (2005) The myth of Howard Gardner's multiple intelligences, *ioelife*, London: Institute of Education, 1, 9.
10. Pashler, H., McDaniel, M., Rohrer, D. and Bjork, R. (2009) Learning styles: concepts and evidence, *Psychological Science in the Public Interest*, 9(3): 105–19.
11. Quoted by Pashler et al. 2009: see note 10.
12. Sternberg, R.J. (1999) *Thinking Styles*. Cambridge: Cambridge University Press.
13. Entwistle, N.J. (1998) Improving teaching through research on student learning, in J.J.F. Forrest (ed.) *University Teaching: International Perspectives*. New York: Garland.
14. Entwistle, N.J. and Peterson, E. (2004) Learning styles, learning strategies and approaches to studying, in C.D. Spielberger (ed.) *Encyclopedia of Applied Psychology*, (pp. 537–42). New York: Elsevier.
15. Vermunt, J.D. (1998) The regulation of constructive learning processes, *British Journal of Educational Psychology*, 68: 149–71.
16. Hargreaves, D.H. (2005) *About Learning*, London: Demos. Available online at www.demos.co.uk.
17. See notes 5 and 6.
18. See note 10.
19. See note 14.
20. Black, P.J. and Wiliam, D. (1998) *Inside the Black Box: Raising Standards Through Classroom Attainment*. London: King's College.
21. See note 10.
22. Gutierrez, K.D. and Rogoff, B. (2003) Cultural ways of learning: individual traits or repertoires of practice, *Educational Researcher*, 32(5): 19–25.
23. At one such conference, one teacher told me that, although she was convinced by the evidence I had presented, she would continue to administer learning styles. Why? 'Well, I have 500 copies of the questionnaire in my room and I don't want to waste them.' So routine and paper prove to be more important than potential damage to students.
24. Sennett, R. (2008) *The Craftsman*. London: Allen Lane/Penguin.

'TV is bad for children' – less emotion, more science please!

Annette Karmiloff-Smith

Introduction

Screen exposure in the form of television programmes and DVDs is occurring at increasingly younger ages,[1] and the press – both scientific and popular – have been engaged in acrimonious debates about this growing practice, claiming that screen exposure is intrinsically bad for children's health, risking an increase in attention deficit hyperactivity disorder (ADHD) and turning young children into mesmerized, mindless zombies.[2] Moreover, in 1997, 2001 and again in 2011, the American Academy of Paediatrics recommended a total ban on screen exposure prior to 24 months.[3] In an endeavour to counteract such emotional reactions, a number of scientists have begun to measure the effects of childhood screen exposure on attention[4] as well as on linguistic and cognitive development.[5] The results have been mixed, however. Some research suggests that language acquisition is delayed in those experiencing greater screen exposure[6] – a study that the British and American press was rapid to headline because it conforms to the popular view. However, other studies have yielded no difference between screen and live learning situations,[7] provided both involve parent–child interaction.[8] Despite its topicality, there are currently few in-depth scientific studies that measure neural, cognitive and behavioural changes induced by screen exposure, but this is likely to be the focus of considerable research in the near future. One thing is clear: however many official bans are announced, children will continue to watch TV and engage in multiple forms of screen exposure and electronic games. Nowadays, even young infants are being given touch-sensitive tablets and are surprisingly apt at using them. So, whether we like it or not, screen exposure occupies, and will continue to occupy, a large part of the majority of children's daily environment.

Children's TV and DVDs: a massively expanding industry

Over the past two decades, some very strong (and usually unsubstantiated) commercial claims have been made about the learning potential and brain changes that are deemed to result from TV and DVDs targeted specifically at infants and toddlers, resulting in a huge increase in child-oriented programming. However, counterclaims have been raised about their possible long-term detrimental effects on child development. So much so that the Walt Disney Company was threatened with a class-action lawsuit for unfair and deceptive claims. Susan Linn, Director of the Campaign for a Commercial-Free Childhood, complained to the US Federal Trade Commission about the educational claims made by the Walt Disney Company about the Baby Einstein series and about another company, Brainy Baby. As a result, both companies dropped the word 'educational' from their marketing. But the Campaign for a Commercial-Free Childhood remained unsatisfied and insisted that Disney refund the full purchase price to all those who had bought the Baby Einstein videos. Disney capitulated and agreed to the refund, with huge financial implications. Indeed, despite the American Paediatrics Association call for a ban on TV for under 2-year-olds, Disney was selling in excess of $200 million worth of the products annually. Reporting on the Disney case in 2009, Tamar Lewin of *The New York Times*[9] suggested that although the Baby Einstein series may have been a great electronic baby-sitter, the unusual agreement by the Walt Disney company to refund their millions of customers appeared to be a tacit admission that the series did not increase infant intellect and were potentially harmful.

Baby Einstein was founded in 1997 by Julie Aigner-Clark, an American housewife, filming sequences in her sitting room. It was one of the earliest players in what became a huge electronic media market for babies and toddlers. The company was acquired by the Walt Disney Company in 2001, and subsequently expanded to a full line of books, toys and flashcards, along with a set of further DVDs including *Baby Mozart, Baby Shakespeare* and *Baby Galileo*. Looking back, it is surprising that they did not invade the second language market with *Bébé Molière, Babino da Vinci* and *Das Baby Goethe*! The videos – simple productions featuring music, puppets, mechanical toys, bright colours and not many words – became a staple of American infant life and was soon to reach the British and other European markets. *The New York Times* reported that in 2003, for example, one-third of the totality of American babies from 6 to 24 months had at least one *Baby Einstein* video. And, even as Disney was refunding parents and the popular press was ringing alarm bells, numerous other companies continued to enter the baby DVD markets around the world.

How much screen exposure?

The main fear with screen exposure is that it will replace more so-called natural forms of creative play, book-reading and social interaction. Yet, at the same time, parents are under pressure to ensure that their little ones begin nursery school already media literate. Unsurprisingly, nursery teachers are confused about whether to introduce screen exposure as part of the nursery daytime activities or to avoid it at all costs. But, to reiterate an earlier point, TV and DVD viewing in infants, toddlers and children is here to stay. It will not disappear because of government prohibitions. On the contrary, it is likely to continue to increase. Recent surveys in the USA (and this is probably true for the UK and many other countries) indicate that by as early as three months of age, the majority of babies have been exposed to regular infant-directed screened media. Moreover, from 12 months onwards most infants and toddlers spend between 1–2 hours in front of a screen every single day. So, the challenge for parents and teachers alike is not how to cut out or replace TV and DVD viewing in preschoolers' lives, but rather how to control its use and make the most of its learning potential. Rather than focus on emotional knee-jerk reactions to its harmful effects or on the unsubstantiated commercial claims of its positive effects, let us take a more scientific perspective.

The digitalized age

While agreeing that many current TV/DVD programmes and electronic games are not appropriate for infants and toddlers, the important question is *why* they are not good and what aspects of screen exposure could, in the right circumstances, make it beneficial to early development.

Interestingly, children's natural curiosity and confidence in experimenting with new objects turns them into some of the most successful (but also most vulnerable) users of new technologies. For example, in her article for the British Psychology Society on digitalization in the early years, Natalia Kucirkova[10] reported that nearly 50 per cent of the top 100-selling Apple apps were targeted at preschool or elementary school-aged children, with approximately 100 new apps released every single day, many of which are designed for babies. What is astonishing is the ease with which babies and toddlers navigate through various apps, without instruction from their parents. In fact, young children are often completely fluent in a digital language that many adults fail to master. Hence the frequent headlines stressing the difference between techno-savvies and techno-phobics: 'Babies are smarter than adults'! Research is still inconclusive as to whether those young infants introduced to DVDs, smartphones, touch-sensitive tablets and other electronic devices – the techni-savvy babies – fare any better in the school years cognitively and socially, but debates continue to rage. As Kucirkova aptly points out, it is currently unclear what is meant by 'being literate in a digitalized world', but the relevance of understanding the positive and negative effects of screen exposure on development cannot be denied.

Those who object to screen exposure and claim that children must have hands-on experience of everything are losing sight of the fact that many children can never experience directly what an elephant or an airplane are, and that seeing static pictures of them in books may be less informative than tracking dynamic images of them moving across a screen. Children in inner cities, for instance, may rarely be able to compare in the real world the biological flight of a bird with the mechanical flight of a plane, so media exposure to these flights may enhance their perceptual knowledge and gradually lead to categorization and conceptual knowledge. Studies by Jean Mandler and her colleagues at the University of California at San Diego have detected conceptual knowledge that reveals itself in the play of babies in the first year of life.[11] Their research showed that if babies are given two almost identical plastic toys, one representing a plane and the other a bird with outstretched wings, they will pretend to make them move in distinct ways: the plane will be made to move in a smooth flow above their head, whereas the bird will be made to make hopping movements on the table, showing that they conceptualize them differently even though they look perceptually very similar. Such knowledge may well have been enhanced by media exposure to birds and planes. Rather than ask whether creative play, puzzles and book viewing are *better* than TV, DVDs and electronic games, we should accept the new technologies and explore how they can be judiciously used to enhance learning within a developmental perspective.

What does screen exposure involve cognitively?

It is often forgotten that learning from screen exposure involves complex cognitive tasks. The first is the translation of knowledge between a 2D representation and a 3D object. Those who complain that screen viewing is all about 2D vision forget that exactly the same applies to 2D images in books! One question that has interested scientists is whether preschoolers are aware of the difference between images on the screen and real-world objects. The findings indicate that they are. For instance, the failure of people on screen to be contingently responsive to the child's reactions is understood early in development. Studies by Philippe Rochat, a French developmental psychologist at Emory University, show that infants differentiate contingent and non-contingent reactions to their own behaviour on a screen.[12] Young children's lack of fear at seeing a wild animal on the screen or their failure to stretch towards objects on screen also suggests that they mark the difference between the screen and real life, although with the advent of 3D programmes, this could indeed change.

Other differences emerge when comparing good versus poor DVDs and TV programmes. First, in most media for infants and toddlers, salient characters and action are featured at the centre of the screen, with the background moving. Our adult visual system interprets this as movement of the foreground, despite the viewer's eye movements being fixated on the centre and thus kept to a minimum. By contrast, real movement rather than inferred movement attracts the infant visual system. Yet, to focus on the central character of most programmes, infants hardly need to move their eyes at all. This makes them very passive observers. Some might object that books are surely better than screen exposure for young babies. However, cognitively speaking pictures in books are static whereas, to reiterate, the infant visual system is attracted by movement. So, while book-reading is of course very positive for parent–baby interaction, the baby is often more captured by the paper sound effects of turning the pages than the actual contents of the book! One might further object that watching a mobile above the cot is dynamic. However, it is important to recall that mobile movement rotates in central vision, so the baby's eyes barely move, whereas tracking an object from one side of a screen to the other involves the complex dynamics of saccadic eye movements, a stimulus to the visual system.

Second, cognitively speaking, babies have to separate foreground from background in films (the same actually applies to books too, of course). This can be problematic because colours on television usually have little high contrast between foreground and background. Our adult visual system has sufficient top-down knowledge to separate the two grounds easily, but infants do not.

Third, it is important to note that sound can be cognitively distracting. One study showed that the imitation abilities of 6- and 18-month-olds infants were disrupted both by the addition of quite simple sound effects during a live demonstration and by background music during a video demonstration. What would seem like mere auditory decoration in the background of screen exposure may add significant cognitive load to the young children, particularly when it does not meaningfully connect visual and auditory content. A nice example of this is in the number domain. Background music while showing pairs or trios of objects to demonstrate the numbers '2' or '3', as in the *Baby Einstein* series, may be more disruptive than playing two drum beats or three drum beats, which match the number of visual objects on the screen, the latter procedure perhaps enhancing learning by providing multi-modality audio-visual representations of the same content.

Finally, adults can learn from a single exposure, whereas infants' developing cognitive systems benefit from repetition. Yet there are relatively few repetitions of event sequences on many television and DVD programmes. In fact, there has been a great deal of infant scientific research showing that repetition leads to habituation, followed by renewed attention anytime tiny changes occur that violate their expectations. So, to be realistic, when a mother or father is momentarily unable to give undivided attention to their baby (and this happens in a busy household), there would be no harm in having a baby see a repetition of a short section of the DVD that he or she had already shared with the parent, because repetition is good for their learning system.

Nowadays, programmers are becoming increasingly aware of the cognitive demands of the infant visual and auditory systems, and how these interact with developing cognitive systems. In my view, the future will witness DVDs and programmes that are inspired by infant scientific research and that make babies active participants in the media to which they are exposed, rather than passive observers.

Age-related differences to screen exposure and the importance of parental interaction

From at least six months of age infants can encode information they observe, keep it in memory over a retention interval and generate an imitative action on the basis of the stored representation. Thus, the expectation that infants and toddlers might acquire new information from age-appropriate video material is not unreasonable. However, it has been found that younger infants and toddlers do not readily imitate actions viewed on video, although they will readily repeat the same actions that they had viewed live. Some scientists have called this the 'video deficit'. At all ages, infants and toddlers do learn more effectively from live models in a direct and dynamic social context, but after 12 months they seem to learn about objects and events very well from screen exposure also. The learning potential of infant-directed video material therefore seems to be less in the first six months but increases over time. However, recent studies also show that if provided with appropriate prompts by a co-viewing adult, the impact on learning increases, even in younger infants. The following facts have been demonstrated, for example: toddlers respond differently to a real toy if the adult on the screen has displayed negative affect to an identical toy; they play more with toys that they saw on TV compared to novel toys; and information conveyed by video alone was able to reinstate a forgotten sequence of toy-play events in 18-month-olds. Research also shows that toddlers who viewed infant-directed videos *with their parents* looked longer at, and were more responsive to the video when the parents provided high and medium levels of scaffolding (descriptions, labelling, pointing), than when the parent simply sat next to them watching. Thus, parent–child interactions play a critical role in ensuring that young children derive the best from screen exposure,[13] thereby enhancing comprehension and learning.

Can language be acquired from screen exposure?

Much of the scientific research on the effects of media exposure has hitherto focused on language acquisition. Here the results seem clear: whether infants or toddlers, children learn best under conditions of live social interaction. One reason for this is obvious. The language-learning situation normally involves what psychologists call 'triadic interaction': mother looks at an object, attracts baby's attention by shifting her eyes from baby to object and back, points and names the object. She contingently responds to whether her baby has joint attention with her and is looking at the object. Screens do not, for the moment at least, respond contingently on their own, although scientists are currently working on such research paradigms whereby the infant's own eye movement will control what happens on the screen. However, as children grow older, they can and do learn new words from screen exposure. In one study, it was shown that 6- and 12-month-olds looked equally at videos with comprehensible (normal speech, ordered speech segments) and non-comprehensible (backward speech, fragmented speech segments) material, whereas 18-month-olds were clearly sensitive to linguistic distortions and preferred the comprehensible content. None the less, word learning has been shown to be successfully supported by TV programmes that incorporate explicit prompting routines to encourage young viewers actually to produce words rather than merely listen passively. However, unsurprisingly, this turns out again to be less positive than learning from a live model in a dynamic social context.

Making the 'bad TV' experience a good one

There is obviously an urgent need to find the right balance between the fact that young children will, come what may, indulge in watching TV and DVDs, and the fact that parents wish to have control over their children's screen exposure and education. If you want babies to reach their full potential, say the so-called experts, do not 'park' them alone in front of a TV screen. But no one questions whether it is acceptable to 'park' babies alone under a mobile in their cots, for instance. As stressed throughout this chapter, we need to examine screen exposure more scientifically avoiding emotional reactions. Below, I list some steps that parents might take to counteract negative effects of screen exposure.

Televisions should never be left on in the background when not purposely watching a programme; it distracts children from their active play. Also, TVs should never be in a child's room; it disrupts sleep patterns and thus the sleep-related consolidation of learning. It is wise for adults to watch any film carefully themselves before allowing children to watch it, to check that its contents are really suitable for their child's age. After all, we do the same with the books and toys we choose for children. A good test of the quality of a screened programme is for an adult to stand behind the TV screen and observe children while they watch. Are they simply mesmerized, with their eyes fixated at the centre of the screen? Or are their eyes moving a lot, and is it possible to detect signs in their behaviour that suggest that they are actually 'thinking' while watching the contents of the film; for example, mouthing sounds, pointing, anticipating what will appear next? As far as possible, adults should try never to leave children alone in front of a screen; that is, using the screen as a baby-sitter! Of course, at times it may be briefly unavoidable (just as a parent would leave a child alone in its cot watching a mobile) but as a general rule, it is advisable for parents to participate actively in the screen viewing with their children and to keep their attention alive by asking them lots of questions about what is happening on the screen now and what will happen next. In summary, it is critical to ensure that when engaged in screen exposure, children are active participants in what they see on the screen rather than mesmerized observers. Judiciously and sparingly used, TV, videos and DVDs can be as educational and enjoyable as books for young children, especially if it is borne in mind that the human visual system is stimulated more by moving stimuli than by static ones – something that is particularly true for infants. So, parents should have moments set aside for books, and other moments set aside for watching the screen with their children. Finally, it is important for even very young children to learn to turn off the TV once they have finished watching something. It teaches them control over their viewing habits, is an excellent training for life, and helps to avoid children subsequently becoming slaves to the TV screen. In my view, TV and children's DVDs are not intrinsically bad if programmes are chosen carefully and if their use is balanced with other child-appropriate activities.

What would make a good DVD for babies? In my view, the following characteristics would need to obtain:

1. frequent use should be made of visual tracking across the screen, with objects reappearing at different places on the screen to make babies search and anticipate;
2. objects should be partially obscured, as in the real world, or displayed upside-down or on their sides, so that the baby's brain has to reconstruct the whole mentally;
3. numbers of objects displayed on screen at a time should be kept between 1 and 3 because research has shown that this is the upper limit of the young baby's understanding of discrete number, and number should be represented multi-modally: in visual images, in *matching* number of sounds, in *matching* number of movements, so that the baby gradually builds up a rich mental representation of what, say, the quantity 3 really means (this is fundamentally different from rote learning to count to three);
4. sequences should be repeated often, to build up babies' anticipation of what will occur, and then a small change introduced to violate their expectations and thereby renew their attention;

5. human voices should change from male to female, adult to child, to match scene changes and to hold the baby's attention;
6. background music should match the tempo of actions: fast when, say, an object moves rapidly across the screen, slowly when the rhythm decreases;
7. tiny mistakes should be purposely made and then corrected (is it a cow? No, a sheep!) to introduce an element of fun, and again to hold the baby's attention;
8. research shows that faces are a particularly attractive stimulus for young babies, so infant DVDs should include lots of close-ups of eyes and full faces.

   In sum, screen exposure for young children should be far more than a display of coloured patterns and music to mesmerize babies; they should be a scientifically designed effort to stimulate babies.

We live in a media-saturated world. It is far better that parents know how to choose the right television or DVD programmes for their children than to make them ashamed at even thinking of ever using screen exposure.

Conclusion

In our modern world of TV, DVDs, computers, Internet, touch-sensitive tablets, electronic games and mobile communication, it is inevitable that most, if not all, children will have had significant experience of screen exposure by the time they start nursery school. Teaching at all levels is becoming increasingly computer-based, even in the early years. Digitalized entertainment is now portable and readily accessible on phones, laptops, touch-sensitive tablets and hand-held games consoles. It is frequently used by parents as a 'portable' means of providing educational entertainment while in the car, on holiday, in restaurants, and so on. In fact, it is common nowadays for toddlers to be more computer-literate than their parents or grandparents, and for somewhat older children to type better than they handwrite – facts that do not always sit comfortably with parents and teachers. Childhood seems to have lost some of its simplicity, and the backlash has witnessed commentators bemoaning the end of innocence, fearing that normal development will be compromised and that machines will be the teachers of the future. But there is currently little evidence to demonstrate that screen exposure is intrinsically bad.

Notes

1. Courage, M.L. and Howe, M.L. (2010) To watch or not to watch: infants and toddlers in a brave new electronic world, *Developmental Review*, 30: 101–15; Wartella, E., Richert, R.A. and Robb, M.B. (2010) Babies, television and videos: how did we get here? *Developmental Review*,30: 116–27; Anderson, D.R. and Hanson, K.G. (2010) From booming, buzzing confusion to media literacy: the early development of television viewing, *Developmental Review*, 30: 239–55.
2. Sigman, A. (2007) Visual voodoo: the biological impact of watching TV, *Biologist*, 54(1): 12–17; Christakis, D.A. and Zimmerman, F.J. (2006) Viewing television before age 3 is not the same as viewing television at age 5, *Pediatrics*, 118(1): 435–6.
3. American Academy of Pediatrics, Committee on public education (2001) Children, adolescents, and television, *Pediatrics*, 107, 423–25.
4. Foster, E.M. and Watkins, S. (2010) The value of reanalysis: television viewing and attention problems, *Child Development*, 81: 368–75; Richards, J.E. and Anderson, D.R. (2004) Attentional inertia in children's extended looking at television, in R.V. Kail (ed.) *Advances in Child Development and Behavior* (Vol. 32). Amsterdam: Academic Press; Stevens, T. and Muslow, M. (2006) There is no meaningful relation between television exposure and the symptoms of attention-deficit/hyperactivity disorder, *Pediatrics*, 117: 665–72.
5. Courage, M.L. and Setliff, A.E. (2009) Debating the impact of television and video material on very young children: attention, learning, and the developing brain, *Child Development Perspectives*, 3: 72–78; Fenstermacher, S.K., Barr, R., Salerno, K., Garcia, A., Shwery, C.E., Calvert, S.L. and Linebarger, D.L. (2010) Infant-directed media: an analysis of product information and claims, *Developmental Review*, 30: 557–66; Kremar, M., Grelat, B. and Lin, K. (2007) Can toddlers learn language from television? An experimental approach, *Media Psychology*, 10: 41–63.
6. Zimmerman, F.J., Christakis, D.A. and Meltzoff, A.N. (2007a) Association between media viewing and language development in children under 2 years, *Journal of Pediatrics*, 151: 354–68.
7. Allen, R. and Scofield, J. (2010) Word learning from videos: more evidence from 2 year olds, *Infant and Child Development*, 19(6): 553–661. Barr, R. and Wyss, N. (2008) Re-enactment of televised content by 2-year olds: toddlers use language learned from television to solve a difficult

imitation problem, *Infant Behavior and Development*, 31: 696–702. Mendelsohn, A.L., Brockmeyer, C.A., Dreyer, B.P., Fierman, A.H., Berkule-Silberman, S.B. and Tomopoulos, S. (2010) Do verbal interactions with infants during electronic media exposure mitigate adverse impacts on their language development as toddlers? *Developmental Review*, 30: 577–93.

8. Barr, R., Zack, E., Garcia, A. and Muentener, P. (2008) Infants' attention and responsiveness to television increases with prior exposure and parental interaction, *Infancy*, 13: 30–56.
9. Lewin, T. (2009) No Einstein in your crib? Get a refund, *The New York Times*, 23 October.
10. Kucirkova, N. (2011) Digitalised early years – where next? *The Psychologist*, 22(12): 938–41.
11. Mandler, J.M. (2004) *The Foundations of Mind: Origins of Conceptual Thought*. Oxford: Oxford University Press.
12. Bigelow, A. and Rochat, P. (2006) Two-month-old infants' sensitivity to social contingency in mother–infant and stanger-infant interaction, *Infancy*, 9(3): 313–25. Marian, V., Neisser, U. and Rochat, P. (1996) Can 2-month-old infants distinguish live from videotaped interactions with their mother, *Emory Cognition Project Report # 33*.
13. Aslin, R.N. (2007) What's in a look? *Developmental Science*, 10(1): 48–53.

Playing with emotions: why emotional literacy trumps emotional intelligence

Brian Matthews

Introduction

Why is it that at times in our lives we all have problems with emotions and yet schools ignore them? Educators sometimes seem to have a split personality when it comes to learning and emotions. On the one hand, most teachers recognize that the children's mental state is important. On the other hand, many feel that cognitive academic standards are what matters most and are uncertain over the introduction of 'whole-child' approaches that include social and emotional development.

A separation of the academic and emotional aspects of education can be seen when whole-child approaches are expected to be covered in Personal, Health, and Social Education (PHSE) but not seen as part of an academic subject's remit. The same separation occurs when teachers do not expect pupils to show emotion. Some people draw a clear distinction between cognitive and non-cognitive (or emotive) thinking. However, this chapter argues that a belief in this separation has led to bad educational practices and that the two are inextricably intertwined.

Emotional intelligence and individualism

Cognitive development has always been seen as an important goal of education. Recently, however, emotional intelligence has come to prominence because there has been a recognition that cognitive understanding alone is not sufficient for people to do well in the world.[1] Better cognitive understanding does not necessarily lead to people having happier lives.[2] Developing pupils' social and emotional expertise in schools should be seen as important for them to do well in their jobs and to be content in their day-to-day lives. To an extent this development is being encouraged in school, but, I argue, in a relatively individualistic way.

The first definition of emotional intelligence was produced by Salovey and Mayer[3] but it was Goleman who popularized the concept and argued that it involves five areas of development. These are:

1. emotional self-awareness;
2. managing emotions;
3. harnessing emotions productively;
4. empathy; reading emotions;
5. handling relationships.

In *Emotional Intelligence: Why It Can Matter More Than IQ*, Goleman (1996: xii; see note 1) pointed out that some people who did very well academically at school often did not go on to use their abilities in society. He asked:

> "What factors are at play when people of high IQ flounder and those of modest IQ do surprisingly well? I would argue that the difference quite often lies on the abilities called here *emotional intelligence*, which include self-control, zeal and persistence, and the ability to motivate oneself. And these skills, as we shall see, can be taught to children, giving them a better chance to use whatever intellectual potential the genetic lottery may have given them (ibid., p. xii)"

Since the publication of Goleman's book, there has been great interest in the concept of an 'Emotional quotient' (EQ) that parallels IQ. If one puts 'emotional intelligence' into an Internet search engine, millions of hits will result including firms advertising an EQ test.[4] These firms believe that emotions can be measured through conventional means, such as pen and paper EQ tests, although there is a lot of variation in how the tests are written and administered.

The tests are used in industry where they can be used either as part of an interview process, or to judge a person for promotion. Clearly, if you believe that a person's emotional intelligence can be measured through a paper and pen test of any form, you believe that emotional intelligence is individualistic; that is, the property of an individual. This is because EQ can be measured without reference to anyone else. It is like saying that the quality of a football team can be accurately judged only by the players' individual ball skills. With this in mind, it is interesting to note that emotional intelligence is often linked to brains, see the quote above from Goleman[6] ... *the genetic lottery may have given them'*. Again, if emotional intelligence resides in the brain, then it is the property of the individual. Also, it is interesting to note that Goleman's summary above only stresses those aspects of emotional development that are more individualistic *'self-control, zeal and persistence, and the ability to motivate oneself'* and does not include more social aspects such as empathy.

Cognitive 'intelligence' is widely regarded as being something that someone has as an individual, and that can be measured through examinations. Some people believe in 'intelligence quotient' (IQ) tests that have no social context. 'Emotional intelligence' and 'EQ' reinforce the idea that emotions can be meaningfully measured as belonging only to an individual. It is interesting to note that the Department for Education (DfE) has proposed that providers of initial teacher training should assess the 'interpersonal skills' of candidates, and their 'sustained commitment, resilience and perseverance', as part of a 'more rigorous' process for selecting teachers.[5] Hence, Michael Gove appears to believe that it is possible to have a written test that can measure aspects of 'emotional intelligence' separate from any social context. If this is the case, it justifies using approaches where emotional skills are identified and then taught to pupils like any other subject material. I will now look at how school practice focuses on the individual to a great extent.

Illustrations from school practice

Research in the USA furthers the argument that approaches to social and emotional learning (SEL) focused on the individual pupil are being used.

Hoffman[6] concluded that: 'SEL in practice thus becomes another way to focus attention on measurement and remediation of individual deficits rather than a way to redirect educators' focus toward the relational contexts of classrooms and schools' (p. 533).

Here are two examples from primary and secondary schools in most of Britain.

(*a*) *The use of 'I'. The Social and Emotional Aspects of Learning* (SEAL) is a project for Years 1–9 developed for schools[7] (see Chapter 9). Secondary schools are provided with three themes for each year (7–9) including one unit on anti-bullying. SEAL has 50 defined outcomes and each starts with 'I'. Here are some examples for years 7–9:

> (3) I can identify my current limitations and try to overcome them.
> (26) I can identify barriers to achieving a goal and identify how I am going to overcome them.
> (30) I can take responsibility for my life, believe that I can influence what happens to me and make wise choices.
> (33) I can see the world from other people's points of view, taking into account their intentions, preferences and beliefs and can feel with and for them (p. x).

Each unit contains outline lessons, with two or three learning objectives to contribute towards the outcomes. I would argue that all these outcomes are valuable for pupils to work at; however, once again the outcomes overemphasise the individual. For example, outcome (3) is almost always achieved through talking to other people and is dependent on the group of people you are with. Also, these outcomes are never fully achieved, but go on developing throughout life. Similar comments can be made about the other three outcomes, each of which could be expressed in terms of working with other pupils, including someone of the other sex who might have a different perspective to bring to bear.

The use of 'I' is also illustrated in a poster for pupils to develop their personal, learning and thinking skills[8] to judge how well they are doing at developing the skills for 'teamwork'. Three levels that mark pupil progress are defined. Here are a couple of them (Table 15.1):

Table 15.1 Developing skills for teamwork

Level 1	*Level 2*	*Level 3*
I am unwilling to lead a group to complete a task	I can help lead a group to complete a task	I have the skills to successfully lead a group of people to complete a task
I have difficulty in taking responsibility and lack the self-confidence to contribute when working as part of a team	I like to take responsibility and feel confident I have something to offer	I like to be personally responsible and feel confident that I have a lot to contribute when working as part of a team

One point to note is that all the statements, yet again, start with 'I'. This style is very common in materials for developing emotional intelligence and is true for all the statements in this example. The use of 'I' focuses on the individual, and yet teamwork is about people being able to cooperate together. As the adage goes, 'There is no I in teamwork'. Rather, one could ask, 'Do other people in the team think that . . . . ?' Similarly, the idea presented above is of a team in which one person takes on the role of leader, so only one person in the group can gain a level 3! This statement could read, 'With the others in the group, I can contribute well to forming a group cohesion'. Similarly, in the second row, the person is graded on *personal responsibility.* The key factor in good teamwork is that people are able to contribute to a group's cohesion so that everyone can feel responsible. What is hidden in this form of presentation is the extent to which teamwork is about the interactions between people and the ebb and flow of ideas.

(*b*) *Relationships*: Here is another illustration. A book for boys by Rae and Pedersen[9] has much to commend it. It has notes for the teacher that makes valid points and indicates overall aims. However, there are certain drawbacks with the approach.

> Problem Scenario **Girlfriends**
>
> **Frankie** has started seeing a girl named Cherie. He thinks she is pretty cool because she likes to just hang out and they like to do the same things. Only problem is that Cherie isn't the best-looking girl at school and the guys are all after Brenda who is

really fit. Brenda has been flirting with Frankie in front of the boys and it is pretty obvious that Brenda is interested in Frankie. The boys have started to tease Frankie about Cherie and say things like, 'Why are you with that when you could have Brenda?'

Solution-focused problem-solving format

How does **Frankie** feel?

What is the problem?

How would **Frankie** feel and behave if this problem disappeared?

How would **Frankie** know that he would no longer have this problem? What would be different?

What 3 things can **Frankie** do now in order to remove this problem from his life? [11: 46–7] ”

The problem is individualized, it is supposedly Frankie's problem. Actually, there is a complex of feelings between Frankie, Cherie and Brenda that is set in a social context about beauty and desire (e.g. Brenda may only be doing this because she does not like Cherie and it is not much to do with Frankie). The attitude of the 'friends' here should also be called into question. In this problem there is a set of social and emotional responses about desire, trust and love that continue all our lives, but it has been reduced to the problem of an individual. What can usefully be discussed are the emotions involved, what principles are evident and how to engage in a dialogue with others to address and make explicit feelings so a path can be followed. The problem cannot simply be 'removed' and the term 'remove' implies that only one individual is involved and that emotions can be denied; yet if Frankie has feelings for Brenda as well as Cherie these have to be faced up to in order to move on. The feelings and motivations of the girls as well as Frankie ought to be opened up. It is also pertinent to consider how one raises with pupils the idea that actions and motives can be due to unconscious feelings. There is no help in the teachers' guide on what to do with answers and issues such as these. Hence, the difficulty of emotional depth is unlikely to be explored, let alone grappled with in meaningful ways such that pupils will be helped to be more emotionally mature in handling situations like these. For example, pupils and adults can discuss sexism, be aware of it, and still go out and behave in sexist ways. So, in this approach by focusing on the individual, emotional development is made less likely.

One difficulty with the above approach is that the lessons are teacher-led. That is, the pupils are expected to respond to a situation with emotions, yet at the teacher's behest. However, even with the focus on 'I' and being teacher-led, the above approaches can be useful in giving the pupils a wider emotional vocabulary, building on their experiences and validating their talking about emotions in schools. Both of these processes are vital to emotional development but there are dangers of the 'taught' approach which tries to make pupils progress in areas of emotional development as if emotions could be learnt sequentially. In an extreme it could lead to even more teacher control over pupils as they feel they are being assessed against the lesson objectives in all areas of their life. It would be virtually impossible for pupils to have achieved the outcomes or objectives in a lesson and this could lead to a decrease in self-confidence as the pupils may feel they are not making the progress expected of them.

A key point is that, currently, the term 'emotional intelligence' is seen and used as being more individualistic than it could be. Another key point is that, as such, it fits into the present discourse of schools and their focus on the individual pupil. Because schools are not centrally concerned with pupils developing socially and emotionally, it does not matter if pupils are separated by gender, religion or social class. Schools are geared to teaching to find out how well pupils achieve individually through tests and exams. Often teaching assumes that information can be imparted to individual pupils using teacher-centred methods. Hence the idea that emotions can be taught to individuals through teacher-centred units fits well into much of the philosophy of schools at the moment. This is summarized in Table 15.2.

When cognitive and emotional learning are individualized then I believe this is 'bad education' because research indicates that this focus on the individual is misplaced. As an alternative approach I now consider what the term 'emotional literacy' can mean, and then relate this to school education.

Emotional literacy

It is possible to view emotional development as being a social process, often called *emotional literacy* rather than *emotional intelligence*,

Table 15.2 Individualistic view of the emotions

1. In society	*2. In schools*
Individual emotional development	The main aim is to develop the cognitive attributes of the individual
Emotions can be measured as property of the person. Emotional intelligence	For emotional development, skills can be identified for everyone, units produced and objectives for each lesson set, along with targets for pupils
Independent of discriminations	Emotions developed so pupils can behave better and do better cognitively
Objective measurement possible	Emphasize exams and cognitive learning
Rational	Cognitive separated from emotional. Subject teachers unlikely to engage in promoting emotional development of pupils *per se*
	All forms of school acceptable, including single-sex, religious and those that separate pupils by social class
	Educators see cognitive development as the province of schools
	Groupwork and use of language not particularly important

although some people use the terms as if there were no difference between them. To illustrate the differences, imagine you are overhearing a group of people talking to each other. The group contains men and women of different ethnic backgrounds and social classes. As these people talk, how would you decide how emotionally capable they were? Clearly, you could see if men and women talked and listened to each other, whether or not there were interruptions and if they supported each other. Similarly, one could judge if a person constantly ignored contributions from people with a different ethnic background. A person from a wealthy (or poor) background may not empathize with some others from different backgrounds. We can see that the components of emotional literacy can only be judged realistically if issues of gender, ethnicity and social class are taken into account. In other words, it depends on who you are interacting with. A person may empathize, listen to and respond well to people of the same sex and religion, but not with people who were different. Hence, emotional literacy is dependent on the social situation.

Previously, I have described emotional literacy as follows:

> Emotional literacy involves factors such as people understanding their own and others' emotional states; learning to manage their emotions and to empathise with others. It also includes the recognition that emotional literacy is both an individual development and a collective activity and is both about self-development and the building of community so that one's own sense of emotional well-being grows along with that of others, and not at their expense. Emotional literacy involves connections between people and working with their differences and similarities while being able to handle ambiguity and contradiction. It is a dynamic process through which the individual develops emotionally and involves culture and empowerment. For example, it includes understanding how the nature of social class, 'race' and gender (sexism and homophobia) impinge on people's emotional states to lead to an understanding of how society could change. Hence it incorporates an understanding of power exchanges between people and a challenging of power differentials.[10]

There are several points that arise from this description. This is an individual-in-group definition of emotional literacy as it places a person within a group social context and involves equity. This means that the social and emotional are inseparable. When people meet and talk, there can be a range of social and psychological concerns at work. Even among friends, there can be some conflict over whose idea gets accepted. When men and women are involved in a discussion, an overlay on the conversation can be one of power and they see themselves as being more in control. In business and industry, people can feel threatened and wish to maintain control and can use a range of techniques to ensure that they retain it. For example, it is not unusual for a manager to block good ideas from a junior if they feel threatened. In this case, the manager could put down the ideas-person as a way of maintaining their self-esteem. On the other hand, a person could put the progress of the group above their personal concerns, accept challenging ideas and be able to support them.

Emotional literacy is about the development of the community as well as the individual. To be able to relate to people both under and above you in this way requires a well-developed level of emotional literacy. It is difficult to be able to accept ideas from other people who may be challenging your authority. One aspect is how one may define one's role. For example, one head of a college who had a very good reputation for the development of information technology (IT) was asked how she did it as a leader. She replied that she saw her job as one of identifying those people under her who were having good novel ideas and then making sure that those who were their direct managers did not get in their way. However, to have the confidence to define one's job as a leader in this way requires a developed sense of relationships and what it means to be in charge. There are of course many types of leaders or managers but some are more inclusive than others. Hence, any definition of emotional literacy should include reference to possible discriminations and power.

What is important to recognize is that in the definitions of 'emotional intelligence' equity is never included, and in discussions of how it is translated into practice, it is rare for awareness of equality issues to be raised in a coherent way. In life, people's interactions almost always include a range of social and gender differences, and hence these and other discriminations should not be separated from ideas of what constitutes emotional literacy. Definitions of 'emotional literacy' do incorporate social issues more, but only the one above explicitly incorporates issues of power and oppression. Hence, emotional literacy can link to community, equality and social justice and can be seen as culturally situated rather than individualistic. I now show how a focus on individualism damages education, first, by looking at its effects on cognitive learning, and then, second, on emotional education.

Constricting education

We live in a fast changing world, the knowledge learned in school is being rapidly replaced and new knowledge acquired[11] (OECD 1999). When knowledge becomes out of date pupils should know *how* to learn.[12] Hence, pupils really require the ability to learn and think by themselves, but are prevented from doing so by the focus on cognitive skills. In order for people to continue to learn, and to want to explore and investigate issues and concerns that arise in their lives, thinking skills are essential. In careers of all kinds the ability to work with others and to be self-motivating is essential, as the Confederation of British Industry (CBI) has pointed out.[13] The CBI found that employers believe that as students enter work their ability to work in a team, be self-managing and problem-solve are all lacking.[14]

Thinking skills involve people working together, irrespective of background or sex, and being able to, for example, consider other views, take on board different viewpoints, accept criticism and be able to have a fresh perspective on things. All of these require emotional literacy to some degree as the exploration of ideas requires self-confidence, being able to discard cherished beliefs and to relate and empathize with others. Also, practically all thinking skills depend on being in a group. This group dependence, which makes assessment difficult as groups change, may be part of the reason why schools undervalue the importance of thinking skills. This is despite the fact that most parents would agree that they would like their children to come out of school being able to get on well with diverse others, being motivated to learn for themselves and be able to be independent learners who can cooperate with others to learn.

The more an education system believes that learning is an individual property, the less likely it is that group learning and lifelong skills will be emphasized. Hence, the view that cognitive learning is an individualistic enterprise is one that restrains and narrows learning. Passing examinations is overemphasized and important thinking skills undervalued. Schooling can then find out using 'objective' measures who is the best student and validate competition of individual over individual. Cognitive individualism makes for a restricted education in the academic realm. Even more importantly, it affects the extent to which emotional development takes place. I argue that the idea of emotional intelligence being individualistic is part of the problem of trying to deal with emotions.

Because of the fast changing knowledge we require an expanding education. As it stands, the world and our society have a number of problems to tackle. Fraser puts this well:[15]

> “Education should critically ensure children, young people and adults are equipped to be unsettled, to be confronted by difference, to be changed, and to effect change. Education is a conduit to different cultures, different places, different times – to different ways of thinking about things and doing things. Education provides us with an introduction to things unimagined and unencountered. It should provide the critical challenge to examine our beliefs, interpretations and horizons, the ability to re-examining ourselves in new contexts, to develop new interests, to review the ways in which we understand ourselves and our place in the world. The purpose of education should be to expand expectations, not to confine them – to support our learners in understanding the impact they can and do have on their world. We cannot expect education built upon, and educators who model, a fixation with certainty and inflexibility to meet the urgent and ongoing needs of pressing social, economic and political change.”

While everyone may not agree with all these points, this view of education requires an extension of the cognitive-based curriculum and to be able to achieve many of the points raised above it would be helped if people had a developed emotional literacy.

Emotional development and communal activities

People develop emotionally because of the experiences they undergo and how they respond to them. For example, to be able to get on with the other sex requires emotional development. A boy or girl may be told not to be sexist, but it is not likely to have much effect on their behaviour. Even as adults we may wish to change, but it takes commitment and effort. To tackle sexism requires boys and girls to get to know each other, to understand differing viewpoints, and be able to empathize, and this can only be achieved with commitment. Emotional literacy cannot be taught through instruction, it can only be developed through experiences and dedication.

Developing pupils' emotional literacy requires acknowledging and using the social and cultural context, ideally in coeducational, multiethnic and multi-social class schools. In such a learning environment pupils may be expected to collaborate, help each other, learn to understand each other across diverse backgrounds and views, and to learn to develop emotionally. Such an environment would require an approach that is contingent rather than taught, such as the approaches that I have developed.[16] The idea that emotions can be taught in units to a whole class, and have assessable objectives for each lesson, can make it appear that emotions are controllable – what can be delivered in a lesson can be controlled. This point is worth reiterating. People often believe that rationality enables us to have control over our lives – we talk about making 'rational decisions'. By this we mean that we make decisions without emotion. Of course, the reverse is true, all our major decisions have an emotional component, but if we can believe in rational emotional thinking, the more we can believe we control our emotions. If this is so, we can psychologically defend ourselves without having to face up to difficulties in our emotional lives.

The more educators focus on the rational individual the more there is likely to be a neglect of emotional development. We can see how this disregard is reflected in our education system. It is possible to argue that emotional development should be central to education. However, schools usually emphasize cognitive development and passing exams. Subject teachers rarely consider that it is their responsibility to develop pupils' emotional skills. People may argue that emotional development is not the province of schools but primarily of parents. This approach can only be justified if cognitive development is seen as being separate from emotional factors and yet we know this is not the case.

Also, many parents would like boys and girls to learn to get on with each other and to learn to face up to social and emotional difficulties. This outcome would mean developing emotional literacy as an individual-in-group context, not as an individual property.[12] In order to achieve this result, coeducational schools that had, as far as possible, mixed backgrounds would help. Groupwork would be seen as important, too.

The more our education system focuses on the individual, the less emphasis we would have to develop pupils' emotional lives in schools. Table 15.3 illustrates the main points.

Table 15.3 Developing pupils' emotional lives in schools

Individualistic view of the emotions in society	*Social/cultural view of emotions in society*
Individual emotional development	Social context of the individual important for emotional development
Emotions can be measured as property of the person. Emotional intelligence	Emotional literacy can only be gauged in the social context of groups
Independent of discriminations	Gender, social class, ethnic all important Power important
Objective measurement possible Rational	
Individualistic view of the emotions in society in schools	**Social/cultural view of emotions in society in schools**
The main aim is to develop the cognitive attributes of the individual	The main aim would be to develop the individual-in-group. This means that the social and emotional are inseparable. The cognitive, social and emotional development of pupils so that they may be able to think, reflect on values, and the problems facing society
For emotional development skills can be identified for everyone, units produced and objectives for each lesson set, along with targets for pupils	Emotional development would be contingent for everyone
Emotions developed so pupils can behave better and do better cognitively	Emotional development is an aim for everyone in its own right Development of the emotions accepted as important
Emphasize exams and cognitive learning	Cognitive learning and emotional development both important and interacting
Cognitive separated from emotional. Subject teachers unlikely to engage in promoting emotional development of pupils *per se*	Emotional and cognitive interact Emotional and social development the province of all teachers

Table 15.3 *(Continued)*

Individualistic view of the emotions in society	*Social/cultural view of emotions in society*
Develop those who misbehave	Develop the emotional literacy of everyone
All forms of school acceptable, including single-sex, religious and those that separate pupils by social class	Coeducational, multiethnic and multi-social class comprehensive schools
Educators see cognitive development as the province of schools	Educators see cognitive and emotional development as the province of schools
Groupwork and use of language not particularly important	Groupwork and use of language essential
	Thinking skills are essential
	Education for participation
	Education for change

Conclusion

The present school system is similar to a factory, where pupils are moved through it to gain as many examination passes as possible, often in competition with each other. Individual cognitive abilities are promoted over skills that would help throughout life and in confronting problems facing society. As a result, education is restricted and narrow. The model of individualistic emotional development fits well with 'factory'or 'banking' schooling system. The system downgrades the importance of our emotions. We discard the value and amazing opportunity of emotional maturing in the school journey. We require a profound emotional engagement with an understanding of our and other's underlying values and perceptions to achieve positive change in schools and the world. We are primarily emotional and social beings.

Notes

1. Goleman, D. (1996) *Emotional Intelligence: Why It Can Matter More Than IQ*. London: Bloomsbury.

2. James, O. (1998) *Britain On the Couch: Why We're Unhappier than We Were in the 1950s – Despite Being Richer*. London: Arrow.
3. Salovey, P. and Mayer, J. (1989) Emotional intelligence: imagination, cognition and personality, 99(3): 185–211.
4. BusinessBall (2011) *Emotional Intelligence (EQ)*. Available online from www.businessballs.com/eq.htm.
5. DfE (2011) *Training our Next Generation of Outstanding Teachers*. London: Department for Education (DFE-00054-2011).
6. Hoffman, M.B. (2009) Reflecting on social emotional learning: a critical perspective on trends in the United States. *Review of Educational Research*, 79(2): 533–56.
7. Banerjee, R. (2010) *Social and Emotional Aspects of Learning in Schools: Contributions to Improving Attainment, Behaviour, and Attendance*. Brighton: University of Sussex; Department for Education and Skills (2007) *Social and Emotional Aspects of Learning for Secondary Schools (SEAL) Guidance Booklet*. London: (DfES). Available online at www.nationalstrategies.standards.dcsf.gov.uk/node/157981. DfES (2007) *Social and Emotional Aspects of Learning (SEAL) for Secondary Schools*. London: Department for Education and Skills (DfES). Available online at www.bandapilot.org.uk/secondary/.
8. Qualifications and Curriculum Authority (QCA). (2010) A framework of personal, learning and thinking skills. 2007.
9. Rae, T. and L. Pedersen (2007) *Developing Emotional Literacy with Teenage Boys: Building Confidence, Self Esteem and Self Awareness*. London: Lucky Duck Books.
10. Matthews, B. (2006) *Engaging Education: Developing Emotional Literacy, Equity and Co-education*, p. 178. Maidenhead: McGraw-Hill/Open University Press.
11. OECD (1999) *Measuring Student Knowledge and Skills: A New Framework for Assessment*. Paris: Organization for Co-operation and Development.
12. Fisch, K. (2007) *Did You Know; Shift Happens – Globalization; Information Age*. Available online from www.youtube.com/watch?v=ljbI-363A2Q.
13. CBI (2010) *Ready to Grow: Business Priorities for Education and Skills* in *Education and Skills Survey 2010*. London: Confederation of British Industry.
14. NUS/CBI (2011) *Working Towards your Future: Making the Most of your Time in Higher Education*. Available online from www.cbi.org.uk/pdf/cbi-nus-employability-report.pdf.
15. Fraser, J. (2011) *The Purpose of Education is to Enable People to Understand, Navigate, Contribute to, Challenge and Change the World*. Available online at www.fraser.typepad.com/socialtech/2011/03/purposed.html.

16. Matthews, B. (2004) Promoting emotional literacy, equity and interest in KS3 science lessons for 11–14 year olds; the 'Improving science and emotional development' project. *International Journal of Science Education*, 26(3): 281–308; Morrison, L. and Matthews, B. (2006) How pupils can be helped to develop socially and emotionally in science lessons. *Pastoral Care in Education* 24(1): 10–19.

CHAPTER 16

The dyslexia debate

Julian G. Elliott and Simon Gibbs

Dyslexia is a problem

Why is dyslexia a problem? Because some children find learning to read very difficult; because parents and children get frustrated and distressed at the lack of progress; because no one really knows what causes it; because no one knows what to do; because someone has got to take the blame; because the problem cannot be clearly defined...

On the other hand, it is a miracle that so many children learn to read English. The way that sounds in the spoken language and the symbols used in writing do not consistently match (through, cough, bough; see, sea), the range of experiences that children have in their early years, the diversity of influences from parents, teachers and policy-makers, the absence of a complete scientific understanding of how reading develops, and what to do when there do appear to be problems, all compound the miracle. No less miraculous, but less often noted, is the multitude of other ways that children find to communicate.

Not being able to read accurately or fluently is a problem. Poor literacy skills disadvantage children and adults. At this point, we must acknowledge that what follows in this chapter might incur the wrath of some who rightly recognize that their child has difficulties with reading and who consider them to be dyslexic. We do not seek to be provocative, nor do we wish to deny the personal and social impact of any difficulty with reading. Clearly, the existence for some individuals of an extreme difficulty to decode text, despite generally sound functioning in most other areas of development, is a reality that has been noted by physicians, psychologists and educationalists for several centuries. Originally recognized as an acquired condition (following some form of trauma to the brain), physicians began to formally recognize its developmental form in the nineteenth century. In one, now classic, case, a British physician, W. Pringle Morgan,[1] described a child of 14 years of age who had failed to learn to read despite normal intelligence and good eyesight. Noting the boy's abilities in other cognitive activities, he observed that 'The schoolmaster who has taught him for some years says that he would be the smartest lad in the school life if the instruction were entirely oral'.

The dyslexia debate, however, does not centre upon whether there are individuals who present with severe difficulty in learning to read; rather, it is whether there is a particular subgroup of these people who can be clearly, consistently and rigorously identified as dyslexic. Unless this is the case, the term 'dyslexia' is little more than a synonym for 'poor reader' and thus can offer little extra information of value for the purposes of assessment and identification.

The problem of definition

Prior to highlighting the many difficulties of definition, it is important to identify which aspects of reading are typically covered by the term 'dyslexia'. Generally, the term is used to describe difficulties in decoding. However, even here there is some difference of opinion as to how broadly this should be interpreted. For some, the term should be reserved to describe those with severe difficulties of single word decoding or word recognition. Single word reading is typically seen by researchers in the field[2] as the best indicator as it removes the contribution of contextual and syntactic cues that may compensate for the core difficulty of letter-sound processing. Others,[3] however, argue for a broader understanding on the grounds that some dyslexics can overcome their decoding/word recognition problems but continue to have difficulties in reading fluently. This emphasis is particularly evident in countries that have transparent languages such as German, Finnish or Italian. Here, reading accuracy difficulties are rare and identified problems usually take the form of slow and laborious reading. While those experiencing problems of accurate and fluent word processing are very likely to experience difficulties in understanding the meaning of what they are reading, comprehension of written text is not usually seen as a key marker of dyslexia.

The fundamental problem is that dyslexia lacks any agreed scientific definition. There is, as we know, a range of definitions but these are somewhat arbitrary, lacking scientifically justified objective criteria for inclusion or exclusion. None of them provides any unambiguous clues about what to do with those labelled as 'dyslexic'. In our view, as a consequence of this ambiguity, the use of the term may also divert resources away from some other struggling readers who might also benefit if only they too could be described as 'dyslexic'.

One of the biggest myths associated with dyslexia is that it should be defined in relation to intelligence. This so-called 'discrepancy definition' of dyslexia recognizes as genuine dyslexics only those whose level of reading is significantly worse than would be expected on the basis of their intelligence (typically measured by an IQ test).

The discrepancy model was dealt a significant blow by a large raft of research studies[4,5] that have convincingly demonstrated that the underlying cognitive difficulties that relate to word reading show no significant correlation with any measures of general intelligence. (We will not here go into the debate about the problems associated with 'intelligence' as a valid and measurable concept, but see Chapter 12.) Interestingly, neuroscience appears to be pointing to the same conclusions; a recent study of brain activation by Hiroko Tanaka and colleagues[6] demonstrated no significant differences on reading-related tasks between (a) those whose reading performance is at a level that one would expect on the basis of their IQ and (b) those for whom there is a significant discrepancy between their reading and IQ. Furthermore, IQ tells us virtually nothing about how likely interventions are to be successful, or prognosis.[7] Indeed, it is now widely accepted that IQ has no relevance for diagnosis in respect of decoding difficulty.

Others have highlighted the moral question that would follow if dyslexia were only diagnosable in bright children: why should supposedly less able children be denied the same intensity of help? We suggest that an answer might lie in claims to social power that just those who think they are 'clever' may assume.

Although scientific research has largely discredited the discrepancy model, the use of IQ for diagnosing dyslexia continues to be widely employed. Several reasons for this apparent paradox are listed by Julian Elliott and Elena Grigorenko:[8]

- The link has a long history and is now steeped in everyday understandings that are not easy to break.
- Those with IQs that place them in the lowest 1 per cent of the population (and who would normally struggle to cope in mainstream schooling because of their intellectual difficulties) often encounter problems in learning to read.
- IQ is often used as a criterion when selecting 'dyslexics' for research studies. However, in such instances, this step is usually taken to help isolate underlying cognitive factors that might not otherwise be easily revealed, not because this is taken as a meaningful diagnostic criterion.
- Some advocate the continued use of IQ in the assessment of dyslexia because of a perceived lack of alternative procedures. Such a position, of course, is hardly accurate or justifiable.
- IQ tests have long been used in the USA and many other countries for determining eligibility for additional education services. Longstanding practices such as these are not easy to dispel.
- There is a clear relationship between IQ and higher-order reading skills of inference, deduction and comprehension. Thus, IQ tests may be valuable for providing understanding of broader learning difficulties;
- The administration of IQ tests is restricted to certain professionals and thus has an influential role in maintaining and preserving professional influence and status.
- The notion that dyslexics are highly intelligent individuals who struggle with decoding (itself a low-level cognitive task) is immensely powerful, particularly for those who struggle to acquire literacy.

For many poor readers, the experience of being treated by peers (and sometimes by teachers) as stupid has had highly negative consequences that have hindered their sense of agency and well-being. It is hardly surprising, therefore, that we so often read in the popular press personal accounts along the lines of: 'I thought I was stupid for much of my life until I was diagnosed as dyslexic. I now realize that I'm not stupid after all'. Here, the core problem is not that dyslexia had earlier failed to be identified but, rather, that an assumption of low intelligence had been made on the basis of the individual's decoding difficulties. Such attributions are complete folly and the fundamental point that decoding difficulties reveal next to nothing about an individual's underlying intelligence must be understood by all, professionals and laypeople. Of course, a failure to learn to read is likely to reduce access to the printed word and this may well impact upon the development of the individual's concept acquisition, vocabulary and general knowledge, all of which are factors that are typically used when we make everyday judgements about a person's intelligence.

Once scientific studies had broken the link between IQ and decoding, defining dyslexia became highly problematic. For some, dyslexia morphed into a general term that merely described those with the greatest difficulties in decoding. This conception was made more complex by growing recognition that reading difficulty lies along a continuum in which there is no absolute distinction between typical and atypical readers; there is no clear-cut category whereby one either has or does not have dyslexia, reading disability, specific reading difficulties, or any other similarly termed condition. For this reason, prevalence estimates of dyslexia range widely depending on where the cut-off point has been applied. There is also much disagreement about gender ratios, with some arguing that the higher preponderance of boys, reported in many studies, merely reflects teacher referral bias because of boys' greater tendency to engage in disruptive and challenging behaviour.

Of course, to identify as dyslexic those scoring at the lowest end of a distribution curve is to place in jeopardy many vested interests, as expensive diagnostic assessments and legal representations would be far less in evidence. However, if one is going to dispense with the argument that dyslexics are merely those who are placed at the lowest end of a distribution curve of poor to strong readers and, instead, see them as representing a subset of a wider pool, it is necessary to provide some form of definition that can guide their identification.

In their detailed review of dyslexia in adults, Rice and Brooks[9] concluded:

> "There are many definitions of dyslexia but no consensus. Some definitions are purely descriptive while others embody causal theories. It appears that 'dyslexia' is not one thing but many, insofar as it serves a conceptual clearinghouse for a number of reading skills deficits and difficulties, with a number of causes."

Some definitions are broad in scope and would seem to be highly inclusive while others reflect a more particularized notion of dyslexia. Reflecting the former approach, a Working Party of the British Psychological Society offered the following definition:[10]

> "Dyslexia is evident when accurate and fluent word reading and/or spelling develops very incompletely or with great difficulty. This focuses on literacy learning at the 'word' level and implies that the problem is severe and persistent despite appropriate learning opportunities."

A similar stance was subsequently taken by the Government-sponsored Rose Report[11] on the identification of dyslexia and literacy difficulties: 'Dyslexia is a learning difficulty that primarily affects the skills involved in accurate and fluent word reading and spelling'. However, the generality of this account was subjected to criticism by the House of Commons, Science and Technology Select Committee[12] on the grounds that: 'The Rose Report's definition of dyslexia is . . . so broad and blurred at the edges that it is difficult to see how it could be useful in any diagnostic sense'.

It has been noted in the professional and research literatures that such general types of definition can result in all children with reading difficulties being considered to be dyslexic, even those with significant intellectual difficulty. Interestingly, others have complained that such definitions are too narrow, claiming that an over-emphasis upon literacy may exclude some so-called 'compensated' dyslexics whose decoding difficulties are minor but who present with other attentional, organizational and self-regulatory problems.

People who consider themselves to be dyslexic (and who have been 'diagnosed' as such by various professionals) often present with a very wide and diverse range of symptoms and difficulties. Commonly offered lists often include: difficulties of phonological awareness, poor memory, a poor sense of rhythm, difficulty with rapid information processing, poor ordering and sequencing, clumsiness, poor concentration, impaired verbal fluency, inconsistent hand preference, poor phonic skills, frequent letter reversals, arithmetical weaknesses, speech and language deficits, low self-image, and anxiety when being asked to read aloud. However, the key difficulty here is that none of these symptoms are necessary or sufficient for a diagnosis of dyslexia (other than the actual reading difficulties themselves, of course). To make matters more complex, such symptoms are found in most poor readers and also in many people who have no reading difficulties. Some difficulties that are commonly believed to be typical markers of dyslexics; for example, letter reversals, are similarly found in younger normal readers who are reading at the same age level, thus reflecting their limited reading skills rather than an underlying weakness. A further complication stems from the fact that many so-called symptoms of dyslexia are also used as indicators of other developmental disorders such as dyspraxia, attention deficit hyperactivity disorder (ADHD) and dyscalculia.

In many ways, diagnosing dyslexia on the basis of such symptoms is not greatly unlike reading one's horoscope. It is highly likely that one can find some elements that can be drawn upon to provide confirmation. The power of the label is great and those who struggle with reading and their family members are often very eager for this diagnosis. This situation can be exacerbated by the fact that the much sought-after diagnosis of dyslexia is often provided by privately funded specialists whose professional livelihoods may be dependent on a steady stream of business.

Biological explanations

Many definitions emphasize the biological underpinnings of dyslexia – that dyslexics are those whose problems are essentially brain-based, rather than environmentally determined. Certainly, genetics and neuroscience have offered a range of insights into reading difficulty, yet our knowledge in these areas is still rudimentary. While it is clear that there is a strong genetic component to reading (and reading difficulty), with about a dozen specific genes so far nominated as potentially influential, we are still a long way from identifying the genetic mechanisms involved in a comprehensive hypothetical model. Furthermore, there are important environmental risk or protective factors (e.g. socio-economic status, family attitudes and behaviour towards education and literacy, exposure to printed material and protected time for reading) that, while unlikely to be causative, appear to be important moderators of genetic risk factors. Thus, in relation to causality, the separation of nature and nurture, as for most aspects of human functioning, is highly complex. It is also important to note that genetic studies have been conducted with poor readers as a general group, not as a clearly defined dyslexic subset.

Neuroscience has provided us with valuable information about activation in the brain during reading. Studies have shown that certain areas of the brain appear to be linked to differing underlying aspects of the reading process and that activation levels are often low in poor readers. They have also shown that activation increases as poor readers become more skilled. However, despite some sensationalist claims, we are still a long way from being able to use brain studies to differentiate between dyslexics (however defined) and other poor readers, or to provide any meaningful information for individual assessment and intervention.

Cognitive explanations

For many, key underlying features of dyslexia are deficient cognitive functions of one kind or another. In general, the three most commonly identified cognitive elements are phonological awareness, verbal short-term/working memory and rapid retrieval of phonological information stored in long-term memory (as exemplified by rapid naming tasks).

Phonological awareness refers to the ability to detect and manipulate the sounds of language. Weaknesses in this respect for early readers appear to be characteristic of many poor decoders. However, phonological weaknesses are not present in all children considered to be dyslexic, and others with phonological difficulties can develop adequate reading skills. Furthermore, while interventions geared to improve phonological skills have proven beneficial for literacy acquisition, the direction of causality is bidirectional, as experience of reading appears to be influential in the development of phonological skills. The role of phonological factors in reading also appears to be less important in transparent languages such as Italian and German where reading fluency, rather than single word accuracy is typically the key issue. Here, a more important predictor would appear to be the ability to name familiar objects as rapidly as possible. As regards the English language, rapid naming has been shown to be deficient in many, but by no means all, children who struggle with reading difficulties, although its predictive power seems to decline beyond the age of nine years.

Poor working memory is another feature commonly associated with dyslexia. This term refers to the ability to store and process information for short periods of time. While researchers have confirmed that many children with reading difficulties experience difficulties of this kind, there are differences between studies with respect to the relative importance of verbal, as opposed to spatial, memory, and it is clear that there is a significant proportion of poor dyslexics who do not experience working or other types of memory difficulties.

Dyslexia has long been associated with visual problems. Thus, personal accounts of distorted or blurred vision and letters 'jumping around the page' are commonly cited in the media. However, it is now widely accepted that the primary problem of those who struggle to learn to read is linguistic rather than visual. While some recent studies,[13] employing rather more sophisticated designs than hitherto, have once more pointed to the presence of visual difficulties, it is generally considered that such problems co-occur rather than play a causal role. Further confusion has centred around the phenomenon of visual stress, a condition where reading can become physically unpleasant. Often individuals reporting such difficulty complain of having sore eyes and headaches, visual distortions and illusions, when asked to read for any prolonged period. This condition, sometimes known as scotopic sensitivity, or Meares-Irlen syndrome, can impair reading fluency to some degree but should certainly not be seen as a causal explanation for severe decoding difficulty.

The problem of intervention

Many would argue that a desire to obtain a 'diagnosis' of dyslexia stems from a belief that an accurate diagnosis will point to the most appropriate form of intervention. The reality, however, is more complex.

Clearly, appropriate forms of reading assessment and intervention are necessary and it is now clear that, in the latter part of the twentieth century, a grave disservice was provided to some children with reading difficulties. During this time, a series of 'Reading Wars' raged between those who advocated a highly structured approach to the teaching of reading with a systematic emphasis upon the teaching of phonics, and others who were swayed by the 'whole language' approaches advocated by writers such as Frank Smith[14] and Kenneth Goodman[15] (and see Chapter 7). Advocates of this latter approach railed against the perceived sterility of structured approaches that they saw as unstimulating, demotivating and a distortion of the reading process. Arguing that the development of reading, like language acquisition, was a naturally occurring activity, they emphasized the importance of story and context and, in some cases, argued vociferously against the complementary use of phonics.

It is now generally agreed by reading disability specialists that the popular child-centred approaches to reading of the late twentieth century did not serve poor readers well. Recognition that written language is a cultural innovation that is not naturally acquired in the way of spoken language has helped us to recognize and understand the importance of explicit reading instruction. Research has shown that while whole language approaches may serve some skilled young readers adequately, these are highly problematic for those who encounter significant difficulties with text. It is now recognized that some children do not 'discover' letter-sound knowledge as a result of reading. As Torgesen[16] has commented, for such children it is essential to provide explicit instruction: '. . . that does not leave anything to chance and does not make assumptions about skills and knowledge that children will acquire on their own' (p. 363).

It is now understood that while all beginning readers require input on print-related concepts, phonological awareness, phonics, the development of reading fluency, vocabulary, spelling comprehension and writing, those who struggle to acquire reading skills will usually require more individualized, more structured, more explicit, more systematic and more intense inputs.

During the last two decades there has been greater emphasis upon reducing the prevalence of reading difficulties by intervening early, rather than waiting for the child to fail and then referring for a clinical assessment. Numerous studies have shown how highly structured programmes delivered to young children early in the school years can significantly reduce the proportion with subsequent difficulties. However, there remains a sizeable proportion of children who still fail to progress adequately, and ways to help this group continue to prove elusive. In addition, there are some who make sound progress in overcoming initial problems in the early stages of reading but subsequently drop back again at the age of eight or nine when reading demands increase substantially. In the USA, it has been estimated that these 'treatment resisters' may account for 2–6 per cent of the school population.

As the child reaches adolescence, the nature of the reading problem often becomes more diffuse. For some, difficulties will persist at the letter-sound level, whereas others may have made progress in coping with simple words but continue to struggle with complex, multisyllabic words. For others, the key problem may now be reading relatively fluently or understanding the content of the text. Motivational problems, arising from years of struggle, and often public humiliation, may limit the young person's willingness to engage with reading. Sadly, even the most structured and systematic intervention studies, based upon our most recent understandings of how best to tackle reading accuracy and fluency, have failed to find ways to overcome the difficulties of a small proportion of children and beyond calling for more intense and individualized approaches the field is still scratching its collective head in a search for more effective solutions.

The perceived need to diagnose dyslexia in poor readers has been further undermined by the 'response to intervention' (RTI) movement that has become increasingly popular in the USA and some other countries. RTI involves the provision of early intervention as soon as difficulties begin to emerge. Such work will typically operate across a range of tiers of varying intensity and group size. Thus, should a child, working in a small group on an academic area of difficulty (e.g. early reading skills), fail to make adequate progress, the number of sessions may be increased and/or increasingly individualized work may be provided. RTI has proven controversial, however, perhaps because by focusing directly on the instruction of academic skills and eschewing the need to assess those underlying cognitive processes that typically feature in IQ testing, it calls into question the value of long-standing and influential psychometric approaches. Advocates of intelligence testing have, unsurprisingly, criticized RTI for its neglect of underlying cognitive processes which, they argue, are important for guiding subsequent action. In response to such critiques, proponents of RTI have argued persuasively that there is little evidence that cognitive profiling can inform individualized reading interventions, or indeed, educational programmes designed to address other academic difficulties.

When one is seeking to help a child with literacy difficulties it is necessary to identify which aspects of the reading process are problematic (decoding, fluency, comprehension etc.). However, unless one were to argue that dyslexia is something other than a general decoding problem, a diagnosis of dyslexia would appear to have little additional utility. If employed as a simple synonym in such fashion, much of the dyslexia industry would be rendered redundant. However, those who oppose this view typically argue that there is a myriad of features (some of which are listed above) that mark out the 'true' dyslexic. Such a position, we contend, is untenable. Not only are such judgements based upon an imprecise and unscientific process, but also there are many questions concerning the particular value of the label as a guide to differentiated forms of intervention. Thus, in relation to the 'dyslexia debate', the key question is whether, within the pool of those who are struggling to acquire reading skills, there is a subgroup (i.e. dyslexics) who require specialized forms of intervention. Such a position would, of course, only be valid if there were clear evidence that differing teaching approaches were efficacious for dyslexic and non-dyslexic poor readers. However, there is no scientific evidence to support this position (despite a proliferation of case studies and personal anecdotes). The evidence we have to date, highlighting the value of highly structured, phonics-based approaches to reading instruction, applies not solely to those labelled 'dyslexics' but to all those who struggle with decoding.

This crucial point appears not to feature in general understandings, a phenomenon that is, in part, explained by the tendency of reading specialists to use the term rather loosely. To illustrate, in the UK, the British Dyslexia Association's '*Dyslexia Friendly Schools*' initiative[17] has received much acclaim. The key areas targeted by this scheme are the development of specialist teaching skills, close partnership with parents, a resource bank of appropriate 'dyslexia-friendly' materials, and a whole school policy for supporting dyslexic children. While a highly laudable initiative, it is clear that the professionals involved are using the term dyslexic to refer to all children struggling with reading rather than targeting an identified subgroup with a particular constellation of underlying weaknesses. Here, then, is a classic example of the evocative power of a label that, in actuality, offers little additional information for professional action. Put simply, the initiative is likely to benefit all children with reading problems: the label merely serves as a means to focus attention upon them.

The problem of our ignorance

Researchers have made great strides in developing knowledge about literacy over the past few decades. However, the field of reading difficulty is still riven with competing theories and understandings. While it is widely agreed that a phonological deficit is a key factor for most (but not all) children who encounter decoding difficulties, there continues to be significant debate as to its precise nature and role. In a recent publication, leading researchers in the field, Ramus and Szenkovits[18] noted that despite more than 30 years of research into the phonological deficit, '. . . we still don't know what it is'. The roles of auditory and visual processing in reading difficulty have both been subject to fierce debate, and periodic fluctuations in their popularity as important explanatory factors are a feature of the dyslexia literature. Explanations that centre upon co-occurring motor difficulties (often pointing to the workings of the cerebellum), together with associated claims for the value of motor skills training, are also frequently promoted despite an absence of sound, supportive scientific evidence.

There is no answer to the riddle, is there?

As long as an arbitrary definition is used to discriminate between dyslexics and non-dyslexic poor readers and to determine whether special treatment is warranted or not, there will continue to be disputes and disagreements. Where there is a belief that a spurious, unscientific 'diagnosis' of dyslexia will provide access to a solution, there will also continue to be widespread public inequity in educational provision and many private disappointments.

Notes

1. Morgan, W.P. (1896) A case of congenital word-blindness (inability to learn to read), *British Medical Journal*, 2: 1543–44.
2. Fletcher, J.M. (2009) Dyslexia: the evolution of a scientific concept, *Journal of the International Neuropsychological Society*, 15: 1–8.
3. Peterson, R.L. and Pennington, B.F. (in press) Seminar: developmental dyslexia, *The Lancet*.
4. Share, D.L., McGee, R. and Silva, P.A. (1989) IQ and reading progress: a test of the capacity notion of IQ, *Journal of the American Academy of Child and Adolescent Psychiatry*, 28: 97–100.
5. Stuebing, K.K., Fletcher, J.M., LeDoux, J.M., Lyon, G.R., Shaywitz, S.E. and Shaywitz, B.A. (2002) Validity of IQ-discrepancy classifications of reading disabilities: a meta-analysis, *American Educational Research Journal*, 39: 469–518.
6. Tanaka, H., Black, J.M., Hulme, C., Stanley, L.M., Kesler, S.R., Whitfield-Gabrieli, S., Reiss, A.L., Gabrieli, J.D. and Hoeft, F. (2011) The brain basis of the phonological deficit in dyslexia is independent of IQ, *Psychological Science*, 22(11): 1442–51.
7. Vellutino, F.R., Scanlon, D.M., Zhang, H. and Schatschneider, C. (2008) Using response to kindergarten and first grade intervention to identify children at-risk for long-term reading difficulties, *Reading and Writing*, 21: 437–80.
8. Elliott, J.G. and Grigorenko, E.L. (2013) *The Dyslexia Debate*. New York: Cambridge University Press.
9. Rice, M. and Brooks, G. (2004) *Developmental Dyslexia in Adults: A Research Review*. London: NRDC.
10. British Psychological Society (1999) *Dyslexia, Literacy and Psychological Assessment: Report by a Working Party of the Division of Educational and Child Psychology of the British Psychological Society*. Leicester: BPS.
11. Rose, J. (2009) *Identifying and Teaching Children and Young People with Dyslexia and Literacy Difficulties (Rose Report)*. Nottingham: DCSF Publications.

12. House of Commons (2009) *Evidence Check 1: Early Literacy Interventions Science and Technology Select Committee. Session 2009–10. HC 44.* London: Her Majesty's Stationery Office.
13. Aleci, C., Piana, G., Piccoli, M. and Bertolini, M. (2012) Developmental dyslexia and spatial relationship perception, *Cortex*, 48(4): 466–76.
14. Smith, F. (1971) *Understanding Reading: A Psycholinguistic Analysis of Reading and Learning to Read.* New York: Holt, Rinehart and Winston.
15. Goodman, K.S. (1970) Reading: A Psycholinguistic Guessing Game, in H. Singer and R.B. Ruddell (eds) *Theoretical Models and Processes of Reading* (pp. 259–72). Newark, DE: International Reading Association.
16. Torgesen, J.K. (2004) Lessons learned from research on interventions for students who have difficulty learning to read, in P. McCardle and V. Chhabra (eds) *The Voice of Evidence in Reading Research* (pp. 355–82). Baltimore. MD: Brookes.
17. British Dyslexia Association (2005) *Dyslexia Friendly Schools Pack.* Reading: British Dyslexia Association.
18. Ramus, F. and Szenkovits, G. (2008) What phonological deficit? *The Quarterly Journal of Experimental Psychology*, 61: 129–41, p. 165.

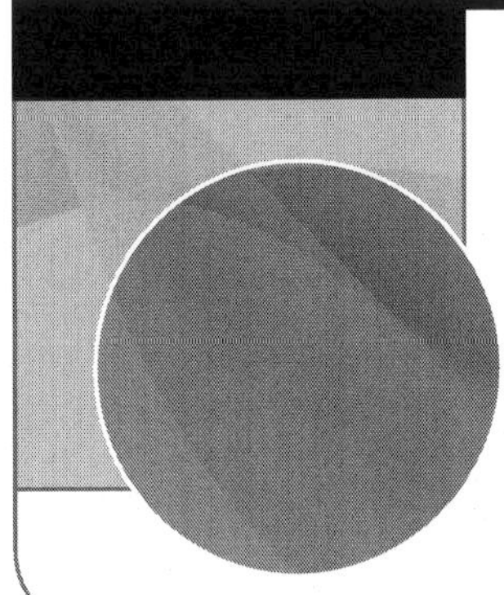

Index

Locators shown in *italics* refer to tables and figures.